THE YOUNG GERMAN NOVEL

UNIVERSITY OF NORTH CAROLINA
STUDIES IN THE GERMANIC LANGUAGES
AND LITERATURES

Initiated by RICHARD JENTE (1949–1952), established by F. E. COENEN (1952–1968)

Publication Committee

SIEGFRIED MEWS, EDITOR

WERNER P. FRIEDERICH   JOHN G. KUNSTMANN   GEORGE S. LANE
HERBERT W. REICHERT   CHRISTOPH E. SCHWEITZER   SIDNEY R. SMITH
RIA STAMBAUGH   PETRUS W. TAX

For other volumes in the "Studies" see pages 185 ff.

Send orders to: (U.S. and Canada)
The University of North Carolina Press, P.O. Box 2288
Chapel Hill, N.C. 27514
(All other countries) Feffer and Simons, Inc., 31 Union Square, New York, N.Y. 10003

NUMBER SEVENTY-FIVE

UNIVERSITY
OF NORTH CAROLINA
STUDIES IN
THE GERMANIC LANGUAGES
AND LITERATURES

Six Essays on the Young German Novel

by

JEFFREY L. SAMMONS

CHAPEL HILL
THE UNIVERSITY OF NORTH CAROLINA PRESS
1972

Der Mensch des neunzehnten Jahrhunderts ist mehr als jeder andere das Product der Umstände und seines Bildungsganges. Das Allgemeine hat die Herrschaft über das Individuum, und wol nur denen, die sich vom Allgemeinen als Dichter oder Künstler emancipiren.

Karl Gutzkow, *Aus der Zeit und dem Leben*

La marche ordinaire du XIXe siècle est que, quand un être puissant et noble rencontre un homme de cœur, il le tue, l'exile, l'emprisonne ou l'humilie tellement, que l'autre a la sottise d'en mourir de douleur.

Stendhal, *Le Rouge et le noir*

PREFACE

The following essays have a dual purpose. It has been my hope to make a contribution to the study of Young Germany (Das Junge Deutschland), a topic that is now of increasing interest. But I also hope the essays will be of value to those not directly familiar with the books here discussed. None of them are widely read and several of them are quite rare and difficult of access; therefore, I have tried to keep the reader in mind who has reason to be interested in the Young German problem but is not extensively acquainted with the primary materials. This purpose obliged me to speak in some detail of the contents of the books under discussion and to quote at length from them, as well as to rehearse some matters that are well known to specialists in the period. I hope that the latter will be indulgent about this and that they will find new perspectives in these discussions.

I am obliged to several persons who have been of great assistance to me. I owe a particular debt of gratitude to Professor Jost Hermand, who has been uncommonly generous with his advice, admonitions, and encouragement, and, on one occasion, with the loan of a book rare enough that I would have thought twice before cheerfully handing it over to another book-lover. I am also deeply grateful to Professor Horst Denkler, who was kind enough to read the manuscript and offer extensive criticisms, which I have taken to heart as far as my native stubbornness would allow and which helped me to make significant improvements. To the companionship of my colleague Professor Peter Demetz I owe much in the way of inspiration and understanding.

A special acknowledgment is due here to George Vrooman, humanities bibliographer in the Yale University Library. Young German materials, because of the onslaught of repression that befell them upon their publication and the generations of neglect afterwards, are very hard to come by and few libraries are well-stocked in this area. Mr. Vrooman, out of his enthusiasm for the purpose, his enormous knowledge of the antiquarian book market, and his astonishing memory for desiderata mentioned to him in months or years past, materially assisted me by acquiring crucial items for Yale's collection and unfailingly calling my attention to them as they came into view. Such people are the unsung heroes of the scholarly enterprise, and I wish most cordially to thank him here. I am also grateful to Mrs. Joan Hodgson of the Library of the University of California at Santa Cruz for assisting me while I was there in gaining access to materials at Berkeley, which has an unusually good collection of Young German books.

A shorter version in German of the essay on Heinrich Laube will have appeared in the *Zeitschrift für deutsche Philologie*, 91 (1972), *Sonderheft* on Heine and Young Germany, 149-163, under the title "Zu Heinrich Laubes Roman *Die Krieger.*" Thanks are due to the editors for permission to republish it in its present form.

To my wife, for her support, indulgence, wisdom, and tact, I can think of no reward other than an uncertain promise not to write another book for a while.

New Haven, Connecticut
July, 1971

CONTENTS

THE YOUNG GERMAN NOVEL

I. INTRODUCTION: ON THE TREATMENT AND EVALUATION OF YOUNG GERMAN FICTION

A set of essays about the novels of Young Germany is more in need of a preliminary defense than is usual in critical studies, for queries arise at every initial point of the undertaking. Is there, after all, any such thing as Young Germany? If so, what is it? Are the books the Young Germans wrote novels, and, if so, is there any justification for talking about them, given their doubtful quality and the small place they occupy in the history of literature? In what spirit and on what premises might they be usefully talked about? It is to these questions that I shall address myself by way of introduction.

It has many times been doubted that the term "Young Germany" is useful at all; Harold Jantz expressed a not uncommon view when he called it an "empty label."[1] As a group, Young Germany was largely imaginary, a fiction put into circulation by the Federal German ban on Heine, Gutzkow, Laube, Wienbarg, and Mundt of December 10, 1835. This was an overreaction of insecure governments, which had made an illegitimate connection between the emphasis that a few writers had put upon their belonging to a young generation and some completely unrelated revolutionary organizations that called themselves such things as Young Italy, or, in Switzerland, Young Germany. Since most of the putative members of the group promptly and vociferously denied either that they belonged to it or that there was any such thing at all, one may well wonder what justification there may be for retaining a term that had so dubious a birth and, in the mainstream of literary history, was often used for abusive purposes. Even if the term is retained, one seems to perpetuate an accident of politics to refer it only to the five writers named in the decree. In recent years there has been much opposition to the splintering of literary history into ever smaller movements and coteries, and much more inclination to seek

1

a synchronic sense of epoch and relatedness. Thus there has been a tendency to look upon Young Germany as an oppositional and dialectical segment of the Biedermeier or restoration period. Similarly, one can expand the concept, if one likes, very broadly; in his edition of exemplary Young German texts, Jost Hermand has included no fewer than twenty-five writers, ranging from the Hegelian critic Robert Prutz to the local Berlin wit Adolf Glassbrenner, and including the young Friedrich Engels.[2]

There is reason in all this, and there is no need to deplore varying usages for various purposes; literary categories are instrumental, not ontological, and may be used as best suits the enterprise in hand. The term "Young Germany" has held on, despite the opposition, and it is, I believe, still usable. Helmut Koopmann, in his recent and valuable study of the subject, argues that the federal decree itself is evidence that the group has a profile of a sort; while there was an unstable and shifting mass of writers of whom one could say that they belonged to the youth movement in literature at one time or another,

> andererseits hätte eine so breite, in ihren Konturen völlig unfaßbare Bewegung gewiß nicht die offiziellen und offiziösen Reaktionen ausgelöst, die wir kennen. Das Junge Deutschland war weder eine Untergrundbewegung noch eine Subkultur. Gewiß gab es Sympathisanten, zeitweilige Mitläufer, literarische Modefans — 'Bewegungen' kennen dergleichen ja zu allen Zeiten. Aber hier, im Jungen Deutschland, konzentrierte sich alles doch immer wieder auf wenige Namen.[3]

I would suggest, furthermore, that there are good impressionistic reasons for maintaining "Young Germany" as a usable term. In the core group of writers there is a special quality of intense urgency. It is strongest in Gutzkow and weakest in Laube, but it is present in all the works I would denominate as Young German and may account as much as considerations of content for the fact that certain writers rather than others found themselves in the baleful glare of government attention. Whenever one moves away from what Koopmann calls the center, whether, say, to a novel of Ernst Willkomm or to the urbane chatter of Prince Pückler-Muskau, one senses a lowering of the stylistic temperature. Other writers on the periphery may acquire this intensity briefly; an example is Ferdinand

2

Gustav Kühne, whom I have included here. In the older men, Ludwig Börne and Heine, the urgency is under firmer rhetorical or artistic control, and when I speak of Young Germany in these studies, I shall not normally be thinking of them, although their involvement with and importance for the movement in general is self-evident. The stylistic quality, moreover, is time-bound, and is restricted for the most part to about a half-dozen years around 1835. The earliest writings of Gutzkow and Mundt, for example, have less of it than those published right around the crisis, and by 1838 it is practically nowhere to be seen. The specific Young German style is *sui generis* and is not wholly captured by attempts to catalogue the terms and slogans that were central to writers' concerns.[4] It is more a matter of pitch and gesture, simultaneously robust and bewildered, crowding insistently close to the reader in the effort to arouse in him some resonance and motion. At the same time, much intellectual pain is communicated, for common to the Young German experience is a powerful feeling of the intolerableness of the world the writers lived in.

Since the toe-to-toe relationship with the reader is the characteristic Young German posture, it sometimes seemed to matter little to them whether they expressed themselves in expository or imaginative writing. Their primary concern was to communicate and disseminate into an age characterized by stagnation and regressiveness what appeared to them to be the best modern thought; therefore the choice of vehicle often seemed to them a practical question only. It is well known, for example, that Gutzkow undertook his novel *Wally, die Zweiflerin* after having been frustrated in his effort to continue Lessing's project of publishing the fragments of the free-thinker Reimarus. The choice of fiction in this as in other cases is motivated by the insistent desire to find a way to smuggle contraband into the consciousness of the public. All the Young German novels and novellas are thesis works of one kind or another. Therefore the question arises whether it is justified to single out the longer prose fiction from the corpus of Young German writing for special attention. With very few exceptions, scholarship on Young Germany has tended from the beginning to draw from writings irrespective of their expository or fictional character, and by and large the Young German novels have not been regarded as such at all, but as fictionalized tracts that pursue the Young German mission by

3

different means. Among the writers themselves there was an extreme and studied vagueness about genre distinctions, about the boundaries between novel and novella, between either and just stories, true or fictional, and between any of these and indefinable mixed bags of fiction, reportage, and speculation.[5]

Yet that the Young German novels are novels can hardly be doubted today. They represent, however, a substantial expansion from what had already become in the 1830's the traditional form of the *Bildungsroman* or the artistic and symbolic novel oriented on the Romantic tradition or Goethe's *Wahlverwandtschaften*. The Young German novel, writes Koopmann, "hatte mit dem überlieferten Bildungsroman allerdings kaum mehr gemeinsam als den größeren Umfang und die ihm damit auferlegten strukturellen Eigentümlichkeiten. Aber er war nicht mehr als rein poetisches Gebilde, sondern als Spiegelbild der Wirklichkeit konzipiert und folgte damit automatisch anderen Gesetzen als denen der tradierten Erzählwerke, die vom Jungen Deutschland als lebensfern und lebensfremd empfunden wurden."[6] Modern readers, who have seen the passing of the well-made nineteenth-century novel form, have become more appreciative of the expanded possibilities of narrative prose achieved by Heine and the Young Germans and are less likely to decry these works as formless. There are serious and largely unresolved formal problems in these books. But, despite the load of propaganda and cultural criticism they bear, they are novels and are accessible to treatment as experimental literary efforts.

The question remains whether they are worth treating independently as such. There is little that can be said for them as enduring works of art, and, indeed, the Young Germans, in their impatience with the *Kunstperiode* of the past, claimed not to intend them to be; Mundt's hero in *Moderne Lebenswirren* asserts that "eines Buches Geist muß in das Volk übergehen, und dann als Buch aufgehört haben zu leben. Es muß wirken und in der Wirkung seinen Geist ausathmen. Die Bücherleiche wird in den Literarhistorien feierlich begraben."[7] If this is the case, it is reasonable enough to regard the novels as simply another strategy in the Young German enterprise. C. P. Magill has argued that literary scholarship is justified in ignoring them: "the eighteen-thirties saw the appearance of works by Dickens and Tennyson, Stendhal, Hugo and de Musset, Lermontov, Pushkin, and Leopardi, Mörike and

4

Grillparzer, and students of the period might well be excused, since their reading-life is short, for giving these priority over Mundt or Laube."[8] The Young German works may be, in their own way, interesting, but that is perhaps not a quality sufficient to justify pursuing them. "Catholicity of taste," David Daiches has remarked, "is a virtue in a literary critic, but only up to a point. ... Of course, bad literature of a previous age has its *interest*; it tells us a great deal about the tastes of the time and may be illuminating sociologically or historically. But there are degrees of interest, and, more important, *interest* is not the same as *value*."[9]

Granting for the moment that the assumptions underlying Daiches' view are valid and that they are applicable to the present case, a turn to the novels is nevertheless justified in a practical sense because, in order to write intelligibly about Young Germany at all, it is necessary to find a focus. The history of criticism on the subject has made this clear. In the beginning, there was an effort by liberal scholars to unearth the buried Young German phenomenon by means of positivistic research. Without the incredibly tedious labors of these scholars, especially those of H. H. Houben, we would have today little to work with. But their books are unreadable. The Young Germans were writers of stupendous productivity and loquacity, partly because they were mistakenly inspired by a goal that they thought near at hand, and partly because the perilous situation of free-lance intellectuals in the early nineteenth century, when the age of patronage had passed and the age of protection through constitutional freedoms and copyright laws had not yet arrived, obliged them to write as though their very lives depended on it, as indeed they did. Houben's efforts to resuscitate all the Young Germans' critical and essayistic writing, the reams of government documents pertaining to them, as well as all their quarrelsomeness and infighting among themselves, were admirable in every respect, but, by the very nature of the subject and material, they produced vast compendia of excerpts and materials that overwhelm the student; and it must be said that the effort to make sense out of Young Germany by organizing innumerable quotations has remained a characteristic of scholarly writing on the subject to this day. Magill remarked, not without justice, that "since recognized literary standards cannot be applied to [the Young Germans] advantageously, the critic of their work may have to improvise a cumbersome apparatus compact of history, philosophy, theology and *Geistesgeschichte*, which generates, more often than not, a smoke-screen of bewildering generalizations obscuring both the writers and their time."[10]

The difficulty of which Magill complains is imposed by the nature of the subject itself, and no one writing seriously about Young Germany will be able to avoid it altogether. Young German writing is hasty, occasional, and, on the whole, impassioned; it therefore lacks compression and is riddled with contradictions and inconsistencies, so that a large amount of material must be gathered in order to draw worthwhile conclusions. The epoch in which the writers found themselves suffered from an overwhelming multiplicity of philosophies and opinions, and they themselves thought this one reason for the general incoherence. "Die allgemeine Verwirrung der Gegenwart," wrote Gutzkow, "läßt sich darum so leicht verstehen, weil überhaupt kein Gesetz herrscht, weil Jeder das Bedürfnis fühlt, sich verständlich zu machen. Jetzt, da kein Gedanke mehr an der Spitze steht vor dem die Völker sich in den Staub würfen und anbeteten, hat eine jede Meinung das factische Recht ihrer Gültigkeit."[11] Or, more succinctly: "Das Uebel ist die Ueberfülle unserer Zeit an Ideen."[12] Since the efforts of positivist scholars tended to reproduce this uproar of ideas and opinions, it became necessary to find an approach that would organize the inchoate material: Houben himself came to concentrate more and more upon the censorship issue, E. M. Butler produced a well-known interpretation of Young Germany as a Saint-Simonian movement, Günter Bliemel analyzed the Young German view of the role and mission of the writer, Walter Dietze and, more recently, Koopmann have looked upon the movement in its relationship to the literary tradition it confronted. There have been a number of other efforts to carve out an angle of vision from the recalcitrant primary material, and a treatment of the novels may modestly take its place among them.

But turning our attention to Young German fiction has, I believe, additional potential virtues. For it remains true that almost all interpretations of the movement suffer from the fact that the Young Germans were unable to find an idiom appropriate to the purposes of their literary and cultural criticism. The abstract vagueness of their concepts has not only long been noticed by all observers, but it also pained the writers themselves, who were, nevertheless, unable to find a way of coping with it. The three

6

terms that recur thematically throughout their writing — *Leben, Zeit, Wirklichkeit* — continue from the beginning to the end to lack concretion despite the efforts to give them content and definition in the process of writing about them. The leading students of the period have performed admirable feats in giving meaning and context to these and other terms of the Young German position; yet the subject has a troublesome way of remaining amorphous. The reason for this lies not only in the weakly anchored abstract terminology, but also in the persistently metaphoric manner of Young German expression, a symptom of a crisis of language with which Heine was also afflicted. I take an example quite at random; it is from Heinrich Laube's inaugural remarks on having taken over the editorship of the *Zeitung für die elegante Welt* on 1 January 1833:

> Keine Pygmäen tändeln vor uns; Adler stürmen daher und bringen den Göttergruß der neuen Zeit. Da ist Alles ernst und bedeutend! Nicht Nachtigallengesänge, nicht den heitern Lerchenwirbel hörst Du. Die Zeit hat ihre Riesenharfe ergriffen und spielt das Lied der Lieder, die Begebenheiten. Nicht das Reich des Schönen und des Reizenden darfst Du erwarten. Die Nothwendigkeit führt den ehernen Scepter.[13]

The passage goes on in this manner at some length. Now, it cannot be denied that it has a meaning of sorts, or, at least, that it expresses an attitude toward contemporary literature and indicates a new beginning with allegiances regarded as more appropriate to the imperatives of the present. So much is clear, but no more. A critical idiom that maintains this metaphorical style permanently becomes, in the long run, uninterpretable. Such writing is characteristic of the major part of the Young German critical and essayistic literature, and reading a large amount of it is a wearing experience. Despite its passionate *engagement*, there is something deeply noncommittal about it, in the sense that one often cannot see why something said in one metaphorical and allusive way could not as easily have been said in another. Interpretation, therefore, once it attempts to advance beyond the general lineaments of the Young German position, is always threatened with foundering in a morass.

It is in the nature of the situation that the style of Young German fiction should not be markedly different from that of the critical

7

and expository writing. Much of the content of the novels is essayistic, clothed in epistolary and dialogue form, and tends to the same characteristics as the rest of the corpus. At times the writers seem to have thought that the boundary between fiction and non-fiction could be erased altogether; they had the universalistic Romantic theory of the novel and the incompletely perceived example of Heine before them. The results, however, show that the business was rather more complicated than they realized. By admitting the dimension of the imagination into their writing, the paradox and ambivalence that were fundamental to the Young German situation and that they were endeavoring to bring under rational control are released, so that the novels and stories have a strong tendency to deviate from the lines that the writers were attempting to propagate. It is therefore frequently inappropriate to adduce evidence from the novels to support interpretations of the general Young German position. The creation of a fiction brings with it a logic different from that of critical or polemical writing. If fiction, as can be reasonably argued,[14] is not natural discourse, but the mimetic representation of natural discourse, then it follows that novels, no matter how didactic, hortatory, or assertive their intent, cannot be tracts, dialogues, or epistolary exchanges, but can only be representations of these, and that consequently they cannot be argumentative utterances, but only representations of such utterances. The consequences of this distinction are several, but the one most important for our purposes is that fiction puts the writer at one additional remove from his subjects and concerns, and frees him to describe, rather than be, the exponent of attitudes and opinions. On the one hand, the will to demonstrative argument becomes weaker, although, of course, it is never altogether absent from Young German fiction; the result is that the confusion of feelings from which the writers suffered is given freer rein, and the search for meaning through expository language yields to a representation of the dilemmas that plague the whole man. The writing becomes process rather than exposition. On the other hand, the very exigency of telling an exemplary story and positing representative *personae* requires the imaginative creation of plausibly recognizable characters and situations; in other words, it involves the writers in the pursuit of realism.

To suggest this is to enter upon a battlefield from which I would gladly be exempted as a conscientious objector. But I do not think

8

that, in talking about the Young German novel, the question of realism can be evaded altogether. The realistic novel of contemporary society is the outstanding achievement of nineteenth-century literature. Its failure to gain a foothold in Germany above the level of industrialized trivial literature, the failure of German writers to bring forth novels that could compare fairly with the achievements of other nations, is the single reason why German literature of the nineteenth century enjoys so little reputation in the world at large, despite its large body of finely wrought novellas, excellent poetry, and relatively few but outstanding dramas. So far as the facts of literary reputation are concerned, it does not help to argue that realism is not intrinsically appropriate to the German literature of the period and therefore should not be adduced as a principle of evaluation, or that the Young Germans were endeavoring to create comprehensive and populist works that transcended well-made forms and purely artistic purposes.

There is wide agreement that realism failed to take hold in Germany because of the backwardness of its society in the early nineteenth century. Ian Watt sees the realistic novel as dependent upon "two general considerations: the society must value every individual highly enough to consider him the proper subject of its serious literature; and there must be enough variety of belief and action among ordinary people for a detailed account of them to be of interest to other ordinary people, the readers of novels."[15] Friedrich Sengle sees the conditions of realism in a similar way, adding the ability to be receptive to the world as it is: "gelassene Welthaftigkeit, die durch den Verzicht auf alle Ideologie und durch die Anerkennung der verschiedensten individuellen und kollektiven Substanzen möglich wird."[16] Günter Bliemel, like the Young Germans themselves, shifts the blame to the conditions of life: "Das Leben selber konnte ihnen diesen Inhalt nicht geben, da es krank war und seine Zustände sich in einem Übergang befanden."[17] Insofar as realism is connected with a capitalist order of society becoming conscious of itself, the preconditions were not present in Germany; as late as 1849 there were 196 rural dwellers for every city dweller in industrial Saxony; and what was to become the mighty firm of Krupp employed in 1846 no more than 122 workers.[18]

That the social and political conditions of Germany were inimical to a modern literature was a widespread and familiar idea in the

1830's. Friedrich Schleiermacher, writing in the previous decade, had observed that the private character of the contemporary novel was due to a major decay of public life.[19] That literature is dependent upon life and that the contemporary conditions of life were too inchoate and feeble to generate worthwhile literature are viewpoints frequently met with in Young German writings. They dominate the argument in Ludolf Wienbarg's *Ästhetische Feldzüge.* In the ninth lecture he asserts that everything in his day is so unclear and shadowy that no valid aesthetic can be deduced,[20] and in the eighteenth lecture he asserts: "Kräftigen, reinen und schönen Stil wird kein Schriftsteller in unkräftiger, unreiner und unschöner Zeit erwerben..., denn der Schriftsteller ist im höhern Grad als ein anderer, oder vielleicht nur sichtbarer, ein Kind seiner Zeit."[21] Consideration of some of the salient features of Wienbarg's argument will help to show the inhibitions that complicated the pursuit of realism at this time.

The *Ästhetische Feldzüge,* which stands at the beginning of the Young German phenomenon as I am using the term, is a disappointing work in many of its details. Not only is much of it patched together synthetically from other writers on aesthetics, but it is also carelessly argued and self-contradictory on crucial issues. Its assertive and aggressive tone, which was responsible for its effect, reflects a posture that is apparently progressive but is seriously adulterated with Wienbarg's nationalistic prejudices and a vitalistic activism that often lacks ethical balance. But, with regard to the relationship between literature and reality, Wienbarg poses an important problem that was to haunt the Young German literary effort. He does this by working a transformation upon contemporary Classical theory. He is highly attentive to the principle of *Humanität* developed by German Classicism; this is outstandingly apparent in the third lecture, where, after having excerpted in the previous one a passage from Herder critical of the Romantic medieval revival, he argues that the test of whether such a mode should be encouraged is whether its spirit is congruent with *Humanität,* a proposition that Wienbarg, in agreement with Herder, denies. It is clear here and elsewhere that Wienbarg has learned from Classicism, but he is nevertheless concerned to draw a set of different conclusions. He has a Classical vision of the whole, free man, but, unlike Schiller in his aesthetic essays, he does not see art as the medium through which

10

such humane freedom can be developed, but rather sees the free, humane, and whole society as preliminary to the development of genuine art; indeed, he argues that the development of a sense of beauty in the characterless man of bourgeois society is damaging, as it may lead to unmanliness and indifference toward the welfare of the fatherland.[22] This difference is of fundamental importance, although in one respect it is not so radical as it may appear to be. For Schiller's aesthetics is also concerned with society — specifically, with the ways in which human freedom might be developed without paying the cost of blood, terror, and tyranny he saw in the example of the French Revolution. This social orientation is one reason why Schiller's aesthetics rarely touches on specific works of art, and Wienbarg's similar motivation appears in his objection to the practice of aesthetics in treating art works rather than the whole organism of society as Plato does.[23] That his aesthetics is related in kind to Schiller's is also shown by the fact that Wienbarg, like Schiller, sees the aesthetic element as a mediating force; in Wienbarg's version it mediates between "Erkennen und Handeln."[24] But his equation is different, for his artist transplants "die Schönheit der Tat, aus dem Leben in eine andere Welt, in die Kunstwelt."[25]

He was not always consistent about this. Viktor Schweizer quotes passages from several other writings indicating that Wienbarg sometimes did entertain the proposition that poesy can have an inspirational effect on life.[26] But for the *Ästhetische Feldzüge* the opposite order of priorities is predominant, and it is an early indication of a problem that was to grow in dimensions in the socially oriented aesthetics of the nineteenth century. The twist on Schiller indicates that Wienbarg was anxious to preserve the humanitarian and libertarian impulses of Classicism without drawing the conclusion apparently suggested by Schiller and Goethe that the existing order of life and society must be quietly accepted until the spirit of man is ennobled. In the long run, Wienbarg's argument pertains to the social responsibility and function of art, as against the tendency of Classical and Romantic traditions to build barriers between reality and imagination. In a newspaper article of 1844 he wrote: "Würden die Künstler den Gedanken an die öffentliche Bestimmung der Kunst in sich wacher und lebendiger erhalten haben, so würden sie ohne Zweifel mit Erfolg die Kunst vor dem Versinken in die Privatsphäre geschützt haben."[27]

On the other hand, Wienbarg's revision of Classical theory into activism and social responsibility poses a problem of a different kind that has some serious dimensions. For the rearrangement of priorities within the context of *Humanitätsphilosophie* introduces an element of pessimism that continually rises to the surface in the argument. Despite Goethe's and Schiller's resigned acceptance of what could not be altered, German Classical thought had an optimistic view of the potential of humane pursuits to prepare humane men for a humane order of society. Wienbarg's postulation of the primacy of life over art makes this optimism impossible to sustain. Gerhard Burkhardt is not quite on the point when he argues: "Im Grunde erliegt [Wienbarg] dabei einem Zirkelschluß, denn er ersetzt die optimistische Kunstspekulation durch eine nicht minder optimistische und utopische Lebensspekulation."[28] First of all, Wienbarg denies the possibility that the impulse for regeneration can come out of art. At one point he clothes this argument in what appears to be a defense against the attribution of immoral influence to art, a live issue in this age of oafish censorship, but the formulation leads to a more radical conclusion: "Nicht die Kunst ist es, die das Leben, das Leben ist es, das die Kunst verdirbt, und zu allen Zeiten, zu den schlechtesten unter Nero, ist diese noch immer besser und heiliger gewesen als jenes."[29] The attentive reader may detect an internal contradiction in this statement, but the operative notion is that it is life that ruins art, not vice versa. For it appears in Wienbarg's argument that a wretched state of affairs in the nation and society obviates the possibility for good art. Such a view tends to call the enterprise of aesthetics into question, and Wienbarg was keen enough to see this. He argues in the ninth lecture that a historical survey shows that aesthetics is always keyed to the respective *Weltanschauung* of the time;[30] this argument, which is clearly tending toward a theory of the dependence of intellectual structures on social determinants, is a little unclear and in several places awkwardly amalgamated with a desire to believe that there are also universal principles of judgment. To pursue this difficulty in Wienbarg would lead us farther into ideological territory than I wish to go here. The passage is followed, however, by the further argument that in Wienbarg's time everything is so unclear and shadowy that no valid aesthetic can be deduced. Quickly, he is forced on his own premises to the radical conclusion that whoever were to presume to provide an

12

aesthetic "müßte vorher . . . eine neue Kunst, ein neues Leben herbei-schaffen."[31] Such a conclusion seems to undermine the sense of offering aesthetic principles at all, and illustrates very strikingly how the theory of the dependence of literature upon life and reality could inhibit the literary enterprise altogether.

At the same time, another problem emerges that stands in the way of the pursuit of realism. The Young Germans often say that life and reality are not being absorbed into literature for their own sake, but to reveal a higher truth or hidden lineaments of the future in the present. In the fifteenth lecture, Wienbarg argues: *"Wäre das Wirkliche der Wahrheit und Schönheit entgegengesetzt, so müßte es der Künstler nicht idealisieren, sondern vernichten, um an dessen Stelle die Schönheit hinzupflanzen"*;[32] and, in the sixteenth lecture: "Nicht das Wirkliche als wirklich will der Künstler nachah-men, sondern dem Wirklichen eine künstlerische Bedeutung ge-ben."[33] Thus, even the concept of realism tended to be, as Theodor Mundt put it in his history of contemporary literature in 1842, "idea-lischen Ursprungs";[34] he describes the literary mission of the present as "ein bedeutungsschwangerer Messianismus der Zukunft, der sich mit hochrothen Feuerzeichen an den Horizont der Zeit gemalt hat."[35] As a practical example of what this means in terms of taste, Mundt's history gives one sentence to Balzac and twenty-eight pages to George Sand. The philosophical atmosphere of the time had much to do with this attitude that the task of art is the representation, as one Hegelian critic put it, "des Werdens des Absoluten in der Zeit, nicht des schönen Seins der einzelnen Menschen."[36]

But it must not be forgotten that Young Germany is a mass of contradictory opinions and instincts pulling and tugging against one another. Friedrich Sengle, in an important section of the recent first volume of his *magnum opus* on the period, has described how the conservative and organic instinct to which the Biedermeier attempted to hold fast is permeated in a convoluted and dialectical way with an increasingly empirical sensibility,[37] and the ambivalent Young German literary situation is an analogue of that complexity. What-ever one may wish to attribute to the Young German viewpoint, the diligent reader can find evidence to the contrary. So it is with realism. The Young Germans were not capable of forming a theoretical principle of realism that could be actively pursued, but the continuous stress upon "life" and contemporary reality itself

13

implies the potential for a kind of literary realism as a solution, and much of the Young German writing suggests at least a longing both for realism and for well-made forms. This longing expresses itself in rather comic form in the criticism the Young Germans directed against one another. Never has there been a literary movement the members of which were more at odds with one another, and this atomization was intensified by the government assault, which splintered the group even further and encouraged the principle of *sauve qui peut*. The annals of Young Germany are full of such mutual criticism, as any reader of Houben's compendia knows, and it all tends to the same point: each writer accuses the other of being too abstract, of allowing ideas and fashionable theories to clog the fiction, of artificiality and excessive introspection, and of failing to produce well-ordered forms. The comedy lies in the fact that these criticisms apply equally well to the works each was writing at the time. But the continuous reiteration of these critical principles shows that there was a perceived gap between purpose and achievement among the Young German writers.

There are also more positive expressions, and they are to be found in large numbers. One of the most curious of them is in Karl Gutzkow's novel of 1833, *Maha Guru*. Suddenly, apropos of almost nothing at all, Gutzkow drops the fictional narration and inserts a personal remark. He tells of a confrontation he had with a government minister who tried to convert him from liberal attitudes. Upon returning to the street, he is especially struck by the details of commonplace reality, which are described in a kind of montage. Two dogs investigate one another's sex; shopkeepers carry on their ordinary business. The author is aware that his shoe pinches and that he has a loose thread on his sleeve. He goes to a store and buys some paper, along with various necessaries like a watch key, two oranges, a hundred matches — "und einen Monat später schickte ich an Herrn Campe in Hamburg meine Narrenbriefe."[38] This passage is uncommonly instructive because of its simple-mindedness. Two significant links are posited: the response to reactionary political pressure is a heightened awareness of mundane reality, of the surface and appearance of things. This heightened awareness then generates a book of modern relevance. Now Gutzkow's *Briefe eines Narren an eine Närrin* has all the qualities of abstractness and diffuseness that the Young Germans criticized in one another, and it is at once

14

incongruous and instructive that Gutzkow should present the inspiration for it as an epiphany of quotidian reality. Later in *Maha Guru*, the author pauses to say: "ich schildere Ereignisse und Menschen, die dem Leben und der Wirklichkeit entnommen sind,"[39] which seems like an odd comment in this imaginary and remotely allegorical story set in Tibet, and it may mean no more than that the *issues* adumbrated in the novel are those posited by life and reality; nevertheless, the fact that the Young German logic is convoluted does not alter the nature of the original impulse.

There are many passages and comments in Gutzkow's writing that could be brought to bear on the question, but there is one more that is of particular interest:

> Es gibt zwei Arten von Schriftstellern. Solche, die vor den Ereignissen kommen, und solche, die nach ihnen. Die Einen sind Vorreden, die Andern Register. Die Vorreden prahlen und versprechen oft mehr, als die Register halten. Die Masse läuft den Vorreden nach und kommt selten über sie hinaus. Die Register, oft so nützlich, sind unpopulär.
>
> Wo man jetzt hinblickt, sieht man Vorredenliteratur.[40]

What Gutzkow says here about the relative popularity of the two kinds of writing seems a little perverse, but the rest is interesting, because it is a repudiation of Mundt's notion of "Messianismus der Zukunft." Literature as an "index" must certainly mean something similar to Sengle's realistic canon of "gelassene Welthaftigkeit." Gutzkow's metaphors of "Vorrede" and "Register" seem to me uncommonly well taken, and if they imply a rejection of almost all Young German writing as such, they express succinctly a major theme of the realism problem.

Laube, of whose views there will be more to say in a later essay, also has a number of scattered comments that are remarkably to the point. In an apologia of his description of Vienna in the *Reisenovellen*, he mounts a defense of the primacy of the disparate apperceptions of reality over the a priori organizing idea:

> Der Leser wird es empfinden, wie man hin und her geworfen wird mit seinen Anschauungen, wenn man nicht nach einer leitenden, starren Idee das Ganze beurteilen will. Dies letztere muß aber meines Erachtens am sorgfältigsten vermieden werden, es bringt nur

eine irrtümliche Einheit in die Betrachtung, das Objekt selbst wird überritten, und man konstruiert eine Stadt aus Forderungen, Möglichkeiten und Antipathien zusammen, wie sie nicht existiert.

Das Recht der einmal wirklichen Existenz muß in allen Dingen geachtet werden, und es kommt weniger darauf an, ob diesselbe vom Darsteller als harmonisches Ganze aufgenommen und verarbeitet, als vielmehr, ob sie ehrlich, unbefangen, auch mit allen scheinbaren Widersprüchen aufgefaßt worden ist.

Die Wahrheit darf hierbei der Kunst nicht einmal untergeordnet, viel weniger geopfert werden, und man hat nur zuzusehen, daß auch die gemischten Eindrücke ein Zusammengefügtes, darstellbares Ganze bilden.[41]

There is an absolute break in these remarks with the tradition of Classical aesthetics, with even as much of it as was retained by Wienbarg. The primacy of perceived *Wirklichkeit* over philosophical *Wahrheit* is asserted with unimpeachable plainness.

It is true that Laube saw realism, for the most part, not as a formal matter, but as one of content adequate to the present. "Warum dulden wir," he asks in an essay on the contemporary novel in the *Elegante* of 23 May 1833, "daß immer noch die alten gestorbenen Interessen abgehaspelt werden; warum verlangen wir nicht vom Romanschreiber, daß die neue Welt sich abspiegele in den Erzählungen! Es gibt in Deutschland kein schnelleres und sichereres Bildungsmittel als den Roman."[42] "Die Gesellschaft," he goes on, "ist eine ganz andere geworden, der Adel ist gestürzt und verlacht, das altersgraue Herkommen ist bezweifelt und angetastet, und die Poesie der Gesellschaft, der Roman ist größtentheils noch der alte"; and he asserts, with comic exaggeration, that only fifteen new novels will be needed to bring modern ideas on their way.[43] Here Laube has fallen into the confusion that Gutzkow later attempted to clear up with his distinction between "Vorrede" and "Register": on the one hand, he asserts that modern times are upon us and it is the novel that is lagging behind; on the other, that new novels are needed to bring modern times upon us. It is a dilemma familiar from the history of Marxist literary theory. But we will have more occasion to advert to the *Elegante* essays when we come to Laube's own major effort in the novel. It will be enough to say here, in view of Mundt's avoidance of Balzac in his history of literature, that Laube on one

16

occasion expresses a view that sounds very much like one of Balzac's fundamental perceptions:

> *Selbst* ist nicht mehr der Mann, aber das Geld. Darum wird es den guten Poeten heutigen Tages so schwer, einen guten Roman oder gar eine gute Tragödie zu schreiben. Sie sind noch immer der Meinung, die Menschen seyen die Hauptsache, und aus diesem Irrthume wächst ihr Unglück. Das Geld ist die Hauptperson, die Verhältnisse des Geldes sind die Nebenpersonen, und die Menschen selbst sind nur die Kleider.[44]

Wienbarg's position, too, becomes more complicated as soon as one looks beyond the *Ästhetische Feldzüge* to some of his other writings. Though probably the least gifted in a literary sense of all the major Young Germans, he felt a yearning for creative writing. In the introduction to the *Wanderungen durch den Thierkreis*, he speaks rather gloomily of a creative flow that refuses to come: "Weiß ich's doch an mir selbst, wie unflüssig und verstockt noch so viele Ideen in mir sind, die zum Strom der jungen Welt gehören, glaube ich doch noch gar nichts gethan zu haben und harre der Stunde, wo die schöpferische Kraft, die in den Tiefen meines Lebens braust, mein ganzes Ich ergreifen und glühend in die harrende Form überströmen wird."[45] Fifteen years later, when his control over the craft of writing had much deteriorated, he exclaims: "Dichter, Künstler zu sein, dazu habe ich Anlage"; he is not born to be a philosopher, scholar, statesman, or demagogue.[46] But this is either whistling in the dark or evidence of a lack of self-knowledge. In keeping with his theory of the primacy of life over art, he lays the blame on the times: "Ich habe nichts geschaffen, was einem Kunstwerke ähnlich sieht. Ich kann antworten, ihr habt nichts gethan, was eines Dichters und Künstlers würdig."[47] But such a statement by a writer on his own behalf is unbecoming and, on the whole, our judgement must be that Wienbarg was, in the first instance, a scholar, essayist, and activist intellectual rather than a poet.

He did, to be sure, have some ideas on the kind of writing that the times required; most of them refer to the novel. In November, 1835, he wrote to a publisher concerning his own novel plans as follows:

> Sie wißen, der Geschmack am historischen Roman verliert sich, und wie in England u Frankreich, der psychologische, zeitgeschichtliche

Sittenroman schon völlig deßen Stelle eingenommen, so wird dieser auch in Deutschland sich Bahn brechen. Gegenwärtig ist freilich noch kaum der Anfang gemacht; die verschrieene, u in der Tat zu flüchtig u in vielfacher Rücksicht unbedacht geschriebene Wally von meinem Freund Gutzkow gehört hieher. Von unsern deutschen Romanschmierern läßt sich in dieser Hinsicht nichts erwarten, denn die ersten Bedingungen des Sittenromans, originelle, feine Konturen, scharfe Analyse der Stimmungen u Charaktere, poetisches Auffaßen der Zeitelemente, wie sollten diese sich vorfinden bei Schriftstellern, die gewohnt sind, mit einer großen Schere in Chronikenstoff hineinzuschneiden u ausgestopfte Romanpuppen daraus zusammenzunähen?[48]

Wienbarg repeated this opinion in his essay *Zur neuesten Literatur*, where he predicted that analytic social novels would become the main branch of literature and displace historical novels.[49]

Although a literary work of any consequence was to elude him permanently, he did engage in a good deal of experimentation, the results of which are to be found in some of the sections of the *Wanderungen durch den Thierkreis*. Most of these items are rather unpromising. One weak effort at a novella, the section entitled "Der Stier," is more profitably examined in the context of Wienbarg's interest in the political system of Norway, and I have discussed it in that connection elsewhere.[50] "Die Jungfrau" is an unprepossessing tale of melancholy and suicide, to which is appended a longish meditation in verse on the subject of passion. Mildly amusing is a Börnesque pasquille in the section appropriately entitled "Die Waage," the name of one of Börne's periodicals. None of these will bear much attention. There are, however, three items of considerably greater interest; they are "Der Wassermann," "Der Fischer," and "Die Zwillinge."

The first of these is subtitled "Die Helgolander" [*sic*] and is a genre picture of the islanders. What is remarkable about it is the degree to which Wienbarg is able to substain a mood that is appropriate to the material and does not seem to contain any overt ulterior messages. It is an impressionistic, almost plotless story. Both the island and its inhabitants are grim and bleak; the pilots of the story are men of courage, passion, and greed, and are without mercy, like the sea. The story, such as it is, tells of an American ship that refuses the local pilot's services; as the crowd ashore watches with grim curiosity, the rejected pilot leads the ship into disaster, even though his younger brother on board begs for mercy. Here there is no idealization of the men of the north; it is an account of a hardy and mean society, the members of which are pleased with the expectation that they will be able to loot the wrecked ship. Spare in its language and unpretentious, it is the best imaginative piece in Wienbarg's writing. Here is an altogether unexpected kind of realism; it is not "poetic," nor is it apparently pervaded by any ideal *Wahrheit* that transcends the *Wirklichkeit*; on the contrary, there is a representation of the cruel and unbeautiful such as was to become the hallmark of much European realism.

Whether Wienbarg would have been able to do any more with it, however, is unlikely; he himself seems not to have grasped its special character, as his further discussion of it lapses into his more familiar attitude. He begins the essay "Der Fischer," subtitled "Faule und Frische Romane," by saying that the Helgoland sketch is the way he would write a novel if he were to write one. This essay is, for the most part, a plea for novels of contemporary setting and relevance and an argument against historical novels, an antipathy he frequently expressed. It begins with some theoretical considerations on the novel, which are unconvincing and of little moment. He then goes on to discuss Walter Scott, whom he charges with a lack of "deutsche Seele" and "Poesie."[51] He sees Scott's value in making the public interested in literature, but there is no poesy in his followers, who lack a central idea; feudal novels, argues Wienbarg, are simply an anodyne. These considerations then lead into a more interesting discussion of Schiller, Jean Paul, and Goethe, and his comment shows his wish that the virtues of the great masters of the recent past might be transformed into a style adequate to the needs of the times: "Ich wünschte, wir hätten von Schillers Hand ein Paar Abhandlungen weniger und einen Geisterseher mehr; und ich wünschte, *Paul* und *Wolfgang* wären Milchbrüder gewesen und Paul hätte etwas mehr von Göthe's Kunst und Wolfgang etwas mehr von Richters überfließender Liebe und Seelenseligkeit eingesogen. Dann besäße Deutschland einen Titan, der meisterhaft und einen Meister, der titanisch."[52] Again he urges writers to reach into their own times and their own experience, and again, as in the *Ästhetische Feldzüge*, the pessimism as to whether the conditions of present-day life are up to producing art asserts itself. "Woher der Stoff zu einem zeitgeschichtlichen Roman? Ich frage aber dagegen, woher entnahm Göthe ihn für Wilhelm Meister? — Versteht mich recht. Um alles in der Welt keinen Wilhelm wieder. Der ist abgethan, der ist Göthe's und seiner Zeit. Was und wer ist *euer*?"[53] Yet, he muses, the present time hardly seems to permit poetic feelings to extend beyond adolescence.

He then attempts to tell how he would go about writing his novel *Johannes Küchlein*, of which the Helgoland vignette is a part, and the incongruence of these remarks with the special character of the fragment itself is most striking. The hero, Wienbarg says, is to be a high-minded theology student who comes to grief "in dem Norddeutschland, wie es ist."[54] The lack of external action would be made up for by psychological penetration. The confusion here is evident, and in the end he seems uncertain whether he will ever do it and, in a somewhat silly way, shifts the responsibility, as it were, onto the Muse: "Und wann wirst du deinen Vorsatz ausführen? Wenn die unsichtbare Hand, die mir die Feder leitet, Erlaubniß dazu ertheilt."[55] Of course, this permission never came. The case, however, is paradigmatic for the way in which the logic of imaginative literature can carry the writer away from his apparent theoretical views.

The remaining item of interest in the *Wanderungen* is "Die Zwillinge," which is the most singular and unconventional piece Wienbarg ever wrote. The twins in question are "Wollust und Grausamkeit," and the piece begins by talking about the destructiveness of children. This beginning sets the iconoclastic tone of the whole. Romanticism, as is well known, made much of childlikeness and of childhood as a lost paradise of innocent sensibility, and it is probably connected with this myth that there is hardly a German writer between Karl Philipp Moritz and Gottfried Keller who can portray children with much verisimilitude. But Wienbarg is not only undertaking to show that lust and cruelty are natural characteristics of children; he is attempting to suggest that they may be virtues, whereby he makes some peculiar and interesting comparisons: "Die Sentimentalität ist bekanntlich keine Kinderkrankheit. Kinder leben, wie antike Dichter, in einer objektiven Welt. Jedes kräftige, lebhafte, geistreiche Kind ist ein kleiner Pantheist, ein kleiner Wolfgang Göthe, der nach Herders zürnendem Vorwurf

20

ewig ein Kind bleibt."[56] It is amusing to see some German cultural obsessions here being turned on their ear. It is also apparent that some of the barbaric quality of Wienbarg's activism is coming to the surface. He goes on to say that children are cruel and demonic. Adults are naturally opposed to these qualities, but it is a lie that adults are more humane: "Ich habe oft darüber nachgedacht, ob es nicht besser, tausendmal besser wäre, die Menschen hätten gar kein Gewissen, als ein so stümperhaftes, invalides, bürgerliches, schwächlich sentimentales."[57] The repressive conscience generates lewdness, malice, sneaky and cowardly sins, and viciousness; far better would be heroic vice.

In this controversial mood, the essay then takes an unexpected turn — Wienbarg begins to talk about the lack of feeling in God and His ironic pleasure at the tragedy of existence. "In ächter Tyrannen-laune schuf er die Welt, um sich an dem tragischen Gaukelspiel des ringenden flüchtigen Daseins ironisch zu weiden. Er zündete die Brautfackeln an, lud die Gäste ein und ließ die Bluthochzeit be-ginnen, die niemals aufhört. Er selber lächelt vom hohen sichern Balkon der Unsterblichkeit göttlich ruhig in die weite ewige Bartolo-mäusnacht hinaus."[58] How wretched it is for people to pray and sacrifice to such a God! "Sie schmeicheln dem Tyrannen in der letzten Lebensminute, die sie auf ewig seiner Willkühr entzieht. Sie bitten ihn um Verzeihung, daß sie sterben müssen, denn sie bitten ihn um Nachsicht mit ihrer Sünde und Gebrechlichkeit."[59] Wienbarg then launches into an extraordinary passage on the absurdity of immortality. But, in the course of it, he suddenly jumps the track of his argument. He had seemingly been talking about the way in which God rules the world, but now it is apparent that this is a God made by man, and Wienbarg chooses to make himself a better one. The tone softens somewhat, and the remainder of the argument is not pertinent to the subject at hand.

This curious essay invites a number of observations. For one thing, its blasphemies and apparent praise of amorality are much more like the image of Young Germany that caused the authorities to respond so immoderately than the usual tone and subjects taken by Wienbarg or any of the others. It is therefore to be regarded as an extreme example of Young German intellectual rebelliousness and not as typical. Secondly, while Saint-Simonian materials have been woven into the essay, in its radicalism it goes beyond those impulses and evinces a spirit more daring and modern than one expects to find even in Wienbarg. Thirdly, it is here that the comparison that has several times been made between Wienbarg and Nietzsche is at its most plausible.[60] This comparison has been denounced by Walter Dietze[61] and indeed should not be pressed too hard, but the evident effort here to send a rhetorical shock wave through bourgeois moral complacency and even to undertake in a cursory way a kind of revaluation of values does remind one irresistibly of Nietzsche. But the writer one really should think of here is Georg Büchner. Hovering over all the social criticism in Büchner's works is a deep and radical mistrust of the moral order of the cosmos. I know of no other place in the Young German literature where the unique tone of Büchner seems to have so clear a counterpart as in "Die Zwillinge." That Wienbarg occasionally had a vision of a literature that would do justice to the merciless and even bleak radicalism of much of this essay appears in the Helgoland fragment, as well as in *Zur neuesten Literatur*, where he rejects Tieck's worn-out irony and humor, and says that he prefers annihilation, madness, pain, and degradation to it.[62] All these things are flickers and impulses; they are not sufficiently developed in Wienbarg to be called programmatic. But they are further evidence of a potential for new directions in literature.

It is clear that Young Germany contains a variety of imperfectly realized impulses. Among these are some tending to realism, in terms of a more immediate representation of experience and perception, and of a desentimentalization, tending to a harsher literature with deeper bite, like Büchner's. I think it somewhat misleading to speak, as sometimes is done, of Young German *Frührealismus*. Realism in Young Germany is, for the most part, an unachieved purpose, and, in talking about Young German novels, our attention will be drawn to those problems and dilemmas that blocked the realistic vision. It is true that the Young Germans, as Friedrich Sengle has pointed out, were to a large extent caught in an irrationalist and anti-empirical tradition. But Sengle goes too far in denying any realistic character to their enterprise.[63] In view of the testimony of the Young Germans themselves, and in respect of a conviction that realism was the appropriate mode at that time for a European literature of any significance, it will not be out of place to use realistic principles evaluatively, both in pointing out the weaknesses of the novels and in assessing strengths where they are to be found. I mention this, and have gone into it at some length, not because the issue of realism is a consistent topic in the following essays, but because interpreters of literature are being confronted these days with demands that they confess their predilections and evaluative principles rather than pretend to scientific objectivity. The foregoing discussion will give the reader some idea of how my evaluations are likely to be made.

Another of my personal predilections, I might as well confess, is a visceral hatred of censorship in all forms, and it is this that prompts me to raise the question of the relationship of the censorship crisis to the fate of Young Germany and the course taken by German literature generally. That Young Germany was a failure in every conceivable respect, no one will deny. Hardly had the writers made a modest move toward bringing themselves together into a genuine literary group than they were flung in all directions and set at odds with one another. Not a single Young German book has maintained itself in the literary canon; their works are read almost exclusively by students of the period. None of the hopes they invested in a new and vital relationship between literature and life were realized; in fact, none of their hopes of any kind were realized, not even their most elementary ideas on politics. Wienbarg preached to deaf ears of his Norwegian constitutional model; and Walter Boehlich has remarked of Gutzkow's plea for universal suffrage in the wake of the 1848 revolution that it took no less than seventy and one-half years for this plain imperative to be realized.[64] The writers themselves were altered by the Young German experience; while Wienbarg, for a time practically an outlaw, drifted obscurely into alcoholism and eccentricity, the others, with greater or lesser reluctance, accommodated themselves to the facts of life and, excepting some of the more remarkable achievements of Gutzkow, faded into the monochrome of nineteenth-century German literary life. Their realistic impulses turned to triteness, their idealism to resignation.

Four explanations for this failure have been offered. One is that the Young German enterprise was, by its very nature, doomed, insofar as the writers attempted to put literature at the service of the issues of the day, thereby making it impossible for them to create works that would survive those issues. A second is that they lacked the literary vocation in the first place, that they were not gifted enough and their brief prominence on the literary scene is due to a more or less accidental constellation of circumstances. A third is that German society was not yet sufficiently advanced to generate and support a modern literary movement; its parochial and splintered character could only yield highly individualized authors working contemplatively on small forms in various corners of the nation. A fourth is that it was government repression that destroyed the potential of the movement. The first of these explanations has little to recommend it; it is grounded in presuppositions concerning the nature of literature that are untenable, nor is it adequate to the Young Germans' self-understanding. They often did speak of writing books only for the moment and in the service of the imperatives of the times, but some of this is bravado; every one of them would have liked to have written a good and enduring book. Günter Bliemel has said fairly that the question of aesthetic evaluation of the works is justified, "weil hinter der Sehnsucht nach idealen Gesellschaftszuständen sich die Sehnsucht nach einer großen Dichtkunst verbirgt."[65] The second explanation has more plausibility. The flame of genius that we cannot fail to detect in Georg Büchner is certainly absent from these men, although it flickers fitfully in Gutzkow from time to time. Neither Wienbarg nor Kühne had any likelihood of becoming good creative writers; they were what Houben called them all, "verdorbene Privatdozenten,"[66] as was Mundt basically, although he was a better writer than either of them. Laube, although he wrote the best novel of the lot, as we shall see, found his true métier as a theater director. But judgment of this kind is difficult and perhaps futile, so great were the obstacles of their environment, intellectual and otherwise. This is why the third explanation has gained ground in recent times: a nation so backward socially and politically could not hope to produce a socially and politically relevant literature of European standards. The question remains whether the censorship, being a concentrated symptom of that backwardness, did not itself exacerbate the situation further and do serious damage to the potential of German literature.

The origins of scholarship on Young Germany are in the late Wilhelminian period, and in retrospect it is clear that the pursuit of this topic was a phenomenon of liberal academic opposition; it is roughly contemporaneous with the first thriving period of Heine scholarship and doubtless should be seen as an effort on the part of scholars to recover the oppositional and progressive literary heritage. At the end of the nineteenth century there was a series of battles in Germany about intellectual and artistic freedom; the attempts to suppress Hauptmann's *Die Weber* and Frank Wedekind's troubles with the law are only among the most outstanding examples. The censorship issue consequently loomed large for liberal scholars, whose work was climaxed by the publication in 1924 and 1928 of the two volumes of Houben's *Verbotene Literatur von der klassischen Zeit bis zur Gegenwart*, a staggering encyclopedia of repression, authoritarianism, mean-mindedness, and stupidity that ought to be required reading for all who work in the field of German literature. In more recent times there has been a rebellion against this approach to the topic; it has been felt that the focus on the censorship issue resulted in the practice of bringing more and more archival material to light without adding to our comprehension. "Damit," complains Burkhardt, "verlagerte sich das Schwergewicht der Diskussion in einem kaum vertretbaren Maße vom eigentlich Literaturgeschichtlichen ins Historisch-Politische. Der Untersuchung der Zensurfrage und des Bundestagsbeschlusses von 1835 wurde ein Raum zugemessen, der diesen bei aller Bedeutsamkeit objektiv nicht zukommt. Der Versuch, die 1835 Gebannten weißzuwaschen, ging wiederum nicht ohne Verzerrungen bei der Beurteilung der Gegner des Jungen Deutschlands ab."[67] It has been objected, first, that the concentration upon the government repression has led to a misinterpretation of Young Germany as a political movement; and, second, that the censorship was more a comedy of errors than anything else: the ban of 1835 was found by Prussia's own bureaucracy to be illegal and had to be moderated; the books continued to be published, due in large part to the infinite resourcefulness of Julius Campe in Hamburg; the actual sufferings endured by the writers were not all that great; and, excepting Wienbarg, they all came out of it in one piece, properly married and at length settled in conventional and reasonably successful lives.

The first of these objections is due to the replacement of one error by another. It is true that Young Germany was not a political movement, as some of the authorities seem at first to have thought, and the political views of the Young Germans themselves were vague, imperceptive, and not infrequently quite regressive; it is easy

25

to make fun of them, as Marxist critics often do. For reasons of conviction as well as tactics the writers frequently disclaimed any political purpose to their publications. But this is to take politics in the narrow sense of constitutional systems, rights, and party allegiances; in the larger sense of politics as the mode by which society is governed, Young Germany was a threat because these writers were endeavoring to make modern ideas more accessible to all classes of readers, in the phrase of the notorious decree of 1835 itself.[68] The key to all the censorship troubles from the Carlsbad Decrees of 1819 on is the governments' determination to inhibit the spread of new and anti-traditional ideas. Metternich, to whom we may grant some understanding of politics, said that the ban of 1835 was necessary to preserve the political structure of the state.[69] The allergy of the authorities to modern thought and even to literacy itself was made plain enough after the defeat of the revolution of 1848, when the Prussian government finally reduced the curriculum in the *Volksschule* to a little arithmetic and enough reading to understand the Bible, banned even the classic authors, put the schools under the authority of the clergy, and moved the teachers' seminaries into villages in order to protect the future teachers from the influence of the "verpestetes Zeitalter."[70]

The second objection comes, I suspect, from a tendency to measure the conditions of those times against the more efficient totalitarianism of the twentieth century. It is true that the technological inefficiency of the police and the inconsistencies and jealousies among the various petty states made the imposition of complete totalitarian control impossible. The Young Germans continued to publish, after a fashion, throughout the troubles, and in the long run they did not suffer real atrocities. But the situation has to be looked at with their eyes. Laube was terrified by his incarceration in 1834, and with good reason; and, although Gutzkow's tougher character was less impressed by his jailing in 1835, the whole sequence of events surrounding his trial and conviction aroused in him a hopelessness about his aspirations and ideals. How can one say that such things are without consequence in literary life? Contemporary observers certainly thought they were; Varnhagen, whose literary connections were vast and varied, wrote to Prince Pückler-Muskau on 26 May 1836: "Die jämmerliche Kreuzfahrt gegen die junge Litteratur ist zwar in sich selber verunglückt, zersprengt und zerfallen, die Nach-wirkung dauert aber unselig fort; und das ganze Gebiet der Litteratur ist wie versenkt und verbittert, der böse Heerrauch zieht über das weite Land."[71] Ulla Otto in her recent study of literary censorship as a sociological problem has argued that censorship can have no long-term effect: "Es ist zumindest kein einziger Fall bekannt, in dem sich ein Buch durch zensorische Maßnahmen völlig und auf die Dauer hätte unterdrücken lassen."[72] Who knows? What of books that were not written at all, writers who did not emerge? She goes on: "Erst wenn die in den Büchern formulierten Ideen ihre soziale Wirkung verloren hatten, verblaßt und vergessen waren, pflegten Bücher erfahrungsgemäß tatsächlich zu verschwinden."[73] As applicable as this may seem to the Young German case, it is simply not sensible if one sees literary history as a sequence, a tradition continually regenerating itself; books and writers that are lost at the time of their relevance, no matter what their long-term stature, must be a wound in the body of literature.

The fact that the Young German writers continued to publish is not proof that the censorship was without consequence. Consider the subsequent career of Gutzkow. In 1837, he was obliged to publish a novel, *Die Zeitgenossen*, under Bulwer-Lytton's name to fool the censor. His comic novel of 1838, *Blasedow und seine Söhne*, was banned. His book of essays entitled *Götter, Helden, Don-Quixote* (1839) was banned. His play *Richard Savage* was banned in Vienna in 1840 because it suggested that it was possible for a noble lady to have had an illegitimate son. In 1841 his publisher Campe was shut down for half a year. In 1843 he was obliged, despite much twisting and turning, to submit to a loyalty oath. In 1844 his comedy *Zopf und Schwert* was banned from the Berlin stage on Tieck's advice. In 1845 all of Gutzkow's plays were banned from the Burgtheater and he himself was forbidden to set foot on Austrian soil because of official displeasure at an essay entitled *Wiener Eindrücke*. In 1846, his greatest single playwriting success, the tragedy *Uriel Acosta*, was banned after its first performance and allowed only after he had revised it to weaken the religious allusions. A play entitled *Die Diakonissin* was banned in Dresden in 1852 and had to be withdrawn and turned into a novel. In 1855 a comedy entitled *Lenz und Söhne* was banned in Dresden because it suggested a parvenu merchant could be appointed to the upper house of the legislature. So it went. Most of these works are probably

27

of small value. Undoubtedly most of them survived the prohibitions and a few may have even benefited from the "banned in Boston" effect. But is one to believe that such experiences were without consequences in a literary career? After all, these works were all written in the hope and expectation that they *might* pass the censor, which in itself cannot be without effect upon literary creativity. Perhaps the passion of Houben on the subject of censorship was overwrought, but it is wrong to bagatellize the matter, and it is wrong to survey nineteenth-century literature without considering these conditions.

The foregoing introduction is intended to indicate the spirit in which I approach the Young German novels. I believe there are reasons for talking about Young Germany in the narrow sense, that there is a style of intense urgency characteristic of Young German writing and by which it is identifiable. The writing of fiction, no matter how much pervaded by didactic and hortatory purposes, liberates the imagination and allows us to see the Young German dilemmas in their most profound and desperate form. While concentration upon the novels lacks some of the virtues of more comprehensive studies of the period, it may obviate some of the amorphousness that is characteristic of the whole Young German corpus and that affects all the comprehensive studies in some degree, despite the great feats of organization and analysis that their authors have performed; I also hope that, by focusing on the novel texts, certain misconceptions that sometimes adhere to less detailed discussions of them can be relieved. There will be no pretense that the novels are structures that can be dealt with by aesthetic criteria of interpretation; on the other hand, I shall not treat them as expository writing in a fictional form, but rather as utterances that involve thought and emotion, argument and instinct in a way that sometimes probes more deeply and deviates from the authors' stated purposes. At the same time, judgments will be made on principles of cohesion and on the adequacy of the various strategies to reproduce reality, because these desiderata are found among the admittedly complex and sometimes inchoate theoretical assertions of the Young Germans themselves and were, I believe, the impulses most suitable to their ultimate goals and their place in literature. Immermann is included by way of contrast and comparison, as a writer coming from a different set of ideological purposes and yet finally coming close to the Young German goals and surpassing the Young German achievements in important respects. Only in the case of Mundt did it seem necessary to speak extensively about his non-literary writings; in the other essays I endeavor to concentrate on the novel texts. The familiar themes of Young German scholarship — the relationship of literature to life and its prophetic mission, the emancipation of women, religious liberalism and Saint-Simonism, and the critique of the literary past — are less central here than the effort to capture the pattern and sense of specific Young German writings.

Finally, the studies have been written out of an attitude that is closer to that of Houben and his generation than that of the more negative critics like Magill or some of the recent interpreters. There is enough silliness, self-indulgence, pretentious confusion, and plain bad writing among the Young Germans to justify anyone's impatience with the whole phenomenon. But they were engaged in an effort to turn the direction of German literature, and for a short, chaotic time they invested a great deal of energy and not a little talent in this effort. They failed, and their failure marks the departure of German literature from the European scene for decades; therefore some attention to their unrealized potential as well as to their achievements seems only fair. The Young German crisis is important and instructive for the fate of German literature and the fate of Germany.

II.   KARL GUTZKOW: *WALLY, DIE ZWEIFLERIN*

The Prussian Postmaster General Friedrich von Nagler, whose occupation it was to open other people's mail, once noted down, after some experience with Karl Gutzkow's correspondence: "Dieser Mensch ist nicht gewöhnlich."[1] Students of the Young German period are bound to agree; Gutzkow clearly possessed the most powerful and resourceful mind of them all, as well as the most rugged character, which carried him through a long and stormy literary life with pugnacious persistence. He labored tirelessly at the literary calling and thought hard about it; he shook the governments of Germany with a novel written in three weeks; and he wrote a string of successful plays, including some of the better comedies in German literature, and a massive experimental novel. It is significant that he is the only Young German who has been singled out for a comprehensive study.[2] For a fleeting moment at mid-century he probably was the leading writer of Germany, only to be promptly overshadowed by the novelists Gustav Freytag and Friedrich Spielhagen and by Hebbel in the drama. He never truly broke through to the first rank of writers. The failures and disappointments of his career are of almost tragic dimensions. E. M. Butler wrote of him: "that a man should undergo all the worst fortunes of the unknown great; that he should imagine himself one of them, know their dark despairs and their spiritual isolation; that he should be their blood-brother in sorrow, yet not their fellow in joy; and akiń to them by temperament should not rank with them by achievement, this is a refinement of cruelty against which one's sense of justice rebels."[3]

Gutzkow should probably be elevated to a more honorable place in the history of literature than he has heretofore occupied. J. Dresch thought him a more powerful social novelist than Freytag, Spielhagen, or even Fontane, though less read than any of these.[4]

Gutzkow's enormous "Roman des Nebeneinander," *Die Ritter vom Geiste* (1850/51) is the most remarkable German experiment in the novel form between Goethe and Fontane and deserves more scholarly attention than it has received. Of his numerous plays, four seem to me at least as readable as many other works in the traditional canon. They are the tragedy *Uriel Acosta* (1846), Gutzkow's greatest stage success, and three comedies of unexpected lightness of touch: *Zopf und Schwert* (1844), a cheerful spoof of court life at the time of Frederick William I; *Das Urbild des Tartüffe* (1845), a literary comedy in the best sense, in which Gutzkow transformed his experiences with *Wally, die Zweiflerin* into a portrait of Molière's troubles with the pompous authorities of his time — the only German comedy I know of that has anything of Molière's spirit; and *Der Königsleutnant* (1849), a witty portrait of Goethe as a teenager that was written for the centennial of his birth and ran into a wall of humorlessness. A comparison of *Der Königsleutnant* with Heinrich Laube's more conventional portrayal of the young Schiller, *Die Karlsschüler* (1846), plainly shows the difference of imagination and *esprit* in the two men.

That Gutzkow never achieved the reputation he potentially deserved is due partly to the Young German crisis: not only because he was forever after type-cast in the victorious ideology as an enemy of the existing order, an unpatriotic rascal, an immoralist, or a degrader of literature to mundane purposes, but also because the brouhaha of 1835 derailed his literary development at a crucial point and obliged him to wrestle for years with a mass of recalcitrant difficulties. But some of the reason lies in Gutzkow himself and in the deficiencies that must be measured against his virtues. First of all, even the most sympathetic observer is frightened off by his incredible productivity, a curse that lies upon the whole Young German generation but upon Gutzkow most heavily of all. I cannot imagine that anyone who ever lived has read his complete works, not even the indefatigable Houben, who remarked: "Wer einen Überblick über seine Thätigkeit hat, kann ihn sich nicht anders als am Schreibtisch stehend und mit hastender Hand die Feder führend vorstellen. Er hat in einem 67jährigen Leben mehr geschrieben als Goethe."[5] This obsessive need to write as much as possible had a catastrophic effect upon his style, which seemed to worsen in the Young German period; I agree with Dobert, who observed that the style of *Maha Guru*, written just before the Young German situation began to take shape, is more refined than that of the later writings, from which Dobert quotes some awful grammatical and syntactical howlers.[6] Gutzkow was aware of his problem and was troubled by it; he wrote in 1836:

> Ich besitze noch immer nicht jenen Abandon des Styls, der die Lectüre meiner Bücher zu einer Erholung machte.... Der Pegasus der Literatur von 1830 lernt jetzt erst Manège reiten.
>
> Das Fatale meiner Schreibart ist ihre Unruhe. Ich scheine oft das Widersinnigste in einander zu mischen, und fehlte doch nur darin, daß ich die Uebergänge zu schwach andeutete.[7]

And, although this semi-apology occurs in one of his relatively lucid and pleasantly written essays, he confesses: "Bei meiner Revision dieses Buches empfand ich recht lebhaft die Betrübniß, daß sich in ihm wieder so viel Verhaue, Verhacke und Gedanken-Anacoluthe finden, und daß ich mich von der Vorstellung nicht losmachen konnte, als wären Bücher, die man schreibt, nur Beschäftigungen mit uns selbst."[8]

"Verhaue, Verhacke und Gedanken-Anacoluthe" is an even more exact description of Gutzkow's style than René Wellek's "fuzzy, flabby, diffuse."[9] Both formulations suggest that behind the problem of style there is one of clarity of thought. Walter Hof has asserted in an exceptionally biting phrase that the expression in *Wally, die Zweiflerin* "krankt, wie Gutzkows Gedanken meist, an seiner miserablen Formulierung, die auf einem seltsam schleimigen Denken beruht."[10] Cruel as this remark is, it is true that his writing can often be quite weird, so that attempting to extract its plain meaning can be difficult and establishing a consistent position in his writings as a whole exceptionally challenging, for his attitudes were extremely mercurial, sometimes necessarily opportunistic, and occasionally rather unprincipled. Though he acquired a grotesque reputation as one of the most dangerous radicals of his time and often seemed to be propagating advanced positions, as early as the beginning of 1835 his statements are interspersed with remarks that show him fleeing simultaneously into the autonomous realm of art. He wrote to Gustav Schlesier: "Meine Narrenbriefe wurden doch geboren in einer aufgeregten Zeit, wo man überall hörte *Qui vit?* u seine Parole sagen mußte: aber später schickt' es sich doch, einzulenken, in die Form, in die Einheit, in die Kunst."[11] To a publisher he wrote about the same time that the writer should not keep concerning himself with the issues of his time, for such literary concern means a great deal less than real deeds; literature is not action, but "ich glaube, daß die Schriftsteller die Zeit nicht zusammenfassen u über sie räsonniren sollen, sondern sie vereinzeln u ihre Eindrücke, als unvergänglich in die Kunst über tragen."[12] This is an example of a typical confused train of thought that arises directly out of the Young German dilemmas. Yet he had the nerve to say of himself that he was, unlike the others, "kein Confusionär."[13]

The abstraction and frequent incomprehensibility of his writings made a bad impression on the reading public; as early as 1831 a reviewer remarked of the first fascicle of his periodical *Forum der Journal-Literatur*:

> Es wird dahin kommen, dass Jeder, der vor dem grösseren Publikum auftreten will, und sich der Schulsprache nicht enthalten, sondern von der "Emanation des Objects aus dem Subject" [the title of Gutzkow's first article in the periodical] und dergleichen schönen Dingen reden will, unfehlbar ausgepocht werden wird. Es muss dahin kommen. Gebildete Geschäftsmänner, und gebildete Frauen, haben aufgehört, von dem heillosen Abracadabra etwas Gutes zu erwarten. Wer sich nicht so auszudrücken weiss, dass man ihn verstehen kann, ohne ein philosophisches Wörterbuch nachzuschlagen, der muss es lernen, oder darauf verzichten, von den Gebildeten gehört zu werden.[14]

This criticism is of some interest because it indicates what the sociological audience of a literature striving to be modern and progressive should have been.

Gutzkow is in some respects the most courageous of the Young Germans; he fought hard to avoid co-optation and submission. When confronted with the loyalty oath that was required in 1842 to free the Young Germans from the special censorship that had been imposed on them in the wake of the ban of 1835, he attempted to protect his integrity by evasiveness and guile. For a long time he refused to sign it altogether. Then he talked the officials into releasing him without a specific promise on his part, but the king intervened. In May, 1843, he asserted vaguely that he had switched to the track of the existing order, but refused to go any farther.

33

Then he produced a carefully convoluted promise to support the existing order "wo die Heiligkeit des Bestehenden mit den Resultaten eigenen Nachdenkens zusammenfällt,"[15] a formulation that, of course, committed him to nothing. On the basis of this empty formula, the authorities, evidently weary of the whole business, lifted the restrictions on him in July, 1843. Frederick William IV attempted to countermand the order, but was unable to do so because it had already been made public. Thus Gutzkow, with his characteristic tenacity, was the only Young German to defeat the loyalty oath (Wienbarg never signed anything, but he had disappeared from the literary scene; Heine was not given the opportunity to release himself by this means).

Yet Gutzkow is also, to my knowledge, the only Young German to have actually written a *defense* of censorship. It appeared in a review of a reactionary book on the press law, which he included in his essay collection of 1838, *Götter, Helden, Don-Quixote*. Here he says that he does not demand "eine zur Unzeit geforderte Preßfreiheit."[16] He continues: "Wenn man nicht annehmen will, daß sich alle gesellschaftliche und politische Ordnung auflöse, so kann die Presse nie in dem Grade unabhängig werden, daß der Staat sie nicht controlire, richte, bestrafe."[17] Gutzkow supports this view by extensive reference to the Hegelian principle that the state is "die vollkommenste Blüthe der Humanität."[18] He is, in fact, arguing against the authoritarian position of the book under review and offers his own draft of what he considers a moderate and reasonable press law: "Preßfreiheit ist der Normalzustand der Literatur; Censur ist eine Ausnahme"[19] — a curious remark by one who at that very time was himself still an "Ausnahme," being subject to the special censorship devised for the Young Germans. While no prince may have the right to abolish censorship, it must be flexible, reticent, and speedy, and, of course, the censors should be literati themselves. They also must have "Scheu vor dem heiligen Autorrechte,"[20] as though justice depended upon the good will of bureaucrats rather than upon constitutional guarantees. This strange and shameful essay is a good example of what has caused those for whom "liberalism" is a pejorative category to present Young Germany as a chain of opportunistic betrayals of the progressive cause. One can easily imagine what Gutzkow's admired model Ludwig Börne would have made of this waffling.

34

As is well known, Gutzkow became insane towards the end of his life. A certain unstable eccentricity of mind and character is evident in him, I believe, from the beginning. There are times when our failure to understand him is not due solely to the peculiar opacity and illogic of his manner of writing; he was himself so unstable, hagridden, and pugnacious that there is reason to believe that his powerful mind was somewhat out of balance. His exceptional belligerence, which was much complained of in his time and which is evident to anyone who has read much of his criticism and correspondence, may be due in part to the social disabilities he had to overcome in order to rise from unlovely proletarian beginnings as the son of a horse trainer in the stables of the Berlin court to a respected and sometimes feared member of the bourgeois intelligentsia. Doubtless the melancholy and sometimes violent environment of his youth had something to do with the foundations of his character, as the tenacity and single-mindedness required by his upward fight had something to do with the formation of it. But we should not put too much stress on the class background. Laube, the son of a poor stonemason, from an environment wholly devoid of cultural inspiration, turned out to be a notably sane and amiable human being. Gutzkow was one of those people one sometimes encounters who are incapable of grasping the distinction between frankness and rudeness. He made a virtue out of the latter; he wrote to Varnhagen on 7 October 1835: "Man sagt, gewissermaßen sey ich von einem angeborenen Instinkt der Aufrichtigkeit so durchdrungen, daß ich Alles ausspreche, was mir vom Hirn auf die Zunge gleitet. Ich freue mich auf dieser Charakteristik; eben sie drückt mein ganzes Wesen aus und macht meinen Stolz."[21]

His fierce independence was, to be sure, a virtue; even in his courting of Wolfgang Menzel in the first fascicle of the *Forum der Journal-Literatur* he stressed to the "pope of literature" "dass ich nicht blos Menzels Anhängsel sein möchte, sondern zugleich Ich selbst."[22] But he carried his individualism to the point where he wilfully destroyed any possibility of literary community. He wrote to Alexander Jung on 7 July 1838:

> Ich muß meine eigenthümliche Stellung in der Literatur, wenn sie irgendwie vorhanden ist, auf das Entscheidenste abgränzen u mir laue Freunde [the other Young Germans] lieber in Gegner ver-

wandeln, als daß ich mich kümmerlich von ihrer matten Toleranz nähre. Dazu kömmt, dß ich die heilige Ueberzeugung habe, weder Mundt noch Kühne vermögen etwas Besonderes u Merkwürdiges zu leisten; wozu sollt' ich mich auf ein Kinderstühlchen setzen lassen? Eine Gemeinschaftlichkeit der *Sache* erkenn ich nicht an in einer Zeit, wo ich nur im schaffenden Talente Heil für die Literatur erblicke; es ist recht gut, dß es dahin gekommen ist.[23]

His denunciatory propensities inhibited the judiciousness of his critical perception, damaged his influence by making him the most generally disliked figure in the literary world, and contributed to the dissolution of Young Germany. Indeed, the very character of his first publishing venture, the negative criticism of all other contemporary periodicals, is characteristic of his strategy in life. His poison pen got so much on the nerves of Heine and Laube that in 1839 they conspired for a while to strike back with "Gutzkowyaden."[24] Yet he was easily hurt and sometimes sorely lacking in self-criticism. Mundt's impression upon first meeting him in the autumn of 1835 was of a man suffering from emotional distress: "Ich halte ihn trotz der Kälte, Ruhe und Besonnenheit, die sich in seinem Wesen ausdrückt, für sehr unglücklich."[25] Gutzkow was at this time smarting from a broken engagement, for which he took revenge in public print, but his grumpiness did not abate much over the years and continually tended to flame into ferocity. When one combines these character traits with the recurring weirdness of his argumentive tactics and the curious contrast between the violence of his opinions and their instability, one concludes that Gutzkow was rather more disturbed mentally and emotionally than the general confusion of the Young German situation can wholly account for. This may be the reason why, despite his large resources of talent and industry, he failed in his long career to produce a literary work that can be read today with unstinting admiration.

It would, of course be unfair to judge Gutzkow by *Wally, die Zweiflerin,* which is only an embarrassing episode in the context of his whole career. It concerns us here because it was and remained the primordial Young German novel in the consciousness of the public, the authorities, and posterity; it is the only Young German fictional work to have been republished in our generation. Just because it was so hastily conceived and superficially written, it exposes some of the problems of Gutzkow's thinking and imagination. Furthermore, it is entirely in keeping with his character that a book of his should have ignited the explosion that, at the end of 1835, blew the Young German movement apart.

This kind of book presents a methodological challenge to literary scholarship that is not easily solved. No one is likely to be impressed by it as an artistic achievement. There are no literary grounds for attempting to save a novel like this for the canon. Indeed, the book is in some respects so bad that it is oddly striking for that reason. Its plot is roughly as follows: Wally is a young and beautiful noble lady who covers her inner emptiness and uncertainty with fashionable pursuits and coquetry. She falls in a sort of love with Cäsar, of whom it is said that he sees everything immediately and abrades what he sees on his own individuality, and that he has transcended idealism and advanced to skepticism. She agrees, however, for a reason not clear, to marry a repellent Sardinian gentleman named Luigi. Cäsar induces her, in order to prove her undying love for him, to reenact a scene from the *Jüngerer Titurel* in which Sigune shows herself nude to Schionatulander as a mutual pledge of immortal trust and loyalty. This was the scene that purportedly outraged and shook the whole moral and political structure of Germany; one police spy reported to Vienna that even eighty-year-old men were lusting after the book.[26] Wally then accompanies her husband to Paris to live a life of empty frivolity. Here Jeronimo, a brother of Luigi, turns up; he has fallen passionately in love with Wally on the basis of Luigi's descriptions of her in his letters. Jeronimo is a weakling and quite out of his head, while Luigi is an avaricious schemer who is systematically doing his brother out of his inheritance. Reduced to penury and lunatic infatuation, Jeronimo blows out his brains in Wally's sight outside her window, an event that she finds extremely annoying, so that she flees with Cäsar, who has meanwhile materialized in Paris. She is unable to hold him, however, as he drifts away to court a young Jewess; and she begins to keep a diary in which she discusses her religious uncertainties. She appeals to Cäsar for help; he sends an aggressively free-thinking interpretation of the life of Jesus, which so shakes Wally's last foundations that she stabs herself to death.

The vulgarity and triviality of this plot are not to be denied. In the second of the three books, which narrates the events and the catastrophe in Paris, the reader has the feeling from time to time that he is faced with a hack writer of the most uninspired kind. Our judgment on the achievement is not improved by the fact that Gutzkow thought he was creating a female counterpart to Goethe's Werther. The narrative strategy at the very end of the book is a travesty of the end of *Werther*; after setting up a similar pattern of introspective writing interspersed with narrator's comments on the activities of the deceased's last day and her appearance when discovered, the novel ends with the same cool, antiseptically objective, and ironic kind of report with which Goethe describes Werther's death and burial. It seems pretentious of the author to call up such a parallel. A similar pretentiousness appears when Gutzkow attempts to reach for symbolism. The novel begins with Wally riding upon a white horse that, unbeknownst to her, is blind. But then the great nemesis that plagues Gutzkow's writing sets in: a convoluted interpretation of symbol and situation appears that lacks all the concreteness and effortless motivation of inspired symbolic writing; and when he begins to speak of traces of fear in the horsewoman not visible to the ordinary man, but perhaps to the jockey, who knows that the horse is blind, the attentive reader is only befuddled. That Wally does not know that the horse is blind, but is perhaps, nevertheless, fearful; that the jockey, who has no further role in the story, knows the horse is blind and perhaps senses the fearfulness — it all crumbles to the touch.

One reason for this poor writing is, of course, haste, the demon that continuously plagued Gutzkow. So carelessly is the book written that on one occasion he even confuses the names of the two brothers in a conversation (p. 174).[27] It is clear that no critical method that seeks for aesthetic unities or hermeneutic interpretations can be applied to *Wally*, for the level of artistic achievement forbids worthwhile results. Therefore the temptation is strong for the scholar to forget about the book as a novel at all. One may well argue that its form as a novel is merely accidental, that Gutzkow had things to say to the public that he was prevented from expressing in any other way, and that what is at issue for the interpreter is not the aesthetic failings of the book as a work of literature, but its character as a vehicle for issues and ideas. When shifting to this tack, one thinks rather sadly of Lessing, especially when one considers that it was the same religious liberalism of the Reimarus manuscripts that inspired Lessing to *Nathan der Weise* and that Gutzkow found nearly sixty years later was still too hot to be published in a straightforward way and had to be re-formed into a literary work. But *Nathan der Weise* is a great play, organized with professional and dramatic cunning and wit, and it is one of the triumphs of the creative intellect over those who would bind it in orthodoxies and repressive ideologies, whereas no such claims can be made of Gutzkow's literary effort. As Dobert not unfairly says:

> Bei Gutzkow ist nichts zu finden von Lessings ruhiger Sachlichkeit, seiner messerscharf aufgebauten Argumentation, hinter der sich nichtsdestoweniger ein großes Temperament ahnen läßt. Bei Lessing ist jeder Satz durchdacht, und wenn er auch den Leser in die Ecke treibt, so beschämt er ihn nicht. Er bringt ihn auf seine Seite, indem er ihm erlaubt, selbst die notwendigen Schlüsse zu ziehen. Mag der Leser sich ruhig einbilden, auf eigenen Wegen zu dem von Lessing gewünschten Ergebnis gelangt zu sein. Auf das Überzeugen kommt es Lessing an! Gutzkow überredet den Leser, er überrumpelt ihn. Er läßt erst gar keine Bedenken aufkommen, daß der Angesprochene verschiedener Meinung sein könnte. Bespricht Gutzkow ein Buch, einen Essay, ein Drama oder nur ein Gedicht, so scheint er selten fähig zu sein, mit unvorgefaßter Meinung an das Werk zu gehen.[28]

Nor is this all. Just as the artistic stratagems of the novel crumble when fastened upon by the literary interpreter, so does the intellectual message of the book give way when approached as an ideological tract. Everywhere one has a sense of inconsistency, of bumbling, of jejune and stilted thinking.

The question is now whether these alternatives — hermeneutic literary criticism and retrospective ideological criticism — are adequate to assess *Wally*. Perhaps one should not take too lightly the fact that it was this novel that finally set off the explosion of 1835. Houben reported in 1911 that he owned no less than forty contemporary books, not to speak of newspaper articles and the like, about the novel, which suggests that the book did challenge the public at the time.[29] Perhaps it is worthwhile to stay with this poorly conceived and poorly written novel a little longer to try to understand how it was capable of generating so immoderate a response.

If one leaves aside questions of literary quality and of ideological perception and reads it just as a human utterance, one feels first of all the impact of a weird and amorphous intensity. That such a book should ever have been written at all, by anyone, is evidence of a fierce crisis, and the earthquake it set off suggests that the crisis was not the peculiarity of one odd individual. In it, paradoxes and dilemmas, rather than being put into an ironic or humorous perspective or being resolved into dialectical syntheses, are strained desperately to the breaking point, so that the book is more than anything else a cry of pain and anxiety, for all that its intention may have been to set out solutions to problems rather than just problems themselves. It is in the nature of the affair that the question of intent should be particularly opaque and elusive. In his rebuttal of Menzel's attack, Gutzkow wrote that the purpose of the novel was a reform of Christianity and an effort to show the nearness of despair to religion,[30] picking up one element (p. 21) of the conflicting messages of the book. In a diplomatic letter to the Austrian ambassador to the Frankfurt Diet of 25 April 1836, Gutzkow naturally trivializes the active thrust of his writing and remarks: "Meine Schriften sind nicht klug berechnet,... sondern es sind Explosionen eines krankhaften Gemüths."[31] Closer acquaintance with Gutzkow, as I have argued, makes one ready enough to believe in the "krankhaftes Gemüth," but reflection on the circumstances suggests that, in this case, the sickness was related to a general condition. What seems in fact to have happened is that a more or less rationally conceived project ran away from the author under the pressures of personal distress, resentment, and haste in composition, and turned out to be something quite different and more threatening than the author himself may have intended.

Although the *Wally* affair was a political one first and last, Gutzkow was ultimately convicted, essentially, of pornography and blasphemy, and if the novel is to be regarded in terms of the events it set off, the real nature of its sexual and religious challenge requires some attention. The search for the link between these two realms will take us through some considerations on the state of society as it is portrayed in the novel. Much has been written, at the time and since, and more unthinkingly copied, about the Young German theme of "emancipation of the flesh," but as an erotic or sensually liberating novel, *Wally* has some peculiar characteristics, to say the

40

least.[32] In line with my initial concentration upon the way in which the book was perceived, I begin with a few words about the notorious nude scene. Its tastelessness lies partly in the fact that it is offered as an episode in a struggle for naiveté and frankness in human relations, while in truth it is extremely stilted and stylized. The force of a kind of perverse Romanticism is felt in it. The passion of the embrace between Cäsar and the betrothed Wally is shifted into literature, and when Wally at first rejects Cäsar's suggestion that she should appear nude before him, he haughtily disengages himself from all feeling for her on the ground that her petty morality has insulted poesy. Wally herself comes to see that the poetic stands higher than all laws of morality and tradition and thus should not be opposed. All this is really a regressive re-Romanticization, which explicitly argues the cause of human emancipation through art and the imagination (pp. 124-125). The appeal to a model in medieval literature also has its Romantic side. Yet the model is wholly inapposite to the tense and modern tone and atmosphere of the book, and its very incongruity tells us something about what is going on in this post-Romantic age. In the *Jüngerer Titurel*, the bond between the lovers is not only imperishable in the face of all obstacles and of death itself, but in the scene to which Gutzkow alludes, it transcends common morality itself, *not* because in general love is higher than morality, but because *this* love is so chaste and constant that sanctions of any kind are not needed and fall away before it. Nothing of the sort is true, of course, of the relationship between Wally and Cäsar. In *Wally*, the relationship is technically chaste, but certainly not constant, and it is hardly presented as love at all, as we shall see. The Romantic effort to recapture an ideal of purity through the aesthetic realm by an appeal to "poesy" rather than to a high but perhaps attainable human condition that the poesy represents is a forced, hothouse endeavor from the outset. In one of the curious narrative gestures with which Gutzkow suddenly distances himself from his narration,[33] he calls the whole scene "ein Frevel; aber ein Frevel der Unschuld" (p. 131). This may be a defensive sop to the prudish reader, but there is something seriously wrong with the scene, given these characters and this frantic story. It is not without its force, for it projects an image of unencumbered sensual beauty against the background of artificiality and disingenuousness that pervades the whole novel. At the same time, the beauty of the nude Wally is aesthetic, distanced, statuesque, marmorean. As Friedrich Sengle not unfairly says, the scene "scheint geradezu aus dem Kloster zu kommen."[34] And here we come to something that has not been sufficiently considered in the assessment of the novel: that its erotic aspect is so exceptionally chilly.

Although Wally falls in love with Cäsar, then marries another, and finally flees with Cäsar, who stays with her for a time, she remains a virgin throughout — as she makes explicit in her diary (p. 217). Although this may strike the modern reader as a strange way to advocate the "emancipation of the flesh," it is consistent with the tone of the book, which is strangulated and anxiously repressed throughout, and, in the account given of the unconsummated marriage with Luigi, oppressively grotesque. Wally's coquetries are from the beginning noncommittal and joyless; she takes a new admirer every month, obliges him, as she puts it, to buy his way into her favor with a ring, and at the end of the year she flings all of the rings to the poor. Interpersonal relations are being acted out in a ritualistic way without any emotional depth. The first love scene between Wally and Cäsar is quite strangely organized. At first it is indicated that a flow of genuine feeling in Wally is released by love. In the next moment it is said that Cäsar is not overcome by love at all, but by "der Gedanke an eine Humanitätsfrage" (p. 75). This is followed by a plea for freedom from convention and prudery, in fact a statement for free love, but it remains unspoken in Cäsar's thoughts. He does not actually address it to Wally in the words reported, thus intensifying the sense of tentativeness and noncommunication felt throughout the book. Then Gutzkow, in another of his distracting authorial gestures, comments that this form of love is a lie, born of the "Zerrissenheit" of the age, and, with another evasion into the realm of "poesy," compares it unfavorably to the truth of Romeo and Juliet.[35]

It is this kind of strategy that makes the book hard to understand in any logical sense. For one thing, although one can often read that Cäsar is a heightened self-portrait of Gutzkow himself, and although the author seemed to think that Cäsar represented the first citizen of a new realm of political and moral freedom,[36] his character throughout is put in a dubious and unamiable light, and his thinking, as here, is subjected to sharp criticism. One might at first think that this is just a trick to hoodwink the censorious reader while smuggling the radical ideas past him. Such I believe is not the case. The problem lies in another area altogether and is characteristic of Young German writing generally: the moral, social, and psychological ideas that are continuously tested and debated are abstractions without roots in living substance. One example of this among several is the edgy debate between Cäsar and Wally on the true character of courage, which remains a logical exercise in manipulating the categories of the faculty psychology of the eighteenth century, to which the young Schiller was much addicted and the use of which suggests the influence of Schiller as an early formative reading experience of these writers. A really striking and illuminating example of this is found in a letter of Theodor Mundt to Charlotte Stieglitz of 26 October 1834. Mundt has just come across the machine called the psychometer, which determines by magnetism whether one possesses a particular personal quality out of a list of 150, a toy Mundt judges to be "eine unendlich wichtige anthropologische Entdeckung."[37] Similarly, the whole matter of love in *Wally* is divorced from any genuine eros and is constantly deflected into abstractions that are clearly desolate and unfulfilling. Gutzkow is no less a prisoner of this insubstantial intellectualism than the other Young German writers, but to a certain extent he is a more intelligent one, for the chaos of abstractions and reified categories is presented in this book as an endlessly revolving machinery that expresses the despair of these characters and the emptiness of their lives and social surroundings. Such things as the negative comment on Cäsar's theories of free love, or Cäsar's tendency to mount sophistical religious arguments, only to laugh at the result of his own proof, indicate an infinite interchangeability of arguments of this kind, which are free-floating and unable to bridge the painfully felt gap between the consciousness of the characters and real life and substance. What I am suggesting is that Gutzkow, far from having written a homiletic, radical tract disguised as a novel, in fact has written, willy-nilly perhaps, an unresolved, rather desperate account of a kind of alienation.

Thus the pursuit of the erotic aspect of *Wally* leads to the periphery of social problems, and some comments may be made in this place about the attitude toward women in the novel. The exceptional interest of Young Germany in the social situation of women has, of course, been much commented on. It would be hard to argue, however, that Young Germany is a kind of women's liberation movement, despite the great admiration for Rahel Varnhagen as the prototypical German-Jewish bluestocking and the morbid fascination with the suicide of Charlotte Stieglitz. Much of the interest in the emancipation of women, in Laube's case notoriously, is a desire that women might be emancipated from their sexual inhibitions in order to make life more pleasant for men. Although Gutzkow suggests something similar in his novel *Maha Guru*, his case is a little different, for he had been deeply scarred and embittered by the negative outcome of his engagement and brooded about the resources of courage and independence in the female character. He took many occasions to speak condescendingly of women; as early as the *Briefe eines Narren an eine Närrin* he mentions his "Abneigung gegen schreibende Damen," and he asserts bluntly: "Zum Empfangen, nicht zum Schaffen sind die Weiber geboren."[38] At the same time he claims to be the warmest defender of the female sex.[39]

One may well ask whether it was wise of him to write a novel from the perspective of a woman, always a challenging undertaking for a male writer even of exceptional gifts, and it may be that Gutzkow, having been impelled into this experiment partly by personal resentment, for that reason wrote so incoherent and unconvincing a book. Much space in it is given over to Wally's own ruminations on the limitations of women, their cruelty and insensitivity, and one may fairly wonder whether a woman would see these things in the same perspective as the jilted male intellectual. There is one moment in which the cause of emancipation is given expression: when Wally broods about the vegetative unconsciousness in which women are kept und asks herself why women should not be allowed to read *Faust* — by which is meant, why women should not be allowed to become acquainted with the dilemmas and issues of modern life. But even at the point where Gutzkow attempts to put Wally in touch with literary issues of the time, something odd happens. Wally is said to find the late Romantic Swabian poets boring and to prefer the second volume of Heine's *Der Salon* (the essay *Zur Geschichte der Religion und Philosophie in Deutschland*), the reason being that Heine's bonbons make philosophy palatable. Referring to the fact that Heine's book was originally aimed at a French audience, Wally remarks: "Welch gesunkenes Volk müssen die Franzosen sein, daß sie gerad' auf der Stufe in den Wissenschaften stehen, wo in Deutschland die Mädchen" (p. 18). The universal polemicist Gutzkow has got three at one blow: Heine, the French, and the intellectual level of women in Germany! Wally is said to be too frivolous and vain to be interested in general topics; she does not try to be a bluestocking because she is beautiful; Cäsar believes her incapable of speculation. This curious emphasis on the superficiality of the heroine is maintained through most of the book and provides a puzzle for the reader, who does not know quite how to take it, for Wally indeed engages in a great deal of speculation, although at one point she must herself laugh at the shallowness of it (p. 97), making one wonder whether Gutzkow is not himself uncertain about the depth and importance of the issues he is raising. Of Rahel Varnhagen, Wally is made to remark that only men are capable of producing anything, even thoughts (p. 242).

Of course, both Wally's subjective failings and her objective troubles are functions of her social situation. Gutzkow, however, does not manage to penetrate to a social typology, probably because of his generalized bitterness at his former fiancée. In one curious episode of the novel, Cäsar tells some fairly grim anecdotes of local love tragedies. Wally finds them unedifying because they do not speak directly to her own concerns. Perhaps these anecdotes that Cäsar recites are examples of a kind of literature no longer important and are rejected because they are not relevant to the modern reader. One of the stories, of a girl torn between two suitors, a trumpeter and a drummer, does seem to suggest some symbolic potential with regard to the uses of art, for the trumpet is a beautiful instrument that drowns out the cries of the wounded, whereas the drum, perhaps like activist prose and perhaps also in consideration of Heine's activist image of the drum major,[40] is both rhetorical and useful; but the knot is never really tied. In any case, Wally's incapacity to sympathize with the sufferings of other women in these stories is claimed by the author to be an example of the lack of feeling true of all women, so that Gutzkow misses the opportunity to develop a social typology.

Despite the muddle and confusion, it is plain that Wally is in a condition of extreme alienation — from other human beings, from her own social context, from any sort of meaningful life and activity. The special problem of women, which is not very precisely defined, is part of a more general situation. A word may be said parenthetically about the fact that Gutzkow puts his story into an aristocratic milieu. It has often been observed that the bourgeois intelligentsia of this time regarded the aristocracy with a combination of class-conscious resentment and envious admiration; E. K. Bramsted has analyzed this complex throughout the history of the nineteenth-century German novel.[41] Houben had argued earlier that "dies zeigt klassisch das Emporstreben einer ganzen Generation in eine höhere Bildungs- und Lebenssphäre."[42] There is some justification in this, but the reason for the aristocratic milieu in this particular case is of a different order. It has to do with the characteristic lack of realistic skills, or, to put it another way, the will to write a modern bourgeois novel is present, but the substance and techniques that made the great European bourgeois novels possible are not available to German writers at this time. The aristocratic milieu is not due, I think, to any particular predilection on Gutzkow's part for the nobility, nor, as Sengle would have it, to the aristocracy's continued visibility and prominence in the backward German society,[43] but is chosen because aristocrats can be presented has having nothing to do, no genuine, differentiated activity that the author would have to describe in a realistic manner. There is a long history in the German novel, going back at least to Heinse, of this kind of setting being used because the creative imagination is capable only of incarnating problems, dilemmas, and ideas, not concrete settings or characters of the class to which the authors themselves belong (Goethe's *Wilhelm Meisters Lehrjahre* is a partial but important exception in this regard). Thus the aristocratic setting is really a capitulation to the unsolved problems of creating a prose fiction adequate to the modern context. Gutzkow was, or came to be, aware of this. In his polemic of 1855 against the mundane, unpoetic material of Freytag's *Soll und Haben*, he confesses that the German novel of the past had been too remote from the world of work: "Jene Goetheschen Gestalten aber und die meisten von Jacobi, Jean Paul und anderen, die bis auf den heutigen Tag die von jenen aufgestellten Persönlichkeiten variierten, scheinen allerdings nur von der Luft zu leben. Sie sind nichts, tun nichts, sie reflektieren nur und folgen den Eingebungen, die ihnen der Dichter gibt, um irgendeine seiner allgemeinen Wahrheiten zu beweisen."[44] But Gutzkow's own practice shows that this mode was very difficult to escape. Even in 1855 he continued to insist that the novel should describe man "in seiner träumerischen und idealen Neigung" and should focus on his "ewiger

Sonntag," "sein Lieben, sein Gefühl für Freundschaft, seine Religion, sein Geschick,"[45] not on his workaday existence.

This is part of a larger problem that we will confront again when we come to look at Laube. Once having granted it, however, we may leave class considerations aside for the time being and concentrate on the exceptional alienation of the characters within their milieu. From the very beginning there is an explicit stress on the disingenuousness, pretense, and affectation in the actions and even the opinions of the characters. Wally's chilly coquetry is one example; Cäsar's calculation, his laughter and scorn as the last residue of an outgrown idealism, his disdainful Don-Juanism are others. One reason that is given for his attitude is that there is no outlet for his activity (p. 10), a problem characteristic, of course, not of the aristocracy, with its avenues to power, but of the bourgeois intelligentsia with its frustrated, boiling energy. The continued emphasis on the insipidness of social relations is not new in literature, and it is one of the specific *Sturm-und-Drang* elements picked up by Young Germany. But here there is another example of how Gutzkow's wayward intelligence sometimes works a little more deeply. For the characteristic *Sturm-und-Drang* posture, as indeed that of Romantic social criticism, is to confront the ossification and dehumanization of society with vigorous assertiveness and intellectual *esprit de corps*. It does not happen here, however, for both Wally and Cäsar are embedded in society and share its diseases. Furthermore, the mindless round of social life is treated, not as a condition to be opposed and defeated, but rather as a form of narcosis for the feelings of helplessness, pointlessness, and lack of guidance in modern life; Wally attempts not to oppose society or escape from it, but to benumb herself in it. This is a perspective fairly peculiar to Gutzkow and it is a notably modern element in what is otherwise a sometimes regressive novel. Wally tries to evade the dilemmas that are undermining her sanity by a flight to the surface of a fashionable life: "Roth oder blau zum Kleide, das ist die Frage" (p. 107). She willingly joins the society of Paris, "eine fleißige Bundesgenossin des großen Feldzuges gegen Natur, Wahrheit, Tugend und Völkerfreiheit" (pp. 136-137), for she has, as the author remarks, no capacity for philosophy; yet it is claimed that her activity is not harmonious with her inner soul. Is there in her, then, a potential for a reunified

47

soul, repressed only by what neo-Marxists would call "false consciousness"?

To say so would be to do Gutzkow too much credit at this point. He is neither a very self-aware proponent of ideology, nor is he a critic of ideology. Rather, like so many of his contemporaries, he broods over the apparent lack of a sustaining ideology in the modern world. At one point, he has Cäsar make a curious remark on Kleist: "die Furcht vor dem Tode, der Schmerz, nicht wie Brutus, der alte und der junge tödten, nicht wie Cato sterben zu können, die Bitte des Prinzen von Homburg, ihn leben zu lassen — das ist das Tragische unsrer Zeit und ein Gefühl, welches die Anschauungen unsrer Welt von dem Zeitalter der Schicksalsidee so schmerzlich verschieden macht" (p. 89). This observation puts the whole issue of skepticism, programmatically announced in the novel's title, in a particular light. Gutzkow's novel is not an argument for skepticism, although that the authorities thought it was, is in the last analysis the reason he went to jail; rather, it describes a condition of skepticism, a lack of deep-rooted ideal allegiance in the modern world, and it treats some of skepticism's spiritual and intellectual consequences.

Now, for Gutzkow at this moment, the consequences of modern skepticism were most severe and agonizing in the realm of religion; this is, after all, what the book was taken to be about and what, in large measure, it is about. For Gutzkow, the lapsed theologian, the religious problem was first of all a matter of personal history; beyond that, it was at least paradigmatic for the generalized feeling that society had lost its compass and anchor. In Wally herself, the resolution of the religious problem becomes literally a matter of life and death. But it only becomes central for her when the external supports of her life are removed. In her diary she says that all doubts can be withstood if the protective love of a man is available; the withdrawal of Cäsar's love requires her to construct a system of religion, which, of course, she is incapable of doing (pp. 217-218). Here, as elsewhere, the religious problem as such is adulterated with Gutzkow's views about women. As long as Wally's life is at least superficially intact, her forays into skepticism are more in the way of an amusing excitation and do not involve commitment or despair. When she finds a misprint in the Bible, she remarks, "Es ist hübsch, in der Bibel Irrthümer zu entdecken" (p. 19). The Bible lies on her table among a number of Young German books, and, at the sight of this contradiction and at the sound of the church organ, she melts into tears. "Diese Thränen flossen aus dem Weihebecken einer unsichtbaren Kirche. Die Gottheit ist nirgends näher, als wo ein Herz an ihr verzweifelt" (p. 21). Here the theme is set that is developed later in the book, for Wally does not experience any genuine religious despair until Cäsar leaves her for another. Indeed, in conversation with Cäsar, his critique of religion frightens her and she evades it (p. 84). Her rather feeble mental activity is derived from "einem religiösen Tik" (p. 91), and it is said that she had no desire to seek for a midpoint in her thinking, but only wished to find the naive, unreflected religion that would give her an occasional vantage point.

Thus the religious problem does not seem to be grave for Wally, merely a mildly troubled preoccupation. Only when she begins to lose Cäsar to the Jewess Delphine does she come to reflect upon it intensely; she envies Delphine's advantage in having been brought up free of any natural religion, with the result that she is neither bigoted nor *zerrissen* (p. 213). Thus, Delphine's love can be "ganz pflanzenartiger Natur, orientalisch, wie eingeschlossen in das Treibhaus eines Harems" (pp. 213-214). This is one of those passages that make so little sense that they must be charged to Gutzkow's inchoate prejudicess and instincts. However, as Wally continues to brood on the problem, the novel becomes more and more an essay on religion, or, rather, two essays, for Wally becomes entangled in the paradoxes of atheism, while Cäsar sends her a debunking historical discourse on the origins of Christianity.[46] Wally's ruminations contain themes that one finds elsewhere in Young German writing; the poverty and frustration of life, she says, should make us angry with God, which reminds us somewhat of Wienbarg's essay, "Die Zwillinge," in the *Wanderungen durch den Thierkreis* (see above, pp. 20-22), and even more of Thomas Payne's arguments in Büchner's *Dantons Tod*, the manuscript of which Gutzkow had received from Büchner a few months before writing *Wally*. She goes on to lament the possibility of asking questions without answers, which foreshadows lines Heine was to write years later in his last collection of poems:

Also fragen wir beständig,
Bis man uns mit einer Handvoll
Erde endlich stopft die Mäuler —
Aber ist das eine Antwort?[47]

But her head spins from all her speculation about nothingness, her desperate effort to think her way through dilemmas without any hold on a world of reality; it is at this point that Cäsar parodies speculation by arguing religious proofs and then overturning them.

The details of Cäsar's argument need not concern us here; they belong to a context of theological dispute that has long ceased to be of interest. They suggest to me that Gutzkow did not have a very sensitive feel for religious matters, as in the place where Cäsar asserts that the admonition to love one's neighbor as one's self belongs neither to religion nor to philosophy, and that because Jesus failed to say, love your neighbor more than yourself, he showed himself unable to transcend his Jewishness. What is significant about Cäsar's argument is that, for its time, it is unusually aggressive and shocking in manner. To describe Jesus as a confused fellow, as not the greatest, merely the noblest man of history, or to say that his miracles suggest a charlatan, not a prophet, and that the account of them is due to the limited intelligence of the apostles is to go farther than David Friedrich Strauss in his theological mythologizing; it is a radical challenge to the sensibilities of the authorities and the public. Gutzkow was, of course, not alone among the Young Germans in mounting such provocations; two years before, in *Die Poeten*, Laube had allowed his radical Constantin to speak of the Bible with similar disrespect: "Auch les' ich jetzt fleißig in der Bibel; ich will doch mit Vernunft über den Unsinn raisonniren, nach 1800 Jahren noch immer ungestört von einem Buch sich gängeln zu lassen, das unwissende Schüler einem großen Meister nachlallten."[48] But this opinion is just an element in the kaleidoscope of attitudes and arguments in Laube's book, whereas in *Wally* it is in sharp focus. Its effect on Wally is apocalyptic: "Das tragische und der Menschheit würdige Schicksal unsers Planeten wäre, daß er sich selbst anzündete, und alle, die Leben athmen, sich auf den Scheiterhaufen der brennenden Erde würfen" (p. 309). Wally's suicide is a kind of partial fulfillment of this sacrifice, performed out of "Haß gegen den Himmel" (ibid.), an act of despair in a world in which the alienation of men can no longer be compensated for by the shared consolations of faith.

Wally, die Zweiflerin exhibits the characteristic problems of the Young German novel in an extreme form. The gap between intent and result is especially noticeable here. All available evidence suggests that Gutzkow intended to write a modern novel, by which the Young Germans meant one that embodies and transmits the most promising modern ideas. A liberating skepticism in religious matters and emancipation from the confining conventions of society are certainly among them. But the choice of fiction as a vehicle has unforeseen consequences. The characters must act out their thoughts and feelings in some sort of recognizable context, and, although a lack of realistic skills obliges the choice of a flimsy and irrelevant milieu, the logic of fiction forces the characters out of a prescribed role as exemplars of liberated man and into a representation of the painful homelessness that is Gutzkow's most fundamental feeling about his relationship to his environment. At the same time an unresolved elegiac idealism generates, not prescriptive criticism, but despair at a society lacking in focus; it is also largely responsible, I believe, for the curious process by which Gutzkow's alter ego in the story turns out to be an insincere cynic and his female Werther a shallow debutante and something of a ninny. All sorts of private matters are dredged up from Gutzkow's disquiet and intermingled in an imprecise way. This runaway fiction indicates a remarkable disparity between thought and feeling. *Wally* shows that the Young German "ideas," which have been so much written about, are not at all congruent with the human condition and environment as Gutzkow instinctively perceived it. The failure to pursue the logic of fiction whither it was leading is the fatal failing of this, as of many other Young German novels and stories. But as an outcry of pain and bewilderment at the alienation of the individual and the erosion of sustaining values in society, it is a symptomatic event of this turbulent year of 1835.

III. THEODOR MUNDT: A REVALUATION

With Theodor Mundt, wrote E. M. Butler in her best trenchant style, we are "face to face with a perfectly mediocre mind and but a moderate intelligence; a fact which moreover is not counterbalanced by any distinctive gift of temperament"; we hear in him "the voice of the normal man."[1] Reasons of several kinds can be found for holding such a view of Mundt. He shares with Goethe and Heine the misfortune of having a wife of whom the critics have not approved. In 1839, while his life was still quite troubled, he married Klara Müller, who under the pseudonym of Luise Mühlbach wrote more than 250 volumes of irredeemably trivial historical novels. "Both husband and wife," reports Butler, "sank comfortably ever lower in the scale of literature."[2] Houben memorably referred to Luise Mühlbach as "ein Papierdrache von gewaltigen Dimensionen."[3] Mundt's friend Kühne complained that she supported and encouraged her husband in his weaknesses.[4] But one would think that a man, even a writer, may be permitted to choose the wife who best meets his needs, as Goethe and Heine did, without being subjected to this kind of judgment. Mundt himself insisted that Luise Mühlbach was nothing like her books, which she turned out only to give herself something to do, complacently adding, to be sure, that his beloved fiancée was rather too plump.[5]

It is also true that he did not distinguish himself by conspicuous bravery during the Young German troubles. But in saying this, one must also recognize that he felt himself improperly named with the group, especially with Gutzkow, whom he did not admire — a sentiment Gutzkow reciprocated. At no time, as far as I can see, was Mundt ever very far exposed on the most oppositional salient of literature. He opened the first issue of his *Literarischer Zodiacus* in January, 1835, with an essay entitled "Ueber Bewegungspartien in der Literatur," in which he vigorously denounced Heine and Börne in favor of "die kernhaften und positiven Elemente dieser Zeitbewegung, für die *Production* zu retten und im *Kunstwerk* zu organisieren."[6] Jost Hermand has called attention to the anti-Semitic aspect of Mundt's frequent critiques of Heine.[7] For Mundt the crisis was purely a difficulty between himself and the authorities, whose proscription hindered him for several trying years from reaching his career goal: a university instructorship. On 29 April 1835, he stood a few steps and a few minutes away from this goal when the door was literally shut in his face. On that day Mundt was to have given his inaugural lecture at the University of Berlin, but Henrik Steffens, who was rector of the university and was peeved at the treatment Mundt had given him in one of his books, caused the lecture to be cancelled.[8] Further stymied by his inclusion in the December ban on Young Germany, Mundt was not permitted to take those last few steps until 1842. During this time he did what he could to put himself in the odor of sanctity, appealing repeatedly to the Prussian authorities and even, on occasion, to the king. He tried as explicitly as possible to dissociate himself from the Young German movement; he wrote, for example, to his publisher on 20 June 1836: "Sie wissen, daß die Ideengemeinschaft, die man mir mit Gutzkow und A[nderen?] aufgedrungen, eine Ungerechtigkeit gegen mich ist, und in meinen bei Ihnen erschienenen Schriften sich nicht wirklich nachweisen läßt. Um so mehr werden Sie daher voraussetzen, daß ich in meinen neuen Büchern, die ich nur unter eine etwas freiere Censur stellen möchte, diese Freiheit nicht dazu benutzen werde, gegen Moral und Religion anzustoßen..., oder mit der Politik des Tages in Conflict zu treten."[9] The road was not easy, however. Mundt vigorously denounced *Wally, die Zweiflerin* in the *Literarischer Zodiacus*, but the periodical was banned anyway for, in the eyes of the authorities, Gutzkow's atrocious book should not have been mentioned at all.[10] With single-minded persistence, however, Mundt managed to publish a variety of works under the special censorship and, in the spring of 1842, freed himself from it by the required loyalty oath.[11] This is to make a very long story short; Mundt's struggles with the censorship fill 135 pages in Houben's *Verbotene Literatur*; of the victims chronicled in the two volumes, only Fichte and his troubles with the University of Jena in the late 1790's take up more space. If Mundt did not distinguish himself as a hero in these years, it certainly must be the effect of living in such a pressure cooker to encourage mediocrity.

53

Perhaps, however, the impression of mediocrity is reinforced by Mundt's manner of writing. Of all the Young Germans, he has the easiest style and the most fluent pen. If toil, trouble, and effort seem too much in evidence in the writing of Wienbarg or Gutzkow, perhaps they seem too little evident in Mundt's, nor does he have the engaging artlessness of Laube. He is glib and resourceful, insouciant about organization, and tends to garrulousness. The light, seamless parlando of Mundt's prose can weaken the confidence of the reader that anything worth attending to is being said. Indeed, his productivity in the very years of his struggles with the censorship is remarkable. By 1837 he had written a large number of journalistic articles, book reviews, and characterizations; a novel, *Das Duett* (1831), several novellas, a collection of essays entitled *Kritische Wälder* (1833), a sort of novel, *Moderne Lebenswirren* (1834), the memoir *Charlotte Stieglitz, ein Denkmal* (1835); the novel *Madonna* (1835), two volumes of *Charaktere und Situationen* (1837), as well as publishing two periodicals, the *Literarischer Zodiacus* in 1835 and *Dioskuren für Wissenschaft und Kunst* in 1836-37, and making continuous efforts to replace them with publications under new names as they were banned. Hyperproductivity was the curse of all the Young Germans at this time, but Mundt's fluency is such that one imagines he would have written more, not less, under more peaceful circumstances. When one reads around among all these publications, one finds here and there achievements of real distinction. He could, from time to time, write pithy and stimulating essays on literary personalities, and a few of them, such as his remarkable analysis of the letters of Rahel Varnhagen,[12] can fairly be called brilliant. Furthermore, he was really a journalist and novelist by circumstance only. Although he continued to write indifferent novels for the rest of his life, his true métier was to be a university professor and his works of an academic nature turned out to be of some value and interest. A few observations on the two most important of them may help to make Mundt's intellectual position clearer.

The first of these is *Die Kunst der deutschen Prosa*, published in 1837.[13] The problem confronted by Mundt in this book was of no little importance for the literary situation of the time. Despite the refined prose art of the late eighteenth century, despite the achievements of Goethe and Heine, there existed at this time a wholly false categorical distinction between poetry and prose, illustrated by the

54

differing evaluation, which is still maintained in our language usage, given to the adjectives "poetic" and "prosaic." The "poetic" is the artistic, the beautiful, perhaps also the idealistic; the "prosaic" is the pedestrian, the common, often also the materialistic. This distinction was maintained quite strictly by Hegel in his treatment of the novel as a genre.[14] It is self-evident that a generation of writers concerned to involve literature with the broad substance of life and the realities of contemporary society must overcome such prejudices if they are not to lose their self-esteem as artists. Heine, although he was acutely aware of the problem and was plagued by it, never quite got his hands on it. His own turn from poetry to prose often seemed to him a necessity imposed by the conditions of the age rather than a breakthrough to a new dimension of literary art. If one believes that prose is a medium qualitatively inferior to poetry, and is aware at the same time that literature reflects the conditions of society, then one is logically bound to think that an age that demands prose is one of degeneration. Heine was never able wholly to shake off this elegiac attitude, and it is a fundamental weakness in him as a writer that still awaits analysis.[15] Mundt, who was of a more sanguine temperament than Heine, makes an effort in *Die Kunst der deutschen Prosa* to undermine the foundations of the prejudice.

He does so initially by making use of the insights of Herder without accepting all the consequences of his position. Mundt is conscious of the value of Herder's views on the interrelationship between language and national life, and announces that he intends to follow Herder's principle that human reason and human language are identical and simultaneous at their source.[16] We are now in an age that requires the development of a refined prose; Mundt quotes Jakob Grimm: "Die *Poesie* vergeht, und die *Prosa* (nicht die gemeine, sondern die geistige) wird uns angemessener."[17] Mundt is concerned to argue that this is a justified historical change, not a pattern of decay. He adverts to the interpretation placed by the then young science of linguistics upon the fact that the morphology of the Indo-European languages has become progressively simpler and less rich in its variety of forms. It was customary at that time to deplore the alleged loss of variety and regard it as a process of degeneration; Mundt appears to accept this interpretation, but he does not really believe that it has a practical evaluative consequence, for he remarks tersely and intelligently: "es [hat] mit dem grammatischen Paradies ohne Zweifel diesselbe Bewandtniß... wie mit dem Unschuldszustande der Menschheit. Man beklagt ihn häufig, aber man vermißt ihn selten."[18]

The importance of this remark, apparently tossed off in passing, should not be missed. With it a Romantic, Rousseauistic ideology that had been imposed upon a set of observed scientific facts is thrown overboard. If it is not necessary to believe that the progressive morphological simplification of language is a process of degeneration from a primeval state of bliss, then it is not necessary to believe that the turn to prose as a mode of literary expression is such a process, either. The pejorative distinction can be removed: "Die Schranke zwischen Poesie und Prosa ist im *Gedanken* durchbrochen, sie bezeichnen nicht mehr verschiedene Ideenkreise, und wenn man auch dem Verse seinen poetischen Heiligschein und die Berechtigung für einen gewissen Inhalt nie wird abläugnen können, so büßt dagegen die Prosa durch dessen Entbehrung keine innerlichen poetischen Vortheile der Darstellung mehr ein."[19] This awkwardly stated point is important; by making verse a sub-category of the poetic and considering communicated content (understood here, of course, in the widest sense), Mundt opens the way toward an acceptance of prose as a form of literary art.

To mount such an argument at all requires an awareness of the relationship of literature and its forms to historical change. Mundt does have such an awareness, but for him the problem lies on a more fundamental level, namely, the condition of the German language. He takes a strongly populist position that undoubtedly owes a good deal to Herder and is not unlike some of the views of Wienbarg. He deplores the state of the language and believes that it is no longer capable of poetic expression directly from the soul, but he argues that this is not due to a degeneration of the national character, but to the nature of German society. Whenever Mundt uses the word "Gesellschaft," he means high society or the social intercourse of the cultured bourgeoisie. Of the human quality of this intercourse he took a dim view. He disliked the concept of "courtesy," for it suggested to him the ossified, feudal, and obsolete patterns of courtly behavior. In a review of a current handbook on etiquette, Rumohr's *Schule der Höflichkeit*, he quotes the observation that in the cities of Italy with a republican constitution the forms *civile* and *civilita* were in use and that similar forms were driving out

56

courtoisie and *courtesy* in French and English.[20] He was no doubt over-optimistic about this development, but he does show an extraordinary awareness of the relationship between language usage and social ideology, as well as an unusually conscious assumption of the role of the bourgeois in the sense of *citoyen*. German "society," in Mundt's sense, is "etwas von den Interessen der Nationalität ganz Abgesondertes, eine für sich bestehende Kalksteinformation unserer gebildeten Stände.... Die deutsche Gesellschaftlichkeit in ihrem gegenwärtigen Zustand ist die Selbstironisirung des deutschen Gemüths."[21] Class distinctions have been calcified in language usage; he argues that it was always the lower classes that revivified the German language,[22] and observes acidly:

> Man höre zu, wenn ein gebildeter und geistreicher Gelehrter, der wenig aus seinen Ideenkreisen herauszutreten geübt, in den Fall kommt, einem gewöhnlichen Bürger oder Handwerker etwas auseinanderzusetzen, was irgendwie einen ideellen Bezug und keine äußerliche Vorstellbarkeit hat; man wird finden, daß er sich bei weitem zu geistig für seinen Zuhörer ausdrückt, zu seiner eigenen Verlegenheit. Diese Trennung der intellectuellen Anschauung und der populairen Umgangssprache liegt bei keinem andern Volke in einem so ungeheuren und beispiellosen Conflict."[23]

In France, Mundt argues, the situation is different; the public character of debate results in a mode of discourse that can be understood by all classes of the population, even the illiterate.[24] In Germany the language is splintered by the barriers between the classes, and its awkwardness of expression is a reflection of the condition of society: "Die Verrenkung der Umgangssprache entspringt nur aus der Verrenkung der ächten Situation, aus der inneren Unbefriedigung der Gegenseitigkeit, in der Ich und Du sich zu einander verhalten."[25] Thus two issues are closely involved with one another: the estrangement of class from class by language, and the barriers erected between one man and another by the artificiality and stiffness of discourse. These issues are urgent because there is so much of value and importance in modern thought to be communicated. This requires a lucid style, which is not merely a matter of decorative rhetoric, for language and thought are an organism: "Kein Gedanke ist an sich schon klar, er wird es erst durch den gestalteten Satz. Bild und Begriff, Phantasie und Schönheit, welche die Werkmeister

57

bei der Entstehung der Sprache waren, sind es auch bei der Fügung des Satzes, der vorwaltend für die Anschauung herauszutreten berufen ist. Der Gedanke tritt durch den Satz in das Gebiet der Anschauung, und so wird der Stil die eigentliche Plastik des Denkens, das Schöne des Gedachten, weil dies in ihm erst an die Sonne hinaustritt."[26] Moreover, the imperatives of the time require a more active and realistic style: "Von einer Zeit aber, in der Alles auf Instrumenten, bis zum Zerspringen gestimmt, seinen Lebenston abspielt, wo unsere Sitten, unsere Speculation, unsere Existenzfragen mit lauter noch unverarbeiteten Elementen geschwängert und überfüllt sind, da verlange man nicht ländliche Schalmeienklänge und Hirtenpfeifen mit Hintergrund friedlich stiller Abendlandschaften, wie in den einfachen rein contemplativen Literaturepochen."[27]

There is a good deal more in *Die Kunst der deutschen Prosa*, but these samples shows that Mundt had worthwhile insights into the problems of language and expression in his time and was able to formulate them lucidly; René Wellek was able to call him the best of the Young German critics.[28] Much of the remainder of the book is given to a history of German prose literature, most of the principles of which have become obsolete by now. Mundt had, for example, no appreciation of seventeenth-century literature and could not be expected to have in 1837. But he traces the problem of style in the period to the deepening class distinctions in the age of absolutism: "Die schroffe Trennung der Stände ließ kein gemeinsames geistiges Band, auch nicht das der Sprache, in Deutschland mehr zu. Die Sprache wurde gewissermaßen etwas Zünftiges. Wie jeder Stand seine Vorrechte, seine Privilegien hatte, so schien er auch ein besonderes Organ des Ausdrucks für sich in Anspruch zu nehmen, das ihm vor den übrigen eigenthümlich war."[29] Besides, there are many judgments that show an instinct for literary quality and that we would share today; he is skeptical, for example, of the achievement of Klopstock;[30] and has, uncharacteristically for his time, a good word to say for Gottsched.[31] When he gets to contemporary times, Mundt has little of much interest, perhaps out of inhibitions imposed by fear of the censorship. He makes it clear, however, that he believes the liberation of language and literature is dependent upon the liberation of the intelligentsia in society:

Der Ineinsbildung von Poesie und Prosa in der productiven Literatur

58

ist an Bedeutsamkeit gleichzusetzen das Verhältniß, welches die Prosa oder die Sprache des wirklichen Lebens zur Weltbildung und den gesellschaftlichen Bedürfnissen aufzeigt. Nur wenigen Schriftstellern verdankt die deutsche Darstellung eine höhere Entwickelung des Welttons, eine weltmännische Freiheit und Feinheit der Bewegung, die schon deshalb eine selten oder künstlich hervorgebrachte Erscheinung unter uns ist, weil nur Schriftsteller literarisch, aber keine andern Einflüsse darauf zu wirken vermögen. Die gesellschaftlichen Mittel, unsere Sprache zu bilden und geschickt zu machen, sind bei uns gering anzuschlagen.[32]

But he fears to be more specific, and at the end of the book he deals with Gutzkow, Kühne, Wienbarg, Menzel, Heine, and Börne in one short paragraph.

Mundt's *Aesthetik: Die Idee der Schönheit und des Kunstwerks im Lichte unserer Zeit* (1845), a set of lectures delivered during the summer semester at Berlin in 1843, is of less interest here, for it falls outside the chronological limits of this study. Moreover, it is a less successful book than *Die Kunst der deutschen Prosa*. It is an example of Mundt's unhappy obsession with Hegel, which he belabored throughout most of his writing career. The obsession is unhappy because Mundt did not sufficiently understand Hegel to mount a convincing critique, yet he himself remained a Hegelian in his terminology and in much of the structure of his argument. Indeed, I would hazard a guess that the difficulty of understanding Hegel is the emotional experience that impelled Mundt to take so eloquent yet ineffectual a stand against him. For he insists, over and over and in many places, that Hegel has imprisoned perception of the world into a dead abstraction and has killed the living sources and wellsprings of poetry and beauty. Mundt attempts to oppose to the Hegelian system something he calls the "principle of directness," which he defines as follows: "Das unmittelbare Leben ist nicht das endliche Leben, sondern es ist das sich *vollbringende* göttliche Leben der Wirklichkeit."[33] Where in this formulation the radical difference from Hegel lies has been difficult for most interpreters to make out, though Mundt flays Hegel with, for him, unusual rhetorical fire:

Hierin liegt der eigentliche giftige Krebsschaden der Hegel'schen Philosophie, in diesem großartig vermessenen, aber auch wieder alle Lebenskräfte fesselnden Unternehmen, ausschließlich in diesem

Vermittlungsprozeß des Gedankens die wahre Wirklichkeit aufbauen zu wollen. Dieser verwegene Griff in die Schöpfung hinein, so titanenhaft er sich auch zunächst anschaute, beruhigte sich doch bei Hegel auch wieder in dem Frieden einer dialektischen Begriffbestimmung, die wie nasser Flugsand sich von dem hohen Meer der Wirklichkeit abgesetzt hatte, und auf deren ödem Strande sich sonst ein Titane mit wirklicher Lebenskraft nicht so leicht zufriedengegeben haben würde.[34]

What is in process in this attack is not a real analysis of Hegel, but rather an involved adumbration of Mundt's main interests. They are: the maintenance of the possibility of religion and of individualism, and the dichotomy of thought and concrete reality in the realm of literature. Eberhard Galley has called Mundt the most religious of the Young German writers.[35] Although his religious concerns were distinctly liberal, he insisted on maintaining them within the context of Christianity. In a letter to Varnhagen of 12 September 1835, Mundt fulminated against Gutzkow's *Wally* as "ein brutaler Ausfall gegen das Christenthum. . . . Dieser Gutzkow taugt nichts für den Fortschritt, er verdirbt uns Alles und glaubt, durch Malice lasse sich die Welt bessern."[36] A Christianity combined with "das ächte Hellenenthum des Geistes,"[37] aware of the obligation toward the poor, admitting pleasure as good, and associated with a just, constitutional state, was Mundt's purpose.[38] He was strongly influenced by Saint-Simonism and, like Heine, he pleaded repeatedly for a synthesis of the spiritual and the worldly; unlike Heine, however, he sees Christ, the incarnated God, as the true image of the genuine unity of the human and the divine,[39] and he urges a new understanding of Christian myth on that basis. In the *Literarischer Zodiacus* of 1 January 1836, he wrote, with a disapproving eye toward the other Young Germans: "Es kommt darauf an, in einer solchen Menschenepoche, wo uns Gott verlassen zu haben scheint, durch doppeltes Aufbieten der menschlichen Productionskraft für Wiederherstellung vernünftiger Zustände zu beweisen, dass ein Gott ist!"[40] This standpoint marks Mundt as a moderate rather than a radical in any sense. So does his insistence on individualism and individual genius, to which he thought Hegelian philosophy inimical. Mundt defines genius as the special power to reveal and form the higher life of "directness." It is the freedom of the highly developed individual, the

"Meister der Wirklichkeit,"[41] who unites idea and form, can penetrate into the world, and make the unity manifest. In this way he acts for all — "höchste Potenz der menschlichen Persönlichkeit."[42] Mundt connects this essentially *Sturm-und-Drang* concept of genius to his religious views: inspiration is sensitivity to the creative force of God; genius is thus prophetic — and good and honorable.[43]

There is not a great deal in these arguments that seems exceptionally original and progressive. Nor is it clear why this definition of genius needs to be defended against Hegel, who made so much of the "world-historical individual," except that Mundt suspects in Hegel's system a determinism that threatens the ideology of individual autonomy. Mundt accuses Hegel of making of art only a sign of thought, "als ob der Dichter und Künstler eine solche schwitzende Pythia auf dem Dreifuß wäre, die nur als ein Werkzeug des Gottes empfängt, aber nicht mit freiem Bewußtsein schafft."[44] On the other hand, in view of Mundt's populist concern with the gap between intellectual and ordinary discourse, already discussed in *Die Kunst der deutschen Prosa*, his view of the dichotomy between abstract thought and concrete reality, although probably not a pertinent critique of Hegel, is not wholly lacking in sense. For Mundt, as for the Young Germans generally, "life" is an unanalyzed, positive term. He asserts that the purpose of his *Aesthetik* is "der Anschauung und Ausübung der Kunst in unserer Zeit das Lebensprinzip zurückzugeben,"[45] and he not surprisingly adverts to Schiller, whose aesthetics he calls "eine Vorschule der politischen Freiheit."[46]

This is a theme that recurs constantly in Mundt, although immediately after the debacle of 1835 it sometimes acquires a resigned tone; a character in one of his novellas is said to have "den schönen Traum von der deutschen Literatur...durchgeträumt. Wie alle jüngeren Talente von Bedeutung war er mit großen Hoffnungen von der Literatur ausgegangen, um sie in eine neue Verbindung mit dem Leben zu setzen."[47] As in *Die Kunst der deutschen Prosa*, Mundt argues in the *Aesthetik* that literature has been removed "aus der Mitte des Volkslebens, wo sie zu stehen hat, und sie ist dafür hineingezogen worden in die Angelegenheiten der heutigen Gesellschaft [meaning, as is usual with Mundt, high society], die Alles entnervende Mode hat sich ihrer zu bemächtigen gesucht und sie soll für den Salon arbeiten, für die Liebhaberei und Eitelkeit des Sammlers, für die exclusiven Vorrechte des Reichthums und der Bildung."[48] This is why Mundt argues that aesthetics must be severed from its dependence on philosophy and turned to the essentials of life, which, he argues characteristically, lie "in der Entwickelung des religiösen Bewußtseins und der politischen Freiheit."[49] Art, he insists, can never be replaced by thought, as Hegel, with his successive ages of religion, art, and philosophy, appeared to mean. But, of course, Mundt's aesthetics is not a purely activist or realistic system; it retains a good deal of Hegel's historical dynamic and is strongly idealistic, as his summary of what he has demonstrated shows: "Wir haben jetzt die Idee der Schönheit auf drei verschiedenen Stufen des Völkerlebens sich entwickeln sehn, und das Schöne darin als die ideale Form der jedesmaligen Lebensunmittelbarkeit erkannt, in welcher die ganze herrschende Weltansicht auf ihren Höhepunkt herausgetreten."[50]

Yet Mundt arrives from time to time at results that point ahead to Marx and beyond. It is quite surprising to find the result of Mundt's premise that, since Christ blessed the poor, he must be seen as the redeemer of the body as well as the soul: therefore labor in the future will be joined to pleasure, anticipating Marx's striking view that in the unalienated society all people could become artists.[51] Not without interest and elegance is Mundt's argument entitled "Die Kunst in ihrem Verhältniß zur Freiheit der Völker." If art is, as Schiller postulated, an expression of human freedom, how does it happen that art has so often flourished in times of oppression and absolutism? This is not a contradiction, Mundt argues; rather, art served in such times as the haven for freedom and the divine creative urge of man.[52] Art thus defends individuality in the face of despotism, which is why — and here Mundt is surely adverting to his own times — despots as often feared artists as they encouraged them. Tyrants, he remarks not without wit, thus are in conflict with themselves; by patronizing art, they acknowledge the force in the peoples that they have suppressed. Conversely, he is obliged to admit that in restoration times art may function as an opiate, a form of "gebildeter Despotismus," thus alienating art from the reality of the people.[53] Mundt anticipates Brecht in his insistence that art must give pleasure; he denounces the devaluation of art as pleasure born of idleness. Pleasure is necessary for man and is his true Muse; the "Drang nach Vergnügen" is as important as the "Drang nach Glück."[54]

These cursory observations do not by any means exhaust the

contents of Mundt's two scholarly monographs. They have been made here, first, to give some idea of the pattern of Mundt's thinking in his mature years and, secondly, to suggest that, despite his limitations, he cannot be disposed of as a mediocre or inconsequential writer. Behind that free-flowing, sometimes careless and imprecise style was a hard-working mind, deeply worried about the contemporary condition of literature and its relationship, or lack of it, to the problems of a society in painful and sluggish transition. Another reason for treating these books in this place is that Mundt's giftedness does not show itself to its best advantage in the literary works that were directly involved in the Young German crisis. Therefore it seemed fairer, before turning to these earlier works, to give some attention to Mundt's capacities where they appear at their strongest. Indeed, Mundt's fiction of 1834 and 1835 seems so harmless that one must marvel as he did that the juggernaut of Metternich's system was rolled over him. A strange age, indeed, when such mild books could disturb the politics of all central Europe. It has to be remembered, however, that Mundt had already acquired a certain public notoriety by his involvement in the most spectacular event in the literary world at this time: the suicide of Charlotte Stieglitz on 29 December 1834.

It is an eerie tale, and although Houben has certified that Mundt scarcely altered Charlotte Stieglitz's letters to him when he published them,[55] it does not altogether make sense. One must suspect a psychopathological dimension to the relationship among Mundt and the Stieglitzes that was beyond the conscious comprehension of the participants. For our purposes, however, psychological speculation is less interesting than what the participants and the public thought was happening, for the affair tells us something about the overwrought emotional state of the literary intelligentsia at the time. Of all the eccentric personalities that emerge in the crisis of the mid-1830's, Heinrich Stieglitz is the most pathetic — a man who either could not, or was not permitted to — it is not clear which — live with the fact that he was not a major poet. Stieglitz, a Jew converted to Christianity in his childhood, wrote in 1831-33 four volumes of poems entitled *Bilder des Orients*, epic and dramatic works inspired by the oriental atmosphere of Goethe's *West-östlicher Divan*. Goethe, with his tendency, so infuriating to Heine, to praise the most mediocre literary works as long as they exhibited allegiance to his own models, spoke well of Stieglitz's poems[56] and undoubtedly did him a very dubious favor. Meanwhile, Mundt had befriended Stieglitz in Berlin and became fascinated by his wife, who was frantically concerned that Stieglitz should rouse himself to poetic genius. While Stieglitz was away in Russia on family affairs in 1833, Mundt corrected the proofs of the fourth volume of the *Bilder des Orients*. Whether he believed that the critic's function is to improve literature by honest evaluation, or for more complicated reasons, he did not, like Goethe, restrict himself to praise of the inconsequential; in May, 1834, he wrote a critical review of some of Stieglitz's poems, and Charlotte was beside herself.[57] Nevertheless, Mundt joined Charlotte in the endeavor to encourage and exhort Stieglitz to higher achievement. On 4 September 1834, Mundt wrote solicitously to Stieglitz: "Dein ganzes Wesen arbeitet an einer schönern und kräftigern Erneuerung seiner selbst, und kein Wunder, wenn in dem Kampfe zwischen den alten und neuen Göttern des Menschen Herzblut schmerzlich dahinströmt"; Mundt urged on him "*Selbstbewußtheit! — Selbstvergessenheit!! — Selbstironisirung!!*"[58]

The correspondence between Mundt and the Stieglitzes in 1834 was a painful analysis of souls according to the old faculty psychology of the eighteenth century, full of idealistic pretensions and demanding a total delicacy of understanding. Charlotte became increasingly distraught; meanwhile, Stieglitz had a dream indicating that it was the marriage that fettered him and prevented the eagle's flight. She killed herself, ostensibly to free him and deepen the resources of inspiration through tragedy. Of course, no such thing happened. Stieglitz was dismayed and embarrassed; Mundt was shaken; and the public was in an uproar: a female Werther had appeared in real life! Gutzkow confessed wryly that without the death of Charlotte he would not have written *Wally*.[59] Upon hearing the news Mundt wrote to his friend Kühne of his magnificent and pure love for Charlotte, and it was not long before he was disgusted with the way Stieglitz trivialized the "Opfertod."[60] Soon Mundt was quarrelling with Kühne, whose apprehension of this love was apparently not holy and pure enough to suit him,[61] although Kühne's account of the affair is not without a kind of pedestrian common sense.[62] But this was a sacred matter for Mundt; at the beginning of *Charlotte Stieglitz, ein Denkmal*, he urges: "Wem sie [these pages] wie ein fremdes Buch in die Hände gerathen, ohne daß sie ihm für sein Fühlen und

Denken etwas bedeuten könnten, der gehe still an ihnen vorüber, wie an einem Monument heiliger Trauer, dessen Bilder und Inschriften ihm wenigstens für unverletztlich gelten."[63]

Kühne's suspicion that there was more to the affair than Mundt had revealed is plausible enough, although, as I indicated, I think it is useless to speculate on the true nature of the relationship because Mundt sublimated it beyond all recoverable psychological reality.[64] Two aspects of it, however, impress themselves on the student of Young Germany. One, noted by Houben long ago, is the apparent recapitulation of the tense, probingly sentimental interpersonal relationships of the late eighteenth century. Characteristic of this revival of *Empfindsamkeit* is a continuous, self-conscious analysis of motive and character in terms of the abstract categories of an undynamic faculty psychology, and the pursuit of a degree of true friendship, true love, total frankness, and total understanding that, as a rule, places a heavier burden on interpersonal relationships than they can bear, for the least real or imagined lapse from complete loyalty and complete empathy creates an uproar that consumes rather than enhances emotional life. This phenomenon occurs when an awareness of the richness of individual culture and moral sensitivity has outdistanced the forms of social intercourse that express human relationships. Such a situation developed in the late eighteenth century, and both the *Sturm und Drang* and the mood called *Empfindsamkeit* are symptoms of it; both find the conventions too confining to permit the communication of a new consciousness and a new sensibility. It is striking that this situation should appear to repeat itself more than a half century later. It indicates that the forms of social intercourse were still inadequate to the modern bourgeois sensibility and were creating nearly unbearable stresses. The political malaise of the intelligentsia at the time is only a part of a much larger dysfunction of society so far as the progressive bourgeoisie was concerned.

The other interesting aspect of the Stieglitz affair is the enormous, emotionally charged prestige attached to artistic creativity. It is an odd situation when a wife and a friend are engaged in pouring all their eloquence into the task of making a literary genius out of a minor poet and that the effort should cost the wife's life. In the Young German period, there was dismay over the state of literature and a conviction that its condition was bad for the "nation," that is, for the cultivated bourgeoisie. Coupled with this was an unanalyzed paradox: although most of the Young German generation was aware of the fact that the unsatisfactory state of literature was related to the unsatisfactory state of society, there was a feeling that this relationship was in some sense reciprocal: that is, if society could not be liberated to the point where it would generate a literature adequate to modern times, then the literature must be created that would aid in the regeneration of society. This may seem a large conclusion to draw from the case of Stieglitz. But that Mundt believed this is indicated by a passage in the epilogue to *Madonna* in which he argues that the "Gesinnung" of his book serves for the time being as a surrogate for unattainable political progress:

> Ich bin und war immer der Meinung, daß die gestörte Bewegung der *Politik* in unsern Tagen in die rastlos durch die Gemüther fortgehende und nicht unterdrückbare Bewegung der *Gesinnung* mit allen ihren Hoffnungen und Wünschen einstweilen übertreten und auf diesem allgemeinen Grunde des Fortschritts doch endlich ihrer größten Erfolge gewiß werden kann. Denn wenn die Politik nothgedrungen in die Gesinnung zurücktritt, wird die Gesinnung, nachdem sie ihre innere Umgestaltung aus sich vollbracht hat, allmälig wieder in die äußere Politik, und dann unwiderstehlich, hinübertreten.[65]

Since "Gesinnung" was regarded as intimately involved with literary creativity, this would explain why a moderately engaged and progressive writer like Mundt should think it so important that a flagging talent be supported and urged to develop. Gutzkow, on the whole, agreed with him. On the one hand, he ascribed Stieglitz's creative paralysis to the impossibility in such times of bridging the causes of beauty and freedom; on the other, he judged that Charlotte rightly saw what is glorious in literary art and was only mistaken in believing she saw it in her husband.[66] But no artist can develop in the kind of hothouse into which Stieglitz was put, unless, like Mozart or Beethoven, he has huge and indestructible natural gifts. There is a tendency in the Young German period to force the end result of artistic creativity, to take the goal of being a creative writer by storm. This is quite different from the distinction that developed in the international Bohemia, born at this time in France, between being an artist and actually creating artistic works. The Young Germans are not poseurs and are wholly uninterested in artistic "life style"; but, having a painful consciousness that artists adequate to the progressive imperatives of the age are needed, they transform this consciousness into an urge to make themselves — or their friends — into these artists.

That Mundt should have been involved in so excessive a display of these problems is a little paradoxical, because his literary writings in the period show only intermittently a real grasp of the progressive issues. Indeed, a review of his novel of 1834, *Moderne Lebenswirren*, praising the book for Goethean coolness and for making liberalism appear absurd, resulted in an invitation from a Prussian minister to enter the state service.[67] How this could be, a year before Mundt's proscription the length and breadth of Germany, appears from an examination of the book itself. Even by Young German standards, it is an exceptionally indecisive and open-ended piece of writing. The author distances himself from the content by presenting himself as an editor of papers for which he takes no real responsibility; he describes the writer of them, the salt-mine clerk Seeliger, as a man of contradictions, but he also emphasizes the pacific quality of the book and its virtue of inconclusiveness.[68]

The satirical tone of these memoirs appears quite promptly. The clerk Seeliger presents himself immediately as a person unfit for practical life, one who wrote twenty-three tragedies as a student rather than learning a profession. His musings are addressed to Esperance, a wise, didactic girl who has become a schoolteacher in order to support her mother and who in the course of the book comes to represent a kind of anchor of reasonableness. Early in the book Seeliger graphically describes the uproar of mind that has beset him since the July Revolution: "Der Zeitgeist thut weh in mir, Esperance! ... Der Zeitgeist zuckt, dröhnt, zieht, wirbelt und hambachert [a reference to the meeting of German liberals at Hambach in May, 1832] in mir; er pfeift in mir hell wie eine Wachtel, spielt die Kriegstrompete auf mir, singt die Marseillaise in all meinen Eingeweiden, und donnert mir in Lunge und Leber mit der Pauke des Aufruhrs herum. Vergebens lese ich in jetziger Stimmung meinen alten geliebten Goethe, um mich durch ihn wieder in die gute goldene altväterliche Ruhe eines literarischen Deutschlands hineinzuwiegen und einzulullen; vergebens brauche ich seine herrlichen Werke, um sie mir gewissermaßen als Aufruhr-Acte gegen meine dermalige Zeitaufregung zu verlesen. Es hilft Alles nicht mehr."[69] Something new must happen to him to give him a new direction because there are too many who are pointing the way: "Die Welt hat heutzutage schon mehr dienstbare Genies, als sie brauchen kann. Wimmelt es nicht überall von Genies, wo man hinsieht, so daß keins vor dem andern mehr zu Worte kommen kann, und sie sich noch alle untereinander vertilgen werden, weil Jeder der Einzige sein will, der den Zeitgeist als Siegerroß reitet?"[70] He fears "innere Bürgerkriege der Genies."[71]

Into this situation, which is an accurate if unflattering account of the contemporary young intellectual at sea, comes a mysterious travelling diplomat named Herr von Zodiacus, who interests himself in the young Seeliger and gives him some quite unhelpful advice on several occasions. It is hinted at occasionally that Zodiacus is a devil, and so he turns out to be: the "Parteiteufel," whose function it is to befuddle the young man with various partisan ideologies. (It is undoubtedly a joke on Mundt's part that he named his first periodical *Literarischer Zodiacus.*) He begins with a praise of liberalism, which the reader, though not Seeliger, recognizes as sardonic. It is a rhapsodic prophecy of the amalgamation of freedom and love, which Mundt was indeed inclined to argue, but it arouses a suspiciously facile allegiance in the young man: "Ich bin mir klar, ich bin frei, ich bin liberal geworden! Ich bin ein Mann der Zukunft geworden!"[72] He starts to incant the word "Volk" as though it were a magic formula: "Volk! Volk! Volk! möchte ich dreimal ebenso bedeutsam ausrufen, als Hamlet seine: Worte! Worte! Worte! Was ist die neue Sache der Zeit ohne Volk? Ich suche, ich will Volk!"[73] The reader cannot fail to recognize a rather heavy-handed satire here, although this strategy is a little puzzling, for it is Mundt's own preoccupations that are being satirized: in one morning Seeliger writes two liberal manifestoes for a publication called *Dampfmaschine für Völkerfreiheit,* one against tipping the hat, the other against the present state of German epistolary style. As it happens, both these antipathies of Mundt are taken up relatively seriously in *Die Kunst der deutschen Prosa,*[74] showing the degree of self-irony in this part of the book. In any case, the experiment with liberalism ends badly, in a quarrel followed by a duel. The pistols are believed to be unloaded, but they become loaded mysteriously, presumably by the "Parteiteufel," and the duel results in the death of one man and the maiming of another.

Seeliger begins to have doubts about liberalism, and Zodiacus reappears with a completely changed line: he now makes a case for servility and absolutism. He praises the past, not the future, and the foundation of life, and argues that a democratic order will not support the arts, although he again becomes obviously sardonic, bewailing the loss of pedantic scholarship and engaging in ironic praise of a number of reactionary figures, including Henrik Steffens, the man who was was to block Mundt's faculty appointment a year later. Again Seeliger is convinced: "O, auch der Servilismus ist süß! Es ist wie mit der Liebe."[75] He praises his own existence as an insignificant official and cancels the political newspapers that, as a liberal, he had subscribed to though he could ill afford them, for now he is an absolutist who stands sublimely above all politics.[76] The curious result of this development is that it arouses in Seeliger a desire to write literature. At this point Mundt loses track of the logic of his narration. The question he has raised is whether there is a connection between absolutist ideology and a flight into the realm of art. He does not pursue it in these terms, however, but rather launches into an essay on literature in which he clearly speaks with his own voice: "Ich will aus dem Ganzen heraus dichten! In einen großen Weltstoff will ich mich vertiefen, und meine eigene Seele soll mich darin überraschen.... In unmittelbares Leben will ich mich tauchen, an frischen, fremden Gestalten gesund werden, und alle greisenhaft wissenschaftliche Anflüge von dem weißen jungfräulichen Körper der Poesie abwehren."[77] He then goes on at some length to argue that art works need not have an eternal existence; they may well reflect the passing needs of the present. It is the task of the present generation, "Pfeile des Geistes in ihre Zeit hinauszuschicken, um das Volk der Deutschen aufzuregen und auf- zuschütteln. Eines Buches Geist muß in das Volk übergehen, und dann als Buch aufgehört haben zu leben."[78] This is a good Young German program, though immured in a satirical context, and it leads Seeliger to consider the possibility of relating politics to liter- ature; and since politics is a word hated by the absolutists, he begins to doubt his absolutist allegiance. He will renounce artistic greatness and write "historisch-komische Novellen"; that is the need of the present.[79] The recognition of this literary need brings him to the conclusion that he must become apolitical. Seeliger's thinking here describes a curious ellipse, from a literary urge to considerations of political relevance to a renewed apolitical literary stance. The reason for this is that the satire has become contaminated with Mundt's own views in an undisciplined way. Although the plan to write "historical-comic" novellas is devised with the same naive hyperbole that characterizes all of Seeliger's swiftly shifting enthusiasms, it presumably does not basically belong to the satirical level, for later, in *Madonna*, this genre is seriously recommended and pursued.[80]

Zodiacus now emerges for a third time, claiming that he was only joking about absolutism; he deplores Seeliger's flight into art and literature, for literature draws Germans away from the present; he recommends writing about railroads, steam cars, and the like, for a new ideology neither of the future nor the past, but of the present: "den Sieg des *Juste-Milieu-Systems!*"[81] Against this argument in favor of the *Juste-Milieu* Seeliger resists most strongly, but he comes to accept it, and the acceptance is coupled with a typical Mundtian polemic against Hegel cast in the form of a dream. In this position Seeliger ends, and the wise girl Esperance seems to encourage the allegiance to the *Juste-Milieu*. The end of the book contains a set of aphorisms and fragments, as though to show how fragmented Seeliger's state of mind is and remains.

It is hardly surprising that Mundt was offered a government position on the strength of his book; it is an irresponsible intellectual exercise, suggesting that the author was potentially employable for any purpose. It is one thing to satirize the excesses and vagaries of ideological dispute, and there may be some justice to Bliemel's view that Mundt meant only to satirize the shallowness of fashionable allegiances, not the true voice of the *Zeitgeist*,[82] whatever that may have been; but to make all such issues the consequence of a demon of partisanship is to satirize partisanship itself and thus to ally one's self with the ideologically neutral position that appeals to conservative authority. Furthermore, the book exhibits an immature intelligence, lacking the confidence of conviction. Positions that Mundt held, after a fashion, are embedded in a generally satiric context that suggests the ultimate interchangeability of all views and an author who is unserious in a very fundamental sense. Such a man, if he is also intelligent and industrious, as Mundt was, makes the perfect intellectual bureaucrat. Surely no one would have predicted for Mundt on the basis of *Moderne Lebenswirren* either a literary career of any consequence or notoriety as a radical dangerous to society. Yet, within a year or so, the Stieglitz affair and the book entitled *Madonna, Unterhaltungen mit einer Heiligen*, accomplished at least the latter.

In form, *Madonna* is substantially under the influence of Heine's *Reisebilder*. The difference in quality is painfully evident. Of Heine's complex sense of form, his skill in integrating themes and images, in weaving together sharp observation and levels of memory, there is no trace. Rarely in Heine, except occasionally in the *Reise von München nach Genua*, does his narration come so close to the flatness of plain, factual travelogue as Mundt's account of Bohemia and of Count Waldstein's Castle of Dux, where Casanova, one of the main topics of the book, spent the last years of his life. The narrator, as Rudolf Majut has perceptively observed, is not a Romantic wanderer, but a tourist in search of diversion.[83] From time to time passages occur which remind the reader directly of models in Heine; an example is the Catholic procession during which the narrator first sees the "Madonna," which recalls a similar description in Heine's *Die Stadt Lucca*. There are also thematic parallels to Heine that will concern us shortly. As is usual in such imitations, Heine's controlled looseness of composition has become indifferent disarray, and as usual, the author attempts to make of this a virtue of the book. In a letter to Charlotte Stieglitz of 26 October 1834, he described the book as "einzelne Skizzen, Humoresken und Phantasiestücke, durch welche jedoch alle nach meiner Art ein gemeinsamer rother Faden geht,"[84] just as Heine spoke in *Die Harzreise* of "die bunten Fäden, die so hübsch hineingesponnen sind, um sich im Ganzen harmonisch zu verschlingen."[85] In the book itself, however, the author raises the question whether it is a novel or novella and concludes: "Ich erkläre mit feierlicher Resignation, daß es eigentlich gar kein *Buch* ist, das ich herausgebe, sondern bloß ein Stück Leben."[86] These ironic disclaimers, inherited from the Romantic tradition, in part via Heine, and amalgamated with the new pre-eminence of "life," are among the most tiresome aspects of Young German writing, for they serve as an apology for every kind of self-indulgence. Gutzkow, incidentally, criticized Mundt in a letter to Varnhagen for the lack of artistic concretion and plasticity.[87]

It cannot be denied, however, that Mundt's critical attitude has stabilized noticeably since *Moderne Lebenswirren*; here there are themes that are unmistakeably liberal. Most prominent among them is the desire to bring movement and progress, urbanity and rationality, into the stagnation of the times. The book begins with a "Posthorn-Symphonie"[88] in which Mundt adverts directly to the stopping up of the flow of ideas by the censorship: "Ich will mir selbst etwas blasen! Jetzt fange ich an, es zu glauben, daß von einer allgemeinen Tonlosigkeit dies unser Zeitalter ergriffen sein muß, denn auch die deutschen Postillons lassen jetzt ihr schmetterndes Mundstück ungenutzt und schläfrig herunterhängen, und jeder sagt mir miß-muthig, ihm sei das Horn verstopft."[89] Do coachmen, the author asks, fear the censorship? The traveller is off on his journey not to see sights or contemplate nature, but to see and talk to the people, to find out how much they are interested in the new times and to encourage peasants and villagers especially to read and to occupy themselves with ideas for a more humane existence. Mundt's rejection of nature as an object of his interest is a rejection of the Romantic tradition: "Der Horizont dieser gegenwärtigen Zeit ist zu bewölkt, als daß man weit ausschauen könnte von den Bergen in die Thäler und die silbernen Ströme entlang, und auf die Kuppeln und Thürme der fernen schönen Städte. Das harmlose, unschuldige Gemüth ist fort, das mit Landschaften und Gegenden sich freute, und ich suche es vergeblich in mir, und finde nichts, als daß ich kein Jean-Pauli-scher Jüngling mehr bin."[90] Nature poetry, Mundt argues, is a symptom of a frustrated and unhappy society:

> Das Unglück geht am liebsten hinaus ins Grüne und unter die Einsamkeit der wehenden Bäume, das Unglück oder die spielende Kinderunschuld. Die Kinder und die Zerrissenen, beide stehen dem Naturelement am nächsten, und beide würden darin verloren gehen, wenn es nicht ein Stärkeres gäbe als das Naturelement, nämlich den historischen Trieb in die werdende Welt- und Völker-Zukunft, die Alle aufreizt, sich zu bilden, zu bewegen und zu versöhnen. Und die Deutschen waren nie unglücklicher, nie innerlich zerrissener, als zur Zeit ihrer Natursentimentalität und Landschaftsempfind-samkeit im Leben und Dichten.[91]

The writer can always call up in his imagination the decorative aspects of nature if he needs them; but imagination will not suffice to make the world of men visible to him; it must be observed.[92] This is a doubtful argument, but one not insignificant for the time, for it suggests a recipe for realism. Mundt's revaluation of the city is a significant aspect of this realistic urge. In a passage of several pages, Mundt speaks of a desire to reverse the logic of Schiller's elegy *Der Spaziergang*, which proceeds from the city into a bucolic landscape and then into a higher realm of elegiac mythological reminiscence. Mundt would like to go the other way and write an "elegy" on the city: "Ich liebe die städtebauende Muse, welche den Nomadentrieb des menschlichen Lebens einordnet in feste Gränzen der beglückenden Harmonie."[93] This allegiance to civilization is the mark of the genuine liberal and is not common in the German literary tradition.

Progressive civilization, motion, future orientation are thus notable aspects of Mundt's attitude in *Madonna*. In his postscript he refers to the novel as a "Buch der Bewegung,"[94] which could be construed, especially by the witch-hunters, as a "book of *the* movement," of a critical and even, from time to time, radical thrust. The part of the book that caused the most offense to the governmental criticism was the long eulogy on Casanova, which the traveller recites to a bigoted and ignorant old schoolteacher in Bohemia. This is, in fact, an extensive literary essay embedded in the narrative, and it shows that Mundt had a good knowledge of Casanova's memoirs, for he knows how they came to be written and published, he stresses their value as perceptive social history, and he calls attention to the wide range of Casanova's intellectual gifts and his indefatigable vitality. But Mundt makes aggressive use of Casanova's role as an apostle of worldliness; he calls him a knight of secular life and a combination of Don Juan and Faust,[95] that is, the quintessence of modern man. His Catholicism, Mundt says provocatively, was "Weltgenuß."[96] Such phrases must have appeared to conservative minds as code words for sexual licentiousness.

It is true that Mundt treats sexuality itself, particularly in the feelings of the "Madonna" figure, with a naturalness that is unusual in this age and is certainly far removed from the cramped and timid treatment in Gutzkow's *Wally*. But Mundt is not making a brief for libertinism, although some of his language was not as carefully chosen as it might have been; he is pursuing his version of the Saint-Simonian reconciliation of the flesh and the spirit. Mundt's views on these matters show numerous parallels to those argued by Heine in *Zur Geschichte der Religion und Philosophie in Deutschland*, which had appeared in January, 1835.[97] The difference, charac-

73

teristic for Mundt, is a greater confidence in Christianity as a liberal religion and as a mediator between the worlds of matter and spirit. This mediatory role of Christianity is a main theme of *Madonna*. The Virgin Mary, for example, is said to be a mediator between a familiar human experience, motherhood, and the divine spirit. There is a long discussion of Raphael, whom Mundt treats, not as the Romantics did, as the epitome of the pious artist, but as the idealizer of Catholicism who painted for the invisible church, a worldly painter who expressed the worldly freedom of thought; he built a bridge from religion to the sensory world.[98] Why this should be especially true of Raphael among all religious painters is not clear, but I suspect Mundt chose this example just because of the way it had been used by the Romantics in their pursuit of an aestheticized piety. These views of reconciliation are curiously combined with a distinctly Hegelian faith in the dynamic of history: "Christus aber schreitet als der Geist der Fortentwickelung durch die Geschichte, und die Religion bildet sich im Geist und in der Wahrheit in die Welt hinein."[99] The overcoming of the dichotomy is described as something already well in process: "Alles wird weltlich in unserer Zeit und muß es werden, selbst die Religion. Denn es kann nichts Heiligeres mehr geben, als das Weltliche, nichts Geistlicheres als das Weltliche. Alles hat jetzt eine und diesselbe Geschichte."[100] Furthermore, for Mundt the gap between the flesh and the spirit is similar to the gap between the people and the cultivated intelligentsia, a concern we have already noticed in *Die Kunst der deutschen Prosa*: "Die Welt und das Fleisch müssen wieder eingesetzt werden in ihre Rechte, damit der Geist nicht mehr sechs Treppen hoch wohnt in Deutschland."[101] While he is not explicit about it, such a parallel clearly indicates that the Saint-Simonian program has revolutionary implications for society. However, he is careful to deny any sympathy with political or class revolution. Lammenais' pioneering effort to devise a kind of Christian socialism meets with strong disapproval; Mundt denounces it as Jacobinism and accuses Lammenais of arming the most dangerous class of the people.[102]

The incarnation of sanctified worldliness is the central figure of the book, Maria, the "Madonna." As a moderate Saint-Simonian, Mundt was of course interested in the question of the emancipation of women. Among the Young Germans, he takes in some respects the least patronizing view of the matter. It is true that he would not meet with the approval of the women's liberationists of today. His apotheosis of Charlotte Stieglitz and his repeated beatification of the "Madonna" as a saint are not unlike that nineteenth-century process by which women were placed on a pedestal and thus elevated out of all significance. In *Charlotte Stieglitz, ein Denkmal*, where he praises Charlotte at length as the paragon of womanhood, he lists his ideals of women: her heart is "ein offener Liebestempel"; what is admirable in women is "das Anschmiegende," "das Dienende..., die süße Magdsnatur im Weibe, die ächt christlich ihrem Herrn die Füße wäscht," and so on.[103] He makes very clear some years later that he thought it an insult to femininity to want women to have any part in the state or in civil affairs.[104] A passage in *Madonna* suggests that Mundt believed a woman could not contend with a man in an extreme situation; it occurs while Maria is resisting an attempt at forcible seduction: "In diesem Moment erfuhr ich zuerst in mir," says Maria, "daß es eine Macht des Mannes gebe, die unserer Natur weit überlegen sei. Er [the seducer] kam mir schön vor in der Gloria des Mannes, wie noch nie, und ich dachte, daß mich nichts mehr retten könne, als Bitten."[105]

The reason for this, however, is Maria's natural sexuality, which in itself is innocent for her, and which at such a critical moment comes into conflict with her abhorrence of her would-be seducer. On the whole, Mundt shows none of the attitude that one senses in Laube, for example, that emancipation of women is primarily a matter of breaking down sexual inhibitions in order to make male life less frustrating and troublesome. Mundt is more genuinely concerned with the way the inner and outer freedom of women is violated in a repressive and bigoted society. When the narrator meets Maria in Bohemia, she is virtually a prisoner in conditions that do not allow her to unfold herself: "Und gerade weibliche Naturen sind es am häufigsten, welche man an ein solches Leben ohne Sterne verbannt findet."[106] Women live in hope, but are worn out and grow old in sacrifice for others. Because Maria is regarded by her father and the neighborhood as godless, she is subjected to humiliating punishments: she is obliged to learn the names of all the saints by heart and to memorize the catalogue of all the outlandish relics collected by Emperor Charles IV. She wishes she were a Protestant — a sign in the Young German context that she wishes to become progressive and modern — and she does achieve this, to her great satisfaction, at the end of the novel.

The story of Maria herself, to which we shall turn in a moment, is evidence enough of Mundt's sympathy, within certain limits, for the cause of female emancipation. He underlines the theme, however, by attempting to give it also a legendary treatment. The legend is based on materials of the Libussa cycle, the ancient tales about the mythical foundress of Prague and her court.[107] A Prague poet, Karl Egon von Ebert (1801-82), whom Mundt, judging from the adventures of his narrator, seems to have met, had treated a part of this material in 1829: the revolt of Vlasta and the War of the Maids after the death of Libussa and the restoration of male rule. Mundt endeavored to make the legend more satirical and to bear more on the question of women's emancipation. The details, which are fairly pedestrian, need not concern us here. What happens in essence is that the women, having been denied the intellectual, cultural, and social equality they had enjoyed under Libussa's rule, become increasingly radical, and are gradually transformed into heartless Amazons and defeated after a bloody war. In the course of the legend Vlasta is made to prophesy the future of women up to the nineteenth century: she tells of the adoration of women in the medieval *Minne* cult, of the fate of Joan of Arc, of the eighteenth century, and of Saint-Simonism and its confusions. In none of these ages are women really free, although Mundt seems to hold out some hope for the nineteenth century. The legend breaks off abruptly, and it is apparent that it was inserted only as a vehicle to discuss the Saint-Simonian issue.

Maria's story is a novella of some seventy pages inserted into the larger work. It is an autobiographical account sent by the girl to the travelling narrator and it is entitled "Bekenntnisse einer weltlichen Seele," in parodistic reference, of course, to the sixth book of Goethe's *Wilhelm Meisters Lehrjahre,* "Bekenntnisse einer schönen Seele." It has some claim to be, I believe, the best of all Young German novellas; certainly it is Mundt's best piece of fictional writing. It is a well-told story — economical, convincing, and psychologically interesting — and the plot contains a startling twist of the sort perfected in the art of O. Henry. Maria is born into impoverished circumstances and is unloved by her parents. (The unconventional theme of a child with unloving and indifferent

76

parents is used by Mundt in another, otherwise undistinguished and poorly constructed novella, *Antoniens Bußfahrten.*[108]) She develops at an early age a longing for freedom and real life; she feels that if she had wings, she would fly right into the middle of life. Just what "life" is she has no very clear idea; she reads about "life" in the Bible and in her school primers, and concludes it must be something going on elsewhere. She prays for it day and night. Then matters take a turn that leads her at first to hope that she is to find life. She is taken to live with her apparently wealthy aunt in Dresden, and the quality of her existence changes dramatically. Here she is amiably treated, lives in comfortable surroundings, has every amenity, and is provided with a good education, which she greatly enjoys. Her happiness is gradually clouded, however, with the growing awareness that it is not her aunt's resources at all that are responsible for her well-being, but the subsidies of a rich count. As she grows older, it dawns on her that she is being prepared for this gentleman's concubinage, and she develops a deep aversion to him. Among Maria's tutors is a young theologian named Mellenberg, who is unprepossessing, bookish, and monosyllabic, but Maria feels attracted to him, as well as to his Protestantism. Eventually the time comes for the count to attempt to collect his investment. Maria resists him in the scene already mentioned, and flees in desperation to the garret room of Mellenberg, now a boarder in the house, in order to hide. The unspoken love between them is made manifest, and Maria spends the night with him. The next morning, in her own room, she feels revitalized, blossoming, more fulfilled than ever before in her life. But soon she receives a note from Mellenberg, in which he apologizes for the great wrong he has done her and informs her that he must take his life out of shame, which he promptly does. Maria, in shattered despair, wanders back to her Bohemian village, where Mundt's travelling narrator makes her acquaintance.

The most striking part of this novella is the fierce irony of its climax. While Maria has found the life she has so long yearned for in her night of love with Mellenberg, he is attuned to an entirely different morality and interprets as an inexpiable wrong what for Maria has been a great blessing. In retrospect Maria interprets this as a mutual failure of understanding: "Er hatte meine Liebe nicht verstanden, und ich seine Religion nicht."[109] But the author Mundt clearly evaluates the case differently. Maria, the worldly "Madonna," the saint, is a wholly positive figure; she is the principle of honest and natural life, whereas Mellenberg's repressive morality is the principle of death that meaninglessly destroys one life and wrecks another. In passing, it might be mentioned that Mundt did something similar in another novella, although with much less success. It is a double-stranded story entitled *Der Bibeldieb*.[110] One strand concerns a pastor who has been imprisoned for political activity; in his great yearning for freedom he escapes and absent-mindedly steals a Bible in order to nourish his spirit from it; this strand ends happily, for it turns out that an undelivered pardon had been issued before his escape. The other strand concerns a crisis between two young people about to be married: the girl finds the young man too frivolous and impious in his opinions; the young man declares the girl is too repressed and prudish. Through a plot complication, the young man loses his clothes while swimming and the girl comes upon him nude. She interprets this as an attempt on his part to humiliate her and drowns herself out of shame. This grisly conclusion to what is essentially a story of comic situations is entirely inappropriate and shows bad taste. It helps, however, to illuminate the more effective climax of the *Madonna* novella. Mundt could be as vague as any Young German about what the "life" was that a truly modern literature ought to represent and celebrate, but he seems to have had a clear idea that its opposite was death. The suicide of Mellenberg takes on symbolic implications; it throws into high relief all the killing repressivenenss of an orthodoxy hostile to the natural vitality of human life. The Protestant Mellenberg clearly has no notion of the liberating implications that Protestantism had for the Young Germans and also for Maria. It is also not without interest that in the one story Mundt lays the burden of repressiveness on the male, in the other on the female; thus he avoids the not uncommon tendency to blame women for resistance to what, in the unfortunate phrase of the time, was known as "emancipation of the flesh."

The story has a few other remarkable aspects as well. One I have already touched upon: the untroubled recognition of the fact that there can be such an affect in a heroine as sexuality, not a very striking matter for our own time, but a promising development in the early nineteenth century, especially because Mundt has his "Madonna" treat it with decorum but without coquettishness or fear.

Maria describes in a fairly graphic way the experience of puberty and the awareness that sexuality is developing in her. She even tells something of her feelings at inadvertently watching Mellenberg, in a room near hers, undressing for bed, although she not unreasonably breaks off this account.[111] Another interesting point is the dilemma in which she finds herself in her aunt's house. Even as a child, she is quick-witted enough to figure out what is going on. She naturally takes a dim view of the situation; the difficulty is that she takes genuine pleasure in the advantages she enjoys; she is delighted to be educated, to live in comfort, to have all the material objects and pleasurable outings she desires. It is unusual that neither Maria nor the author sees this as a moral defect. One is given rather the impression that it is good for a human being to have pleasurable and urbane surroundings, to acquire cultivated accomplishments and love handsome possessions. Mundt's strategies here remind one of Heine's dislike of Jacobin puritanism and his belief that the reformation of society should bring more joy to more men, not less. They are a not inconsiderable virtue of this novella.

Another is Mundt's characterization of the count. Although he is engaged in a scheme that is deeply disrespectful of the personal freedom of another human being, attempting literally to buy and breed Maria as though she were a pet, he is not presented as a monster, but rather as a pleasant, urbane, and vaguely well-meaning gentleman whom Maria does not really hate; she is indifferent to him personally and dislikes passionately only the dehumanizing situation into which he has put her. With a surprising realistic instinct, Mundt here avoids a melodramatic pitfall. There is one additional and effective moment in the novella. Mellenberg's suicide and Maria's helpless despair at it occur simultaneously with a religious riot in Dresden, caused by the refusal of the Catholic authorities to allow the Protestant population properly to celebrate the tricentennial of the Augsburg Confession. As Mellenberg's death is caused by allegiance to obsolete religious principles, so the whole of society is thrown into disorder by primitive and obsolete religious passion. The Augsburg Confession had, after all, been negotiated in 1530; that society should be still tormented by it must have seemed as absurd to Mundt as the religious conflicts in Northern Ireland seem to us today. With this juxtaposition, Mundt achieved a meaningful integration of a private fate and a wider social incongruity such as is rare in Young German fiction.

These virtues of Mundt's story do not make of him an outstanding writer, nor do they suggest that, under differing circumstances, he could have become one. They do indicate that the predication of mediocrity to one of the struggling young writers of this period is beside the point. Mundt's *Madonna* shows that there was enough intellectual and realistic material at hand in 1835 to make competent and worthwhile literary writing possible. If not by Mundt, then by another; but the real issue is not the failings and limitations of Mundt, but those of a ruling class of society that strangled these beginnings in their cradle.

IV. FERDINAND GUSTAV KÜHNE: *EINE QUARANTÄNE IM IRRENHAUSE*

Ferdinand Gustav Kühne was more on the periphery than in the mainstream of the Young German movement, although from time to time he applied the label to himself. He was not named in the proscription of 1835 and, as far as I know, became involved in the mill of the censorship only twice: his *Klosternovellen* were not permitted to be published in Mundt's *Dioskuren* in 1837[1] because of their anti-Catholic tone, a theme that Kühne pursued vigorously in later years in the spirit of the *Kulturkampf*; the other occasion was a series of proscriptions and fines in the early 1850's, for Kühne became a genuine "forty-eighter," if a middle-of-the-road one, whose periodical *Europa*, which he took over in 1846, published a number of the important *Vormärz* liberals, and he fell afoul of the repressive measures of the authorities after the failure of the revolution.[2] He did grieve at the censorship under which the Young Germans suffered; he wrote to an elderly lady friend in 1837: "Die Maßregeln gegen die junge Literatur haben mich nicht vernichtet, aber gelähmt. Es ist eine böse, böse Zeit. Der innere Mensch ist so gut, warm und kräftig, aber die Objectivität der Welt erdrückt ihn. Der innere Mensch möchte auferstehen wie ein weltlicher Christus, aber der Stein über dem Grabe will nicht weichen, die Engel, die ihn heben müßten, sind verscheucht, die Engel der Unschuld, Milde und Liebe — und der Stein bleibt von der Polizei versiegelt."[3] Kühne had some fleeting acquaintance with Gutzkow, but his main line of contact to Young Germany was Mundt, with whom he maintained a life-long if not untroubled friendship beginning with their school-days together in Berlin. If we have quarrelled with the predication of mediocrity to Mundt, it is difficult to do so in the case of Kühne, for, though not insensitive or unintelligent, he was a fairly ordinary soul, almost a philistine in the mundane conventionality that underlay the superficial lability of his thought and feeling. Although he wrote

81

prose works all his life — historical novels, mainly — and some drama and occasional verse, he seems, by the standards of a Gutzkow, a Laube, or an Immermann, to have been almost wholly devoid of literary gifts. A more justly forgotten writer is hard to imagine.

In 1835, however, the year of the crisis, Kühne published a novel that gives us a tour inside the head of a chafing young liberal of the time, and for that reason it is of value for our investigation. Kühne himself regarded it as a major breakthrough after a series of unsatisfying novellas and later called it a book of "blutige Schmerzen."[4] It is entitled *Eine Quarantäne im Irrenhause* and its plot is as follows: the unnamed hero is the son of an aristocratic mother and a bourgeois father. His mother's brother, the prime minister of a small principality, dislikes him because of this odious mésalliance and is suspicious of him for other reasons. The hero pursues the intellectual life without making any effort to take up a useful occupation, and his brooding and thinking upset his uncle, who, a former Jacobin enthusiast, has become a fanatic absolutist and persecutor of youthful demagogues. Even worse, the nephew has become attached to an opera singer named Victorine Miaska, a patriotic refugee from the crushed Polish revolution. The uncle has his nephew and, shortly thereafter, Victorine, incarcerated in a madhouse to cure them of their deviant attitudes. The hero escapes with Victorine and three other characters. Victorine returns home just at the moment when her ill mother, in despair at the rude treatment she has been receiving from the authorities, shoots herself; Victorine, while wrestling with a policeman for the pistol, is shot and killed. The uncle, meanwhile, in his fanatic hatred of the rebellious younger generation, has become genuinely insane and must be confined, although in a lucid moment just before his death, he reconciles himself with his nephew. This action, which is reported in a day-to-day diary so extensive that it is impossible to imagine its author would have had time to participate in the events described, covers eighteen days.

There are a few other complications, but this, in essence, is the story, and one can easily see that so plain if melodramatic a plot cannot account for a novel of 335 pages. It does not, although the plot itself has some clear symbolic significance. The attachment of the young liberal to the patriotic Polish girl has an obvious ideological import, as does the policeman whose grip on her is likened to the grip of Russia on Poland. The Soviet-style effort to repress dissent by ignoring its content and ascribing intellectual deviation to insanity is an acid commentary on the atmosphere of the time; it is a telling coincidence that, during the crisis at the end of 1835, the Saxon government proposed that all Young Germans be put into prison or into the madhouse.[5] It cannot be determined whether the persecuting, lunatic uncle has any reference to the Prussian censorship official, Gustav Adolf von Tzschoppe, who, as was well known within the government and to some extent outside it, suffered from serious mental disturbance, but Kühne's strategy appears apposite in retrospect. However, such observations do not define the character of this novel, which, much more obviously than Gutzkow's *Wally*, is a vessel for its author's thinking processes — one sees easily in reading Kühne's letters of the time that his hero is a more extreme case of his own bewilderment and alienation.

The main purpose served by the fiction is to permit the intellectual discourse to run on and round about without logical restraint. It is not fundamentally a question of genre, but of the quantity of interest that this interminable verbiage holds for the reader: "Für den heutigen Leser," remarked Houben sixty years ago, "ist Kühnes Buch eine ziemlich schwere Lektüre, und man kann dieses Chaos von mehr oder weniger geistreichen Paradoxien, redseligen Betrachtungen, historisch-politischen Reflexionen usw. nur überwinden, wenn man eine sehr intime Kenntnis der Zeitgeschichte, ihrer Blüten und Auswüchse zur Kontrolle gegenwärtig hat."[6] Equally to the point is the critique that the novelist Heinrich König wrote to Kühne in 1854 of his novel *Die Freimaurer*, for it shows that Kühne was never able to find his way to a more objective narrative form or to overcome his discursive, intellectualized style:

Indem Sie aber eigentliche "Familienpapiere" geben, haben Sie — absichtlich oder aus Instinkt — die weiteste und bequemste Form poetischer Darstellung für ein so mächtiges Material gewählt, und müssen nun freilich auch hinnehmen, was dem Dichter, wie Sie wissen, zu begegnen pflegt, daß er sich nämlich seine Leser nur in dem Maße fesselt, als er sich selber bindet.... An concreten Erlebnissen fehlt es zwar in Ihren Mittheilungen auch nicht, aber nur einzelne sind wahrhaft lebendig und hinreißend ausgefallen und dazwischen kommen wieder Strecken vor, über welche hin der Erzähler im Bündel seiner *Erlebnisse* zu schwer an den *Studien* des

Dichters über Literatur und Leben zu tragen hat. Die Betrachtungen sind geistreich, treffend; gute Laune und Witz fehlen nicht, aber man fühlt zu oft lebhaft, daß alles dies Eigenthum des Dichters ist, das die wechselnden Erzähler als eigenes Gepäck tragen müssen.[7]

Similar objections can easily be made to *Quarantäne*, in which both action and characterization are submerged in the philosophical brooding of the twenty-eight-year-old author.

Quarantäne is a book about madness, not primarily in a clinical, psychological sense, although there is some concern with that. (Kühne's father was a difficult, both tyrannical and morbidly dependent person who became mentally unbalanced after his wife's death.) But its chief concern is to describe a pathology of the intellect and the times. Kühne wrote to his publisher on 26 December 1834 that the "Novelle, obwohl sie in Form eines Dichtwerks erscheint, eigentlich eine Pathologie des modernen Lebens genannt werden kann."[8] The pathology is related in a complicated way to the repressiveness of the times, of which the madhouse, a kind of compassionate prison, is a symbol. In one of the rare moments of compact writing in the book, Kühne describes an inmate who loses his grip while digging potatoes: "Einer der Arbeiter schwang plötzlich seinen Spaten wie ein grimmiger Türke über den Kopf. Er stieß ein lautes, wieherndes Geschrei aus: es war wie ein Angstruf der verzweifelnden Menschheit, die nach Ruhe schnaubt. Der Aufseher, der ihm zur Seite stand, griff ihn aber hart an die Brust und schüttelte ihn tüchtig. Da besann sich der Arme wieder und grub hastig nach seinen Erdäpfeln weiter" (p. 28).[9] The question of how the madhouse and its inmates relate to the world and the general condition of mankind is one matter of interest in trying to understand Kühne's book.

The initial question, however, is that of the sanity of the diarist himself. Almost his first assertion is that he is sane, although he admits to a physical fever and delirium from which he is now recovering. But both the validity and the meaning of this assertion are quickly called into question by the subsequent course of the narrator's brooding, which zigzags in unresolved antinomies and revolves round and round with pedantic, almost lunatic persistence. The asylum's doctor, after having read part of the diary, says not without justice that it contains "bei manchen lichten Intervallationslinien viel mystische Hieroglyphe, viel dämonisch irres Getriebe, nicht ohne Methode, aber überwacht, übernommen, mein Verehrtester" (p. 185). Persistent argumentation with constantly shifting premises was apparently a characteristic of Kühne; in a touchy letter of 1828, Mundt complained of Kühne's heat in disputation and that "Du oft den Streit um wichtige Gegenstände in precäre Kleinigkeiten concentrirt und Dich mit der Sache selbst in einem sophistischen Zirkel herumgedreht [hast]."[10] The perpetual inner monologue in *Quarantäne* is not unlike this way of arguing, although here it is objectified into a distracted and representative individual, of whom it is said in the "editor's" preface that he is a self-tormentor and a negative example of the delusion of the times (pp. v, vi). The question of the meaning of sanity is raised immediately with the hero's claim that he is sane; here, as elsewhere, it is indicated that sanity is a state of harmless normality enforced by repression; at the same time, the hero claims such normality for himself, while indicating ironically that this is hardly the whole truth and suggesting an uneasy balance between his intellectual speculations and his remoteness from active life.

At the outset of the novel, there is a certain eccentric shrewdness in this nervously oscillating self-presentation. The best way to show the character of this prose is to quote a passage at considerable length. The hero is trying to figure out the reason for his sudden incarceration:

> Ich hörte auf der Reise viel munkeln von Verhaftbefehlen gegen Alle, die nur jemals im Geruche der Burschenschafterei gestanden; die frankfurter Unruhen [the storming of the constabulary in April, 1833] hatten zu dieser Maßregel einen nur zu triftigen Beweggrund gegeben, oder nicht Beweggrund, Veranlassung, Befürchtungsgrund, nicht Beweggrund. Großer Gott! Bewegung! verruchtes Wort! Wie kann ich Bewegung den Verfolgern der Bewegung zumuthen. Den Grund boten die frankfurter Trivialitäten; auf den Grund wollte man der Sache kommen, selbst wenn sie bodenlos sein sollte. Aber ich für mein Theil war nie Burschenschaftler gewesen, ich konnte nicht verdächtigt werden, ich konnte vor Gericht nichts aussagen, ich bin weit unschuldiger noch als Staberl, der mit einem Flüchtling den Rock wechselt und so dessen Signalement auf seinen Rücken nimmt. Ich war zeitlebens ein viel zu timider Mensch,

85

ich war zu geizig mit meinen Gedanken, um einen einzigen derselben für zehn Revolutionsideen umzutauschen. Ich lebte in B. so still wie eine Kirchenmaus Jahr aus Jahr ein. Stille Kirchenmäuse zernagen freilich oft die Hostien im Tempel und zerfressen die Sacramente des Lebens, allein man stellt Gift hin neben die heiligen Dinge und ist dann sicher gegen den Zahn der Kritik so kleiner Wesen. Auch für den Zahn der Zeit hat man Gift genug; man kann ruhig schlafen und Alles gut sein lassen. Politische Zeitungen hatte ich gelesen, politische Gedanken im Kopfe gehegt, des Völkerlebens Lust und Leid im Herzen getragen, allein nie ein Wort hinausgesprochen aus der verschlossenen Brust; Gedanken und Gefühle waren unausgebrütete Eier geblieben unter den schirmenden Flügeln einer policeilichen Stiefmutterhenne. Mein Ich hatte ich selten hinausgedrängt auf den Markt des Ruhmes; ich hatte mehr als eine Persönlichkeit, mehr als mein Ich suchen wollen und war freilich so vereinsamt geblieben, daß ich doch nichts hatte und behielt von all meinem emsigen Forschen und Grübeln, als die mein armes, kleines, winziges Ich. Ich schien der gefahrloseste weil unbrauchbarste Mensch im Staate, ich war von je der stillste Bürger dieser Erdenwelt. Elegien könnte ich schreiben über die mein stilles wissenschaftliches Vegetiren: warum mich gefänglich einziehn? Blos auf mein ehrlich Gesicht hin und mit einem kraftgültigen Paß versehen, hatte ich mich in das Ausland, d. h. in ein deutsches Ausland, hineingewagt. Meiner Schulden wegen konn ich nicht gefänglich eingezogen werden, denn mich drückten kein ein Engagement hatte ich nicht, wie reisende und ausreißen Künstler, im Stich gelassen, denn mich band keines; wegen ve säumter Amtspflicht konnte ich auch nicht eingezogen werden, de ich war ja in meiner Heimat ein eben so amtloses wie harmlos Individuum. Ich wollte eine Vergnügungsreise machen, sowie i überhaupt zum Vergnügen lebe und zum Vergnügen sterben w wenn's sein muß. Ich lebe in meiner Heimat, wie man so zu sag pflegt, ganz frei und ungebunden, amtsfrei und — so lange G will — schuldenfrei. Sollte man diese Freiheit nicht erlauben

Ich bin in B. blos Mensch, Doctor der Philosophie, auch Magis der brotlosen Künste. Wäge ich diese drei Würden gegen einand ab, so fällt auf die Menschenwürde das meiste Gewicht. Ich l nichts, rein nichts, man kann mich nicht verhaften. Philosoph beargwöhnt man, sie haben oft falsche Begriffe von der Freih verbreitet. Advocaten und Doctoren der Philosophie standen an der Spitze der neuesten trostlosen Bewegungen. Allein ich als Philosoph demonstrire Jedem, nach Hegel, daß Freiheit und Notwendigkeit identisch sind, und bin demnach ein gefahrloses Wesen. Ich bin sonst ein stiller friedlicher Mensch, aber wenn man mich reizt, so habe ich einige dialektische Fünffingergriffe bei der Hand, die ich dem Inquisitor um die Ohren schlage, daß ihm seinerseits die fünf Sinne vergehen. Ich kann als Philosoph nicht arretirt werden; auch lebe ich nicht von der Philosophie, vielmehr lebt und zehrt der Philosoph in mir vom Menschen in mir; als absoluter Philosoph will ich nichts Anderes sein als ein absoluter Mensch. Bin ich nun als absoluter Mensch unschuldig: wer will mich verhaften? Als Magister der brotlosen Künste sterb' ich mehr als daß ich lebe Aber gesetzt ich hätte mein Brot von den brotlosen Künsten. bedauern mögt ihr mich; wer will mich aber verhaften? Ich lebe nur zum Vergnügen, und wenn mir Einer beweist, ich würde, falls ich länger des Vergnügens wegen lebte, vergnügenshalber umkommen, so beweist das noch nicht, daß ich vergnügenshalber gefänglich eingezogen werden darf. Das ist kein Privatvergnügen mehr, das greift in die Sache der Gerechtigkeit und Staatsverwaltung, und die Zeiten sind vorüber, wo Recht und Gerechtigkeit blos zum Vergnügen der sogenannten Großen dieser Welt gehandhabt wurden. Lebten wir in einem *ancien régime,* so wüßte ich, daß es *lettres-de-cachet* gäbe und tröstete mich dann mit dem nicht unbedeutenden Range eines Wirklichen Geheimen Staatsgefangenen; allein in dem Bewußtsein, weder innerlich noch äußerlich etwas Burschenschaftliches an mir zu tragen, glaubte ich sicher meines Weges gehen zu können und bin doch bitter getäuscht.

Aber wie trug sich die Sache nur zu? — Während ich darauf sinne, merke ich erst, wie absorbirend ein Fieber auf die Gedächtnißkraft wirkt. Das klare Denken hält noch schwer (pp. 3-6).

It takes a long passage like this to see Kühne's manner most clearly, for each element or segment of it is influenced by what comes before or after; what appears to be a series of statements in discursive prose is actually a continuous floundering about in a sea of unstable attitudes and feelings. Stylistically, the prose is haunted by the pale ghost of Jean Paul: the oblique allusiveness, the continuous punning, the onrunning chain of associations, and the frantic grasp for the integrity of the peeling, splintering self all indicate that model. The change in tone and purpose, however, is just as evident. There is no liberating humor here, very little wit, no aesthetic playfulness with language; it is all dead earnest and quite desperate. Its principle quality is an elusive irony that seems to imply more than it says. The hero insists he cannot be arrested, when in fact he has been; he appears confident that he is not living in an arbitrary *ancien régime*, but he is indeed the victim, although he does not know it at this point, of something rather similar to a *lettre-de-cachet*. He is insistent that he is by no means a revolutionary, although his side glances at contemporary political repression are bitter and the queer simile of the churchmouse introduces an attitude of critical opposition and adverts to the poisonous defenses of the status quo against it. His quietude and harmlessness are forced upon him, his philosophy condemned to inactivity, yet somehow he has come into conflict with authority despite his apparently private character. With all its irony and allusiveness, the prose is, in a sense, rich, yet, at the same time, it lacks density; what presents itself as thinking and concentration is in fact the running on of a mind threatened with diffuseness and a failure of logical control — and, one must add, an intellectual narcissism that hinders the effort to find solutions to the problems because it is part of the causes of them.

The writer of this prose is bleakly self-ironic. In another place he describes the scene of his arrest: "Der Himmel hatte sich schwarz umgezogen, ein Gewitter kündigte sich in lauten Schlägen an, der Regen goß in dichten Strömen. Das gehört zur abgenutzten Romantik der Entführungsgeschichten" (p. 12). Reactionary life imitates obsolete art, yet the writer of these lines is victimized himself by the conditions under which he tries to think and cannot get out of the maze of abstraction and disembodied conceptualizing. His intellectual equipment continually carries him away from rather than toward clarity and reality. At the beginning of the second day of his diary, he tries to mobilize his "inner freedom" in order to be "ideally" not in the madhouse (p. 21), and he experiments with a version of Fichte that turns out to be parody: "Ich bin ich, das ist das Staatsgrundgesetz des psychologischen Menschen, das Ich hat Alles in sich, begreift, beherrscht Alles. *L'état c'est moi*" (p. 22). He continues twisting and turning in this vein, again punning from dilemma to dilemma, with similes always on the periphery of critical allusion, until he is indeed incarcerated. The style, therefore, can be intriguing, but after many pages of this the reader becomes distressed and wearied, not only because the interminable paradoxes seem to revolve more and more pointlessly and the jejune self-absorption of the memoirist gradually causes us to lose interest in him, but also because one gets less and less the feeling that there is a controlling intelligence behind it all; the gap between narrating author and narrated character shrinks to near zero, and what appears at first to be a kind of shrewdness in representing intellectual bewilderment turns into hopeless bewilderment itself. The author, the reader comes to feel, is permitting himself too much; the lack of discipline of which Heinrich König complained leads to self-indulgence.

The theme of madness is turned over and over, dissected and reassembled, and set into dialectical puzzles. The narrator, for good reason, fears for his own sanity. He becomes curious about the doctor's methods of treatment and thinks of pretending madness, but senses immediately the danger he is in: "O Hamlet, Hamlet! Du *wurdest* was Du schienst! — Mein Gott, führe uns nicht in Versuchung!" (p. 30). Later, after a curious disquisition on the relationship of suicide to madness, he remarks strangely that he could forgive a suicide, but would avert his eyes from a madman, because "ich hasse sein Bild meinetwegen; meinetwegen, ich fürchte, gerade weil ich ihn liebe, die Ansteckung" (p. 74). The suicide is a martyr of error, he says, but madness is "ein Vergehen gegen die Weisheit unserer Tage" (p. 72). But this statement is ironic, for competing definitions of sanity are at stake also. In arguing with the doctor, he finds his vigorous efforts to prove his sanity only make the doctor more suspicious, and he concludes that men and nations should reason less and accept more; then they would be thought mature. In this view, sanity is defined by convention as accomodation to authority: "Ich sprach von meiner gesunden Vernunft wie ein Volk, das plötzlich emancipirt sein will. Grade das Drängende der Über-zeugung duldet man nicht" (p. 31). Later he determines, in order to please his doctor-jailer, to be "fromm und sanft ... wie ein Lamm" (p. 148). Thus there is a tendency for sanity to take on a pejorative aspect as a kind of normality that accepts repression and avoids all creative, imaginative aberration.

But the alternatives are by no means clear. One of the patients is a demented clergyman who is obsessed with water as a panacea for all the ills of the time. He is the kind of grotesque eccentric that Karl Immermann was to make a speciality of in his two major novels. He derives soul and temperament from climatic conditions — a satirical anticipation of Taine — and wants to cure the world with laxatives. Like Immermann's characters of this type, the clergyman is not only an object of satire, but also a vehicle of it: "Philosophie, Poesie, Politik," he observes, "Alles ist bis zu einem Wahnsinnsgipfel hinaufgedrängt und möchte sich von oben kopfüber hinabstürzen" (p. 93). But the hero, in one of the idealistic rhapsodies to which he is prone, denounces the clergyman for the materialism of his views. On the other hand, the doctor recommends to the hero for emulation the clergyman's successor, whose philistine moderation is rather too pedestrian:

> ein solider Seelsorger für seine Bauern, ermahnt sie zu rechtschaffenem Wandel, tauft, traut und beackert nebenbei sein Feld, hält Land, Leute und Vieh in guter Ordnung und läßt Gott einen guten Mann sein, der im Himmel sitzt und thut was er will und was kein Mensch weiß. Der vernünftige junge Pfarrer wirft die Schöpfung nicht kunterbunt durcheinander, sucht nicht in Gott die Natur, nicht in der Natur den Gott zu deuten und hält Alles hübsch auseinander, das blöde Geschlecht der Vierfüßer, den dummen Erdenkloß, Mensch genannt, und den allmächtigen Herrn der Welt. So bleibt er fromm und moralisch gut und hält sich den Wahnsinn vom Leibe (p. 105).

Such, apparently, is the goal of mental health. Kühne's hero rebels against it; when the doctor has certified him as sane, the hero sardonically speaks of himself as now "abstract verständig, tugendhaft nüchtern" (p. 190), but he quickly becomes bored in this condition, which he identifies as one devoid of passion and imagination, and he launches, as is his wont, into a long, purple rhapsody on this theme.

These variations are complicated still further, however, so that one is eventually at a loss just how to interpret and judge the question. For it occurs to our author also to make madness a function of modern civilization, which is teetering at the height of intellectual perception between being and non-being, while just below the animal part of man threatens, Mephisto lurks, and with him, madness. "Es ist ausgemacht, daß die Zahl der Irren mit den Fortschritten der Bildung bei allen Völkern steigt" (p. 58). The doctor, for his part, suggests that the whole world should establish itself as a mental institution (p. 209), and he lectures the hero on the increase in madness that has accompanied the progress of modern philosophy (pp. 177-184). On the other hand, it may be that the conventional life of society is a refuge against madness — and, simultaneously, a flight from feeling and imagination, a view not dissimilar to that found in Gutzkow's *Wally* (see above, p. 48). The doctor flirts with the female patients because "er mochte überzeugt sein, daß es zweckmäßig sei, die Reconvalescenten allmälig an den gesammten Unsinn des Gesellschaftslebens zu gewöhnen, und er hat Recht, sehr Recht, denn wer sich mit seiner ganzen Persönlichkeit in die Manieren des Visitenlebens hüllt, der hat eine gute Schutzdecke um sich gegen alle Gefährnisse der Gemüthswelt" (pp. 108-109). If a young lady has a little religion, dabbles in manners and fashions, knows a little of languages and love, reads a little Schiller and Goethe, "wie soll da ein Wahnsinn in solch einer erbärmlich zerstückelten und verflachten Seele seine Rechnung finden?" (p. 109); the madness would die of boredom. But, our hero pontificates, woe to you when the Lord asks you to give an account of the content of your life: "welches Gefühl war der Leiter, welcher Gedanke der Träger Eurer Seele im Wandel der Vergänglichkeiten?" (ibid.). There must be something in us, even if only an eccentricity or a whim, to live for; the life of society is only a homeopathic cure. If the reader thinks he understands this, two things militate against that conclusion. One is that the hero, as often happens, winds up his whole argument by denouncing it; he criticizes himself for drawing constant distinctions between madness and reason, whereas in fact everything is a mixture (pp. 110-111). The other concerns his view of the narcotic emptiness of social life; for, as it happens, the hero's childhood was spent in salon society and is pictured as bright, happy, and full of stimulation.

The possibility mentioned above that madness might be a function of contemporary philosophy and intellectual life is yet another tangent. The reason, apparently, that this philosophical brooding cannot come to rest is because it is, by choice or by necessity, out of touch with living reality. This is perceived as a specifically German problem: "Die geistige Cultur unsrer Zeit ist so mit Dampfapparaten in die Höhe getrieben, daß mehr Wahnsinn in der Welt herrscht als man denken sollte und nach dem System der speculativen Vernunft-Wirklichkeit [whatever that may be] zu denken gestattet ist.

Und eben dies Denken und Denken-Sollen ist es, an dem wir Deutschen einen Narren gegessen haben, um nicht gefressen zu sagen. Andere Nationen werfen sich auf reelle Stoffe, und ihre Narrheit wird von dem Materiellen bezwungen" (pp. 39-40). While other nations discover new worlds, travel through the air, invent railroads and steam engines, the Germans have "wässerige Moralsysteme, luftige Naturspeculationen, eisenharte Begriffsbestimmungen und qualmige Theorien" (p. 40). Thus the hero would seem to be caught in a vicious circle, for he is committed to philosophy, yet this commitment is involved with his perilous mental state. The hero's effort to cure himself and to emancipate himself from philosophy through philosophy is one of his fundamental ambivalences.

There are many others. Pertinent to our purposes are particularly those dealing with the social and political context. In the constantly shifting dialectic of these musings, it is not promising to look for a coherent social and political position, but one can keep one's eyes open for a certain instinct, for Kühne, in the course of time, did develop a clear position: one of classical bourgeois liberalism, anticlerical, pro-parliament, national, and decidedly opposed to any revolutionary movement on the part of the lower classes. Kühne was shocked by the killing, during a popular demonstration, of two right-wing members of the Frankfurt parliament in September, 1848, General von Auerswald and Prince Lichnowsky, and he welcomed the use of soldiers "gegen die ehrlosen Räuberhorden und Barrikadenhelden, die sich Demokraten nennen";[11] on the other hand, the lawless execution of the moderate democrat Robert Blum in Vienna drew from Kühne an "objective" judgment, the main point of which was that Blum's death was his own fault.[12] These results in Kühne's maturity may be usefully kept in mind in what follows.

There are passages in *Quarantäne* that reveal some traces of an apocalyptic longing for revolutionary violence, in which revolutionary war appears as the poetic war of our time: "Nach der Liebe ist der Haß die schönste Leidenschaft. Jemand hassen, der die Krone des Lebens stahl und mit frecher Hand in dein Heiligthum griff, das macht dich zum Halbgott. Religionskriege sind die blutigsten, aber auch die schönsten, und wäre der Gott, der die Gemüther entflammt, auch nur ein Dämon, ein Phantom — die Poesie der Leidenschaft redet und tönt in tausend Zungen" (p. 9); and the passage goes on to remark that freedom is the religion of our time. Another facet of this longing is an argument recurring from time to time that sin, violence, and the diabolical are necessary to keep the dialectical forces of life in motion. Life is a tragedy, it is argued, and sin is a necessity; "die Tugend ist ein Abstractum, der lebendige Mensch in Kampf und Noth ist das Concrete" (p. 236). "Ohne Teufel [e.g., Napoleon] keine Weltgeschichte!" "Das Diabolische hat Jeder in sich: sehe nur Jeder zu, daß auch sein innerer Christus miterwache!" (p. 237). With this last phrase, of course, Kühne's closet diabolism drifts back into harmlessness. The same theme is involved in the hero's passionate defense of Don Giovanni and his dismissal of the avenging Stone Guest as a philistine: "die Philosophie, die das Leben besser gemacht hätte, die die Sünde blos verketzert und in dem Bösen und seiner Verlockung nicht vielmehr den Impuls, die Erectionskraft [!] der Menschengeschichte sieht, ist eine falsche Philosophie" (p. 239).

Once in a great while these effusions spill over into the realm of the relationship between literature and politics, with which is involved an ambivalent view of Börne and Heine, who are mentioned, usually paired, several times in the book. At one point the narrator launches upon a breathless rhapsody on the need for democratic exchange of ideas: the world is in an uproar, poets fling their verses out into the open air; the diabolical Börne sits on the ruins of the state and Heine on the ruins of Christianity (pp. 131-132). But such experimentation with radical rhetoric causes an automatic shift to a more moderate stance, for the hero then inquires plaintively whether bourgeois society must be destroyed in the process, and goes on to assert that reason is democratic, not Jacobin, it is oppositional in itself — if only its workings were not so slow (p. 132). Typically, the passage ends with the complaint that the hero cannot revolutionize anything but his own head (pp. 132-133). The turn to an inner, harmonious religiosity is characteristic of Kühne throughout *Quarantäne*. An example of this, and of the way in which each little action in the novel generates a weighty gloss, is the hero's meditation on the fact that he has put a note from Victorine in his breast pocket on the left side: "Die linke Seite ist in der Welt oft genug die rechte, die Oppositionsseite oft genug die Seite der Wahrheit. Nur das Gesuchte, das Absichtliche darf nicht hervorstecken als der Stachel des *diaconus diaboli.* Die Linksmacher sind auch immer die Rechtsverdreher. Alles muß wie eine Blume sein auf Gottes freiem Felde, keine Treibhauspflanze. So die Politik, Poesie, Philosophie, das ganze volle Leben" (p. 205). Much that is characteristic of Kühne is concentrated in this passage: the timid assumption of and then withdrawal from an oppositional posture, the punning and the strained metaphors, the insistence on keeping a religious context intact, and the drift into portentous banality.

Young Kühne shared with the Young Germans and much of the liberal movement generally a weakness for monarchy. In a discussion of the false extremes of patriotism, his hero asserts that true patriotism "huldigt der Persönlichkeit des Monarchen und lebt in der Idee, die der Staat welthistorisch dermaleinst in der Wirklichkeit zu erfüllen berufen ist" (p. 33). The Hegelian jargon points to another problem that will be touched upon presently; the difficulty with such sentiments is that it was hard to locate real kings deserving of such veneration, and, indeed, some years later, in Berlin in 1843, remarking upon the general unhappiness and depression of the atmosphere, Kühne is obliged to remark of Frederick William IV: "Der König steht schon ganz isoliert. Es wäre nicht so unerhört, machten ihn die Zustände zum deutschen sechzehnten Ludwig. Er ist so characterlos und so liebenswürdig wie dieser."[13] But when it came to liberal agitation and revolutionary threats, Kühne, despite his apparent willingness to accept the violent and chaotic as part of the dialectic of life, was by and large of a negative disposition in *Quarantäne*. It is not quite certain whether this reflects an anti-democratic attitude or whether it was that liberal behavior aroused in him a Heinesque sense of the absurd. At one point, harping on the theme of madness, the hero reflects that a general insanity might take over mankind at the height of civilization. "Ein ganzes wahnsinniges Volk gäbe ein Schauspiel, das noch nicht da war im Lauf der Geschichte!" (p. 59). We who have seen this show in our century may well be struck by this passage, but unfortunately it turns out that it is liberal and egalitarian phenomena that presage this development. One symptom of the incipient madness of civilization is the convention of German liberals at Hambach in May, 1832, "ein Haufe Menschen, die einigen Irrenanstalten entlaufen sind" (ibid.). The mad society will be one in which class distinctions are erased and the Saint-Simonian doctrine will gain the upper hand: "Jeder Lump von der Gasse wäre Souverain, die Könige knieten im Kothe vor ihm und küßten den Saum seiner

Fetzen"; everyone would be a sans-culotte and run around without trousers, nature would be the highest divinity, the rehabilitation of the flesh would be the first religious and political principle; instead of gods there would be only goddesses and women would be held in common; all life would be a "Ragout von Sodom und Gomorrah" (p. 60). One would take this to be a piece of reactionary, un-Young German satire, were it not that positions and attitudes are only tasted and tested in this work and are nowhere firmly founded; a feeble, unclear irony is characteristic of the book, and on the other occasion on which Hambach is mentioned (pp. 168-169), there is a more ironic treatment of freedom as *Schein* in the German double meaning of "shine" and "illusion."

The general tendency, however, is toward a critique and suspicion of the most exposed salients of the liberal opposition. Young Germany itself the hero apostrophizes as follows: "Junges Deutschland! ... Dein Leben scheint mir hektisch, eine rapide Schwindsucht! Du bist engathmig, Du keuchst. Tanze und rase Dich nicht zunichte und zu nichts; Deine Galopade ist weiter nichts als eine Gallomanie. Nimm Dich in Acht, daß Du nicht zu früh alt, in Deiner Jugend schon alt wirst, und dann nichts mehr jung bleibt als die alte Vernunft, der ewig alte und ewig junge Phönix deutschen Denkens und deutschen Dichtens" (p. 232) — a good passage for demonstrating that neither Kühne nor his hero know what it is they mean. Real revolution is certainly suspect in this perspective. The reactionary, absolutist uncle is said to have been, in his equally radical, Jacobin youth, a "Freiheitsschwindler" (p. 319). The metaphorical association of Kühne's hero with a patriotic refugee of the Polish revolution is not without its ambivalence, through which the typically liberal theme of sympathy for the fate of Poland is modified. Victorine is committed to the madhouse because she physically resisted an arresting officer and for that reason was thought to be mad; self-defense against arbitrary authority thus appears to be a symptom of madness, and, after a long disquisition on Poland's lamentable fate, the hero indicates that the Polish desire for freedom was a form of insanity (p. 271). This suggests, as do other aspects of the text, an ironic despair at the suppression of liberty, but it is also indicated that the suffering of the Poles is due to their own deficiencies; Victorine is said to be typically Polish, strong and firm, but unsteady and excitable in mood, unable to distinguish friend from foe (pp.

95

274-275). In retrospect, one must in fairness think that in 1830/31 it was a little difficult for the Poles to discern who their friends were.

What is detectable in all this is a steady, though perhaps not wholly conscious drift into the Biedermeier attitude: a retreat from these exacerbating dilemmas into private virtues, private relationships, and privately maintained harmonies. That this process did in fact take place in Kühne is indicated by his love-letters to his fiancée, which Edgar Pierson published at embarrassing length. In one of them Kühne asserts plainly that "es ist lohnender Wenigen viel zu sein, als Vielen wenig. Daran schließt sich mein Glaube, daß das Familienleben wichtiger ist für Herz und Geist als das Gesellschaftsleben."[14] The attractive force of private virtuousness and harmony is evident in the novel itself. After having described the mad society of lost class distinction and Saint-Simonian emancipation, the hero goes on to predict that in such a society those who pursued the old-fashioned virtues, pieties, family life, and idealism would be preserved as antiquities in madhouses that would serve also as museums; the writer of these memoirs is already there. In this context, madness is not the longing for unattainable liberties, but the maintenance of conservative virtues, and it is positive, not pejorative. It is this sort of thing that puts the novel beyond any clear ideological definition. In the very few places where it raises the question of the cure for madness, however, the conservative tendency comes into the foreground. In denouncing the clergyman with his materialistic philosophy of the constipated age and the need for a purifying water cure, the hero asserts that madness can only be cured by something harmonious, like music, which in turn is an indication of "eine tiefere Musik . . ., eine Musik der Poesie, die unserer Zeit fehlt, eine Harmonie der Gefühle, die uns Deutsche allein zum Verständniß unserer selber bringt und zur Überzeugung, wir seien Ein Volk im Denken und Dichten" (p. 99). Man can be above the animals only, he continues, if the spirit exists "selbständig als Ursubstanz für sich von Ewigkeit zu Ewigkeit" (p. 101). In this connection, the hero accuses the pastor of being "ein grober, ein *deutscher* Saintsimonist" (ibid.). And it turns out at last, with the example of Mozart's *Don Giovanni*, that it is art, just as the Romantics thought, that contains in its eternal verities of the imagination and the spirit the cure for modern man: "Die Kunst muß heilen vom

Wahnwitz des Lebens, sie selbst ist der schönere, der göttliche Wahnsinn. In ihr müssen wir uns Alle wieder zurechtfinden, wir Alle und alle Völker der Erde. Es bleibt der Welt nichts Anderes übrig" (p. 279).

There is another alternative to the perilous state of the modern mind, however; parallel with the longing for ordered, private, aesthetically elevated circumstances is the longing to escape from this perpetual conceptualizing and to overcome madness by entering the real world. The hero becomes weary of metaphysics, which has not made him wise or brought him to the quietude of abstraction; it only urges him toward life, and teaches him that "das Leben selber sei der Inbegriff aller Wahrheit" (p. 148), a locution that strongly recalls Wienbarg. The longing for reality generates simultaneously a desire to evade it and flee from it: "Seitdem die Empirie so verschrieen ist, wird Alles früh alt in Deutschland, schrecklich früh schrecklich alt. Das macht der speculative Gedanke! Die Empirie erhält frisch und geschmeidig, die Speculation verzehrt schnell des Lebens Öl — und da thut man immer wohl daran, recht bald in eine Klause zu kriechen, wie die Schnecke sich in die Schale flüchtet und im steinernen Häuslein selbst versteint, daß Gott erbarm'!" (p. 234). It seems that the living of real life, beyond speculation, is so unthinkable in present circumstances that the retreat into the inner realm is the only possible recourse. This is a form of social criticism, but it takes on so desperate a character because the hero's demands on life are so absolute and all-encompassing: "ich kann und will nichts Vereinzeltes im Leben, ich will das Leben selbst, will die ganze Oper einstudiren [he is refusing a role in a performance of *Don Giovanni*] und in mir tragen, nicht eine einzelne Partie" (pp. 241-242). This pursuit has frustration built into it from the outset, and it is not surprising that the hero not long afterward exclaims: "Es lebe die Freiheit des innern Menschen! Das Bischen andere Freiheit schmeckt nach Wermuth!" (p. 259). As though these issues were in any sense resolved, the memoir and the novel end with the words: "Ich selbst glaube dem Leben, seinen Freuden und Schmerzen anzugehören. Ich ziehe weiter durch die Welt" (p. 334).

The distracting and wearying effort to transcend philosophy by means of philosophy is one of the fundamental ironies of the book. There is a curious combination of faith in the labors of the intellect,

97

allegiance to the "spirit," with a recognition that there is no exit in this fantastic maze of concepts and antitheses. After having concocted with his friends a really down-to-earth, practicable, and, in the short run, successful plan of escape from the madhouse, the hero, in his euphoria at this unwonted activity, is plunged into sarcasm: "Wir fühlten uns Manns genug, gegen die ganze Welt mit unserer Vernünftigkeit zu Felde zu ziehen, wir hätten Jeden zu Tode debattirt, dialektisch zermalmt, wäre uns Einer entgegengetreten als Opponent, um zu bezweifeln, wir seien nicht ganz gescheit" (p. 280). Everything in this sentence is completely short-circuited: one does not know whether "rationality" refers to practicality or to philosophical speculation, whether the plan devised rouses this sarcasm because it is efficient or because it is illusory, whether they might be accused of being not quite right in the head because they have presumed to think a way out of their incarceration or because they are pursuing the illusion of freedom, whether or why they are deluded.

One could pick this problem apart in the novel for pages without becoming any wiser about it. A few aspects of it are striking enough to deserve some commentary, however. One is a dream experienced by the hero while still in a feverish state. He is being interrogated by his uncle as to why he is only a useless *Literat*, just lurking about "um auf der Tafel des Lebens nichts als kritische Randglossen zu verzeichnen" (p. 15). The hero attempts to answer with a complex comparison of the free *Literat* with moths that lay thousands of eggs for the coming of a new age. For this simile he is flung into a torture chamber; his inquisitors remove his entrails and read his secrets in them; even though he was isolated from the world and undertook no active life, they find black sins and crimes in him, because with his knowledge and thinking he has absorbed all the crimes of history; he has eaten of the tree of knowledge and become critical of what is sacred; he has relived all the atrocious rebellions and revolutions of history in his soul: "Eine Ideenassociation verbrüdert Dich mit allen Aufrührern, allen Neuerern" (p. 20). He is an ideal Robespierre, lacking only opportunity. He is condemned as an absolute man, a radical, and executed.

This dream is one of the few passages in *Quarantäne* that exihibits a degree of imaginative power. It is simultaneously satirical and desperately anxious. The concept of intellectual guilt by association argued by the inquisitors is grotesquely extreme, but as a caricature it was certainly not irrelevant, for all the censorship and repression of the time was motivated by a fear of new knowledge and new ideas, and it is plain to the student of the period that the conservative ruling class would have liked best to keep the largest part of the population in a state of permanent ignorance and backwardness. But the claim that the hero is, or is trying to be, "der absolute Mensch" recurs as a refrain throughout the novel. Just what it means I have not been able altogether to puzzle out. At times the stress seems to be on the "Mensch," on the striving for the wholly humane or, at least, if one takes into account the adumbrations upon the necessity for the strife between good and evil, the wholly human. At other times, and more frequently, the stress is on the absoluteness, which seems to suggest the striving for total, organic comprehension by means of metaphysical speculation and thus becomes caught in the ambivalence that adheres to the philosophical enterprise throughout the book. Three *personae* in particular play a role in connection with this theme of the absolute man: Faust, Shelley, and Don Giovanni.

The Faust motif is ambivalent and elusive to the point of incoherence. The Faustian element is introduced as a threat to mental equilibrium. Faust's drive for absolute understanding, argues the hero, should lead to madness — or he will petrify, as the objective world around him vanishes into dust. "Wir müssen entweder den Faust in uns sterben lassen oder wir werden mit ihm zu Stein!" (p. 42). What this means I am not sure, but is clearly bears upon the conflict of internalized philosophical speculation with a living subject-object relationship toward the world without. The most recent work of Faust, the hero argues in a not uninteresting passage, is Hegel's system (pp. 42-43). Hegel seems to be a kind of monster haunting Kühne in this book as he haunted Kühne's friend Mundt. As in Mundt's aesthetic writings, there is a continuing resistance to Hegel in a context that would be unthinkable without Hegel's philosophy. Mundt, in fact, saw Hegel's philosophy as the fundamental issue in Kühne's book.[15] It is not many pages after the passage alluded to just now that Hegel's essence and dialectic are praised, although they must be freed from their container, which the hero, picking up the petrification image used in connection with Faust, calls "ein steinernes Beinhaus" (p. 45). Hegel's God, the narrator says, "ist die absolute Bewegung, die ewig strömende Immanenz des Geistes im Stoffe" (ibid.), a formulation not inconsistent with the rather sentimental pantheism that seems to be the basic element of the narrator's endlessly involved speculations on religion.

Elsewhere, however, Hegel is regarded less positively. Later, the hero goes on for eight pages in a highly metaphoric critique of Hegel, which in itself is an interesting document for Hegel's effect on this generation. At first, the hero seems to align himself with the philosopher by writing rhapsodies on world-historical individuals, on the depth and daring of great thinkers, and on the dialectical temporariness of any philosophy. His diction seems to stress, as Heine did, the revolutionary implications of Hegel, who marks in the narrator's life "eine Revolutionsepoche, auf die für meinen innern Menschen noch keine Restauration erfolgt ist" (p. 142). But these implications turn out not to be so positive after all. Since studying Hegel, the hero says, he has never been happy or whole-souled, and he injects, with obscure significance: "Mag die Welt hierüber lächeln; ich kann es ihr nicht wehren, ich bin ein armer Mensch im Irrenhause" (p. 143). Hegel's philosophy disturbed his faith in Christianity and erected a new but joyless god of reason. Hegel, he goes on, again reflecting a view of Heine's, has the same role in Germany as the revolution in France: "Der nackte, absolute, radicale Mensch foderte seine Rechte und zerschlug die Gestaltungen des Lebens mit grausamer Hand. Er kannte keine Liebe, keine Hingebung, keine Freundschaft, keine persönliche Größe, keine fromme Andacht, keine Verklärung in Kunst und Poesie; er beraubte Alles seiner Idealität, wie Hegel's absolute Vernunft" (p. 145). Here the absolute man, the modern, revolutionary man of reason and philosophy, is seen in a pejorative or at least in an elegiac perspective, for the hero goes on to say that though subjective idealism — apparently the antithesis to Hegelian absolute, objective reason — rages vengefully through the world at present, this may be its last battle, and with its end will come the end of poetry (p. 147). Thus a tragic inevitability is postulated for the Faustian Hegelianism with which Kühne's narrator appears to be out of harmony.

Kühne's tendency to pin every aspect of these dilemmas upon every representation of them without any integration makes the Faust *persona* less clear than the Hegelian parallel might at first suggest. In a delirium, the hero carries on a conversation with Faust, in which he urges Faust to rejuvenate himself and attempts to galvanize him by a kiss; but Faust does not permit this; he urges calm and vanishes in a "metaphysische Nebelkappe" (p. 50). Just as Goethe's Faust discerns a flash of fiery red in the wake of the black poodle that stalks him on Easter Sunday, so there is a flash of red as Faust vanishes here, the red of a Jacobin cap and Mephisto's feather, images put into significant parallel. Subsequently, the hero muses that Faust has become Satan in Börne; Faust and Mephisto have become one and haunt the people — the revolutionary implications of the Faustian absolutism are connected with radical evil — although it may fairly be doubted whether poor, honest, well-meaning Börne, whose name hardly ever appears in this book without the adjective "diabolical," is an apposite incarnation of this alliance. The hero's next endeavor is to undertake a loose parody of Faust's inconclusive exegesis of the opening words of the Gospel of John. Characteristically, he overreaches himself and sets himself the task of working out the problem "What is truth?" This question he determines to answer in a modern vein, without recourse to any of the thinking of the happy, untroubled generations of the past, for the hero knows of the pain, the dynamic striving of reality, "das Unglück des alten Faust, des alten absoluten Menschen" (p. 54). His first answer is: "Wahrheit ist das Sein Gottes in mir" (ibid.), a formulation that leads him in a mystical direction, for he quotes several lines from Angelus Silesius. Then he tries: "Christus ist die Wahrheit" (p. 55), which leads him to despair, for he does not feel Christ reborn in him. At this point we hear that *Christ* is the absolute man, for his truth is in every soul and he is the prototype of self-redemption. Here the concept of absolute man, having become adulterated with Kühne's individualistic Protestantism, goes wholly out of focus. Before abandoning this enterprise, the hero concludes with the rather obscure formulation that truth is "das *Sein meiner in Gott*" (p. 57). A final incongruity is that Faust, after having been brought into connection with Hegel, with the absolute intellectual striving of modern man, and with the demonic force of revolution, is also identified with the absurd clergyman who desires to cure the constipated world with water and whose pedestrian successor is referred to as his Wagner (pp. 104-105).

Insofar as the absolute man suffers from the Sisyphean labor of pursuing absolute spiritual clarity, Shelley is also made a part of this context. It may seem somewhat incongruous that so fundamentally conventional a spirit as Kühne's hero should assert a spiritual intimacy with the likes of Shelley, but the English poet is used as a demonstration of the relationship of pure speculation and madness: "bei all diesem redlichen Bemühen nach Klarheit und Frieden mit sich und der Welt, [hing] der Wahnwitz nur an einem Haar über seinem Haupte. . . . So wenig nutzte ihm sein Denken" (p. 70). How Shelley's profound battle with the conventions of society is to be assessed in this context is not clear, but it is fair to say that Kühne does not express the same enthusiasm for the revolutionary aspect of Shelley that Friedrich Engels was to exhibit a few years later. Of Don Giovanni there has already been occasion to speak, in connection with the tragic and dialectical need for energy and sin in order to transcend and transform present reality. As the active version of the absolute man, however, Don Giovanni's tragic rebellion exhausts itself in the sphere of the private and the personal; he fails altogether to penetrate the shell of his own self and come to some kind of viable subject-object relationship with the world.

Whatever absolute humanity may be, Kühne's hero fails to attain it. Towards the end of the novel he calls himself instead "ein gattungsloser Mensch, ein Mensch an sich, ein radicaler Mensch, nichts weiter, wahrhaftig" (p. 314), which seems to be a reductive, more negative version of the absolute man. At length he must recognize that he has not mastered life and cannot draw a sum from his inner experiences and that no resolutions are remotely in sight: "Warum soll ich die Dissonanzen für mich lösen, da sie in unseren Zeitläufen harmonielos durcheinander tönen? Ich will mich nicht täuschen und einen Frieden, den ich nicht erlebte, mir nicht mit künstlichen Tractaten zusammenstellen. Es gibt provisorische Zustände in der Literatur wie in den politischen Constellationen der Welt; ebenso gibt es auch provisorische Menschen. *Sie sind das Product einer Krisis*" (pp. 317-318, my italics). These provisional men were, in a few months, to have a name forever after — the *Epigonen* of Karl Immermann's novel. Kühne was not a writer who had the gift of naming things with precision. In view of the extreme lability of feeling and opinion in this, as in other novels at the time, it is strange indeed that his friend Mundt could write in January, 1835, that "heute . . . uns kein ächter Dichter ohne Grösse und stählerne Kraft der Weltanschauung, mithin ohne Einheit und Schwerpunkt des Daseins mehr denkbar ist."[16] The novel is better described by the general observation of Ruth Horovitz: "In den anarchischen Romanhelden verwirklicht sich nicht das Bild einer anderen, neuen Gesellschaft, sondern der jungdeutsche Zerrissene zeigt die alte Gesellschaft nahe der höchsten Stufe ihres Zerfalls."[17] But the crisis that generated Kühne's book was a real one, and, if nothing else, it shows spectacularly how inadequate were the resources within the reach of a normal young doctor of philosophy of the time to cope with it. It shows also how dubious it can be to mine these novels for quotations in order to elucidate the thinking of the time, without considering how shifting are the sands in which it is mired.

V.   HEINRICH LAUBE: *DIE KRIEGER*

Heinrich Laube was not the sort of man who should have got into trouble in any moderately sane social and political environment, and that he should have suffered the most harrowing punishment of all the Young Germans is evidence of the grotesque conditions of the time. Laube's personality positively exudes good health and good cheer; Rudolf Majut has written of him that he was "kein 'armer' wie Heine, kein 'grüner' wie Keller, sondern ein wahrhaft 'junger' Heinrich."[1] So robust and athletic that he was once offered the post of university fencing master, he is of all the Young Germans least "sicklied o'er by the pale cast of thought." Sengle's opinion that Laube was the liveliest and freshest of the Young German writers because he had the least understanding of philosophy has much to be said for it.[2] He was also the most amiable of them by far, and remained so long into his old age. While Gutzkow's autobiographical memoirs make generally unpleasant reading, with their convoluted self-justifications and his by then pathological belligerence toward all and sundry, Laube's — which are concerned largely with his long career as manager of the Vienna Burgtheater and are important source materials for the history of the theater — are charming, good-humored, and not infrequently even wise. While he was never to become a major writer, his career and œuvre, measured by Young German standards, rank second only to Gutzkow's, and a comprehensive study of his life and works would be a welcome contribution. Gutzkow thought him a critic of crucial importance: "Die Kritiken, welche H. Laube in einer von ihm redigirten Zeitung schrieb, wurden Mittelpunkt aller der jugendlichen Kräfte, die den Geist einer neuen Literatur ahnten und an seiner allmählichen sichtbaren Erscheinung selber mitarbeiten wollten."[3] The periodical in question is the *Zeitung für die elegante Welt*, which, in the period of Laube's editorship from January, 1833, until his arrest in July, 1834, contains a great deal of interesting and instructive literary criticism ("literature" understood in a broad sense, including books on history, current events, etc.), and these essays themselves would deserve a separate study. Houben remarked that their "prickelnder, schlagkräftiger Stil und die mühelose Erfassung moderner Lebensprobleme im Anschluß an literarische Fragen stempeln diese anderthalb Jahresbände unter Laubes Redaktion zu einem der wichtigsten Manifeste des 'Jungen Deutschland.' "[4] When one considers that the formal experimentation of Laube's *Reisenovellen* has drawn the critical attention of Reinhold Grimm;[5] that Houben thought several of his later works, including the novella *Die Bandomire* (1842) and the nine-volume novel of the Thirty Years' War, *Der deutsche Krieg* (1861-66), worthy of admiring notices,[6] and that, as I am about to assert, the middle part of his trilogy *Das junge Europa* is the best of the Young German novels, it seems that he may be deserving of rather more respect than he has been accorded in recent times.

It has clearly been difficult to regard Laube's role in the Young German crisis without a queasy feeling. What is distressing is not so much that, for both private and tactical reasons, he abjured any connection to the calumniated movement, but that he did so with such obtrusive insistence, that he repeated his recantations so often and falsified his own recent past. "Wie ein Held," Houben was obliged to remark, "hat sich Laube gewiß nicht benommen."[7] But the moral outrage directed against him has sometimes exceeded reasonable limits. Walter Dietze calls him the type "des böswillig-verschlagenen Mitläufers und Karrieristen . . ., der sich nur nach außen hin radikal und 'stürmend' gebärdet, in Wirklichkeit aber seine Kampfgenossen beinahe Tag für Tag aufs neue verrät."[8] In other places he uses terms like "politische Charakterlosigkeit," "Renegat," and "gemeiner Gesinnungslump."[9] This manner of expression is entirely out of place for several reasons. For one thing, Laube never endangered anyone by his official statements, nor did anyone ever suffer any harm because of him. Furthermore, Laube's views had been moderating noticeably before his arrest, which made the whole proceeding seem senseless to him, as indeed it was. E. M. Butler, in regard to her negative judgment on Laube's early activist writings, concluded that his liberal commitment had never been intrinsic: "If a man of twenty-six in the grip of a great enthusiasm cannot produce something worth reading, there are only two conclusions to be drawn. Either he is incapable of literary expression, or he is following after alien gods. Laube was not incapable of literary expression, as his next book [*Die Poeten*] and his subsequent life were to prove; it seems therefore as if, in making himself the exponent of liberal and revolutionary ideals, he had mistaken his true vocation. And this I believe to have been the case."[10] By 1848 he belonged, as he said, "Zum Centrum u. zwar mit einer Neigung nach rechts";[11] the change in his convictions in the early 1830's can be traced,[12] and one recent student sees the coincidence of the breakdown of his progressive allegiance and his arrest as purely accidental.[13] However that may be, there can be no doubt that the fright he got at the hands of the authorities strongly reinforced his desire to live at peace with existing society.

The story bears a quick retelling here for two reasons: it illuminates aspects of the nineteenth-century literary environment to which scholarship has given too little attention; and, since Laube had a bit of luck in the long run and the affair turned out less badly than it could have, there has been a tendency to make light of it, without considering how it must have looked to him at the time or the probable effect of it upon the courage of the whole literary community.[14] The reason for the exceptionally difficult time Laube had in jail was due, paradoxically, to the fact that the authorities had great trouble finding something to charge him with. Laube's critical writings in the *Elegante* and the first volume of *Das junge Europa*, *Die Poeten*, had attracted the ill-will of the Prussian censors. His praise of Heine and Börne and his view that democracy was the basic idea of Christianity had been found especially offensive. The first problem in coping with him was to get him out of Leipzig and onto Prussian territory. The authorities at first attempted to get him drafted, but, comically, the former student athlete was rejected for nearsightedness. They then pressured the Saxon government to expel him, which it was eventually obliged to do, although the Saxon authorities indicated to Laube that some way might be found to avoid this decree and suggested in a friendly way that he not go to Berlin. But, with the cheerful insouciance characteristic of him, he went straight to Berlin to confront his accusers. He called on Varnhagen, who had been following the whole business with sympathetic concern and was shocked and amazed to see Laube turn up of his own volition in the lion's den. Sure enough, he was arrested on 26 July 1834.

He freely admitted his literary sins and defended them adeptly; they really weighed too lightly to justify imprisoning him, and anyway, he argued, he could not be legally punished in Prussia for books that had passed the censorship in Leipzig, which was true. The minister in charge of these matters, Rochus von Rochow, was by August actually on the point of ordering Laube's release. But the ineffable Gustav Adolf von Tzschoppe intervened, for he could not bear the thought of setting one of these dangerous fellows free once he was in custody. Tzschoppe countermanded the order to release Laube on the grounds that he was suspected of activity in the *Burschenschaft*. According to the Carlsbad Decrees of 1819, membership in the *Burschenschaft* was punishable by six years of fortress imprisonment. Frederick William III, however, had later amnestied all members of the *Burschenschaft* whose activity fell in the years before 1830, provided that they had behaved properly since then and not done anything else punishable; if they had, the old sentence could be invoked. Tzschoppe was determined to meet this condition, to find any kind of transgression, no matter how minor, that would permit Laube's conviction under the old law. Thus literary misdemeanors that were not in themselves of sufficient moment to justify legal action against Laube were to be used to convict him for a crime for which he had been amnestied, as there was no evidence that he had any connection with the *Burschenschaft* after 1830. For eight months, while Laube was held without trial, the authorities combed his writings and personal connections for evidence against him.

Those who make light of Laube's plight neglect to consider two important aspects of it. One is that even a relatively short period of solitary confinement under the conditions to which he was subjected, without visitors or companionship, without books, writing materials, or any diversion other than an occasional interrogation, is a quite terrible experience that has been known to break stronger men than him. Laube felt himself being brought to the brink of madness and was in a condition where his thoughts, as he wrote later in his memoirs, "einander gleichsam in die Haare [fallen], man faßt seinen Kopf in beide Hände, als wollte und könnte man verhindern, daß er im Wahnsinn auseinanderspringe."[15] The other

107

aspect is that he could have no assurance of when this torment would end, indeed, if it ever would. There was no such thing as "civil rights" in restoration Germany; the citizen had no natural rights at all, only legal ones, the interpretation of which lay with the government authorities. There was plenty of precedent to cause Laube to take a doleful view of his prospects, and one curious coincidence may have contributed to his terror. In the *Elegante* of 3 May 1833, he had included an anecdote about a political prisoner in France who had been in solitary confinement for forty-three years and who, "um nur einen Augenblick das Sonnenlicht zu genießen, sich mehrmals mit solcher Täuschung todt gestellt, daß man, als er endlich wirklich gestorben, es nicht habe glauben wollen. Es liegt wirklich etwas Schauderhaftes in dieser Sehnsucht nach dem Licht bei 43jährigem dumpfem Hinbrüten in einem unterirdischen Loche ohne Beschäftigung und Gesellschaft."[16] One can imagine that this gruesome story went through Laube's head a year later when he found himself in a similar situation.

Laube's many asseverations of loyalty while in jail and while free under indictment must be judged in the light of these considerations, and the fairest observers have always done so. Houben maintained that an experience of this kind is "eine Probe auf den Charakter, über die nur derjenige triumphiren sollte, der eine gleiche durchgemacht hat";[17] Butler made a similar judgment.[18] Even Varnhagen, who had grounds to be out of countenance at Laube's apparent defection, found his way to a generous view:

> Der Heldenmuth, lieber unterzugehen als sich zu beugen, ist groß und schön, wir müssen ihn bewundern, dürfen ihn aber nicht fordern. Galilei widerruft seine eingesehene Überzeugung, ohne daß wir ihn deßhalb verachten dürfen. Auch die größten Könige bequemen sich zu schmachvollen Friedensschlüssen. Die Freundschaft, welche der König von Preußen nach dem Frieden von Tilsit gegen Napoleon heucheln mußte, ist nicht schlimmer noch besser, als die, welche von Laube gegen Tzschoppe bezeigt wird.[19]

Nor should one draw any conclusions about the general situation from the fact that Laube's seven-year sentence was reduced to one and a half years and that he was able to pass it in relative comfort under house arrest on Pückler-Muskau's estate. The first relief was due to Tzschoppe's unpredictable arbitrariness and the second to the personal influence of Frau Laube's connections. Laube told Heine in a letter of 19 August 1837, perhaps as a sardonic joke, that the reason for the commutation to house arrest was that all the fortress prisons were full.[20] There was nothing in either piece of good luck to comfort the literary generation that was watching the affair. Laube had been in a very dangerous situation and one cannot judge his behavior in it without recognizing this. In any case, moral or political disapproval of his failings should not block the view into his literary achievements, the most important of which at this time is the second volume of *Das junge Europa*, begun, probably, during his incarceration but not published until 1837.

I hold this opinion despite the fact that the novel has received relatively little attention. Houben once characterized it fleetingly as the best of Laube's youthful works.[21] One could go farther and maintain that *Die Krieger* is, in certain respects, the most successful of all Young German prose works. The reason that the value of this novel has never been appropriately stressed is connected with the kind of question previous interpretation has put to it. The concern with content and ideas has so occupied the study of Young Germany that the inner connections between the sociological situation and questions of literary form have not always come into focus.[22] Insofar as the purely artistic achievement of Young Germany was generally quite mediocre, such a method has its justification. When the trilogy *Das junge Europa* is examined from the point of view of ideas or sociological relevance, the tendency is to look upon it as a continuing process and to put the stress upon *Die Poeten* as the starting point and then upon the Biedermeier resignation at the end of the third novel, *Die Bürger*. Since both those works exhibit a rather modest degree of artistic value, it has apparently been difficult to separate *Die Krieger* from their company and examine it more carefully. Therefore, a few words about the general problem of the trilogy may be helpful.

In the third part, the hero's correspondent Hippolyt writes the following about the English novel: "Wie arm seid Ihr [the Germans] dagegen! Wo nicht ein Lehrgedanke das Faktum, die Schilderung, die Begebenheit unterstützt oder gar rechtfertigt, da meint ihr Unnützes zu treiben; das Thörichte nennt ihr Romanhaftes, darum besitzt ihr auch den reinen Roman nicht, ihr seid verdorben für reine, bloße Bilder, die nichts sein wollen und sein sollen als Bilder."[23] Whether this attribution of self-sufficient images to the realistic English novel is an adequate interpretation does not concern us here; but we cannot fail to hear in these lines an uneasiness on Laube's part with regard to Young German experimental prose. For the lack of substance and the meagerness of characterization are just the weaknesses of a novel like *Die Poeten.* The epistolary form — "diese schwatzhafte, uranfängliche Form," as Laube later judged[24] — is chosen because it is the easiest to manage for a writer embarrassed for lack of material and substance. In this case, the figures become abstract types and the plot exhausts itself in an opaque snarl of criss-crossing love relationships, the purpose of which is to illustrate Enfantin's two categories of constancy and inconstancy in the character of men and women.[25] The ideas and the involved interrelationships that are illustrated in the book are not without interest, but the novel form itself is sadly regressive. To Heine, Laube spoke of it timidly as "die *Exposition* einer modernen Novelle."[26]

Of Laube's intimations of realism something has been said in the introductory essay. A few more of his remarks can be adduced here. Realistic standpoints appear repeatedly in his criticism in the *Elegante.* He requires "blut- und lebensvolle Darstellung" and "lebendige Romane," "irdische, materiell-poetische Substanz" and "moderne Erzählungen" in contrast to the historical novel.[27] He criticizes a minor contemporary writer this way:

> Aus dem Blute der Personen können und sollen Ideen, Meinungen, meinethalben Systeme hervorgehen, wenn denn einmal eingeschachtelt werden soll, aber aus den Ideen springt im Leben kein Blut.... Das ganze Verfahren unsers Verf. ist das eines Philosophen, welcher geschickt und gewandt raisonnirt, und zu größerer Deutlichkeit hier und da mit lebendigen Figuren etwas beweist; aber es ist nicht das Verfahren des Dichters.[28]

Such remarks, of which there are many, represent consciously or unconsciously a critique of Laube's own first novel. If his memory did not betray him in his old age, Laube was concerned to avoid pale abstractions when writing *Die Poeten.* "Handlung schien mir das Suchenswerte.... Nicht bloß Raisonnements! dachte ich; das bloße Besprechen war mir in dem Tumult der Meinungen unerquicklich geworden.... Mit einem Worte: erzählen muß man lernen — das war wohl damals mein Grundgedanke."[29] But in the same passage he intimates why he did not succeed in doing this, although he does not seem to have the problem quite in focus: "Die verschiedenartigen Meinungen um mich her versinnlichten sich mir in verschiedenartigen Menschen, und alle diese Menschen bildete ich mir aus zu eigenen Persönlichkeiten, zu Charakteren, wie man's nennt, und jeden ließ ich sprechen."[30] But opinions can be concretized into characters only with an extreme degree of artistic ability. Even the fact that Laube constructed his characters out of his own circle of acquaintances did not prevent the dissolution of reality into a mental game. A lurking conflict with reality is latent in *Die Poeten*, to be sure. Karl Häberle observed accurately: "Die Maßlosigkeit des subjektiven Anspruchs, die Erfahrungsfremdheit und der überfliegende, antizipierende, hastende Eifer werden der Begegnung mit der Wirklichkeit nicht standhalten."[31] The weaknesses of *Die Poeten* did not escape the other Young Germans and, as usual, Gutzkow was at hand with an acid comment: "So geht die Handlung die Kreuz und Quere, die Neigungen tanzen Quadrillen und Kontertänze, verschlingen sich bald hier, bald dort, so daß man sich in der Tat in einen Kaninchenbau, wo Vater und Tochter sich heiraten, versetzt glaubt."[32]

Things are even worse in the third novel of the trilogy, *Die Bürger*. It seems to me plausible that Laube had lost interest in the project altogether in the meanwhile, which would not be surprising, as the original plan could not be kept intact through the tribulations of 1834 and their aftermath. In the autobiography that Laube produced in jail, the original plan was described as follows: "In dem zweiten Theile beabsichtigte ich die Leute durch allerlei Inconvenienzen zu führen und zu erläutern, daß die Bildung nach allgemeinen Principien selten zu einer ruhigen körperlichen Existenz leite und daß es wichtiger sei aus dem Einzelnen herauszubilden, das Nächste zu beachten und statt der Allgemeinheit das Individuum ins Auge zu fassen.... Das Ganze sollte ein Entwickelungsroman nach Art des Wilhelm Meister werden."[33] Of course, Laube was here attempting to put the novel in what he thought would be the least provocative light for his persecutors, but that the direction of it should have changed under the circumstances is not surprising. Formally, the result is altogether a catastrophe. Laube returns to the epistolary form, which is then broken in two by the long narrative report of the imprisonment of the hero, Valerius. This part taken by itself is a considerable achievement. Laube drew from his own experiences

111

in solitary confinement, and the account of a man who is brought near to mental collapse by the complete absence of any intercourse with another human being is genuine and convincing. One might even fairly be reminded of Kafka by a sentence such as this: "Das Verhör allein kann uns fördern, den traurigen Zustand ändern, wenn nicht in einen besseren verwandeln, denn im schlimmsten Falle ist Strafgefängnis eine Erholung gegen den Untersuchungs-Arrest — und doch fürchten wir Alle das Verhör, wenigstens die Ankündigung desselben, das Klopfen, den Namensruf, das hastige Ankleiden, den Gang durch die dunklen Corridore."[34] The virtues of this section in style and content are obviously due to Laube's opportunity to make use of profound personal experience. It is a little paradoxical and ironic, however, that what is here given such impressive literary expression is not something in or of the world, but the frightening loss of an objective and responding world.

Among the evidences of loss of coherence in this novel is the fact that Valerius' correspondent Hippolyt does not react to this heart-rending account with a single word of sympathy or acknowledgment; he seems to take no note whatsoever of Valerius' sufferings. So far as the trilogy as a whole is concerned, this insensitivity cannot be accounted for by Hippolyt's demonic egoism; in the first novel, for example, he helps one of the correspondents out of an embarrassment with a loan.[35] It is rather that, in *Die Bürger*, two fates are presented that are hardly connected with one another, apart from Valerius' critique of Hippolyt's radicalism and the contrast of social attitudes that is to be revealed. The content of these contrasting views is important enough in itself, but they do not yield a novel. Much in the plot and language of the book indicates increasing carelessness of composition. Hippolyt's own affairs are melodramatic and absurd, full of lurid seductions, duels, and whatnot. He is finally murdered by a jealous rival in the midst of a racial disturbance in New York, a scene that may touch our present sense of the relevant, but that in fact shows how issues of great gravity get introduced into this kind of writing in an inadequate and haphazard way. What has happened is that Laube's ideological horizon has become too foreshortened to contain Hippolyt's radical anarchism. The Young German intellectual substance is a kind of colloid in which widely disparate standpoints can be held in suspension; thus the figure of Hippolyt could maintain some plausibility among the various incarnated viewpoints of *Die*

Poeten. Now, however, that Laube's own ideological tolerance has shrunk toward the center, Hippolyt's attitudes and doings appear increasingly outlandish and the dialectical link with the perspective from the center of the novel, that of Valerius, has snapped. The return to the epistolary form also suggests, in my opinion, that Laube had exhausted his material and that only two masses remained: the account of his experiences in jail and the ideological contrast between Hippolyt and Valerius.

Apart from the autobiographical account of solitary confinement, there is little in either *Die Poeten* or *Die Bürger* to suggest that Laube had realistic gifts. Yet, in the middle novel of the trilogy, a will to realistic form and the actual achievement are more congruent than in any other longer work of fiction among the Young Germans. Laube himself recalled in his old age: "[Ich] ging entschlossen ab von der Art des ersten Buches: 'Die Poeten', welches in doktrinärer Absichtlichkeit befangen geblieben; ich meinte der vollen Roman-form, der reinen Erzählung mich ganz hingeben zu können und in ihr einen Fortschritt für mich zu finden."[36] It is interesting that here he did not attempt to draw from his own personal experience. Although the novel is about the Polish revolution of 1830/31 and deals extensively with regular and guerrilla warfare, Laube himself never saw Poland beyond the boundaries of Silesia and never took part in any fighting engagement off the fencing floor. But such direct experience was not necessary. It was the knowledge of concrete context that he and his literary contemporaries lacked. Laube was able to acquire it when he had a burning need to do so. We know from his own account that he interviewed a wounded Polish nobleman at great length and extracted from him exact details about the atmos-phere and the events of the revolution; later he studied the materials on the revolution that Jean Paul's nephew Richard Otto Spazier had collected in Leipzig.

The subject of the novel was a fortunate choice. It is true that there had been other novels in the past describing enthusastic German youths involved in the revolutionary struggles of other nations — Hölderlin's *Hyperion* is an example — and Wolfgang Menzel scorned them bitterly as examples of the inability of the Germans to pursue modern imperatives in their own country.[37] But Laube's choice of this strategy had specific theoretical advantages, because it preserved the virtues of the historical novel without what the Young Germans perceived as its drawbacks. When realism is in a primitive stage, the historical novel is an obvious genre to develop. Since the surrounding world and society cannot yet be comprehended with precision, the concrete materials of history offer a substitute for the lack of abundance in perception of the contemporary environment. An additional virtue is the element of adventure that holds the reader's interest and enables the writer to find a resonance in a larger public — an advantage of the historical novel that even Wienbarg, though he was very opposed to the genre, was obliged to admit.[38] In Wienbarg's view, however, the orientation on the past is bad. Instead of capturing contemporary life in a critical perspective, the author of historical novels is largely supplying opiates to the people.[39] Thus it is clear what Laube gained by choosing the Polish revolution as a subject. The excitement of adventure retains this advantage of the historical novel, while the relative contemporaneity of the revolution, which was watched from Germany with much interest, gives a suitable context for the ideological crisis through which Valerius must pass. The artistic assimilation of the current-event material with Valerius' *Bildungsroman* is, to be sure, not altogether complete; especially in the second part there is a tendency for the narrated historical and political events to separate themselves from the internal fabric of the trilogy. But complete success was hardly to be expected under the circumstances; what Laube accomplished is remarkable enough.

It is in characterization that Laube's movement in the direction of a more modern realism is most evident; Rudolf Majut, speaking of the trilogy as a whole, went so far as to draw a parallel with Thomas Mann's *Zauberberg*.[40] The contrast between *Die Krieger* and *Die Poeten* is perhaps more profound than Laube himself could know, for it exemplifies a vital change in the representation of types. Peter Demetz has distinguished between the Romantic type and the realistic type as follows: "Der romantische Typus ... in-karniert zeitlose Laster, Tugenden, Energien, Kräfte und Leiden-schaften in mehr als menschlichen Gestalten, welche die relativen Konturen des Humanen zu sprengen drohen; der realistische Typus soziologischer Relevanz, der aus der Praxis der Naturforscher her-vorgeht, repräsentiert viele einzelne Menschen der analogen Gruppe in einer Figur, der nichts Menschliches mangelt."[41] These definitions fit Laube's two novels with but a single adjustment: the characteristics of the "Poeten" are not "zeitlos," but explicitly time-bound. However, the character of each functions almost exclusively as the heightened incarnation of the quality ascribed to it. In *Die Krieger* this is no longer so. Here the characters do not, in the first instance, incarnate concepts or qualities, but rather represent types that occur in a specific and concrete social and historical situation. The gain in human substance is quite remarkable and could be shown by the example of Valerius down to the manner of his language. But the transformation that Valerius undergoes has already been sufficiently analyzed by previous interpretation; furthermore, it must be said that the presentation of this unheroic, bourgeois, indecisive hero can hardly, when one thinks of Goethe's Wilhelm Meister, be regarded as an entirely original breakthrough on Laube's part. The progress is more clearly shown by considering the ancillary characters.

It is noteworthy and, for the reader coming from *Die Poeten*, somewhat surprising that the first person who emerges at the beginning of the story is an old Jew. Opening a novel by concentrating our attention on a relatively minor character — he is hunting for his son on the field of a recent battle — is an instinctively realistic device. It draws us *in medias res* and gives an opportunity for setting the scene without obtrusive authorial presence; it also places us in that perspective below the level of high policy and decision that we all share when looking upon events as they transpire. Here, however, Laube's strategy does more; it shows us that we have left the hermetically sealed pseudo-society of letter-writers passing their limitless leisure in amorous intrigue and have entered a socially more differentiated world. The prominent role of the Jew and his son can, in addition, be taken as a modest liberal challenge. That may be a speculation, but it seems to me less speculative to suggest that the Jewish characters are symptomatic for the artistic virtues of the novel.

Even in the Young German context, Laube stands out as exceptionally philo-Semitic. The Jewish anti-Semitism that flickers from time to time in Börne und Heine is notorious; it is a partly psychological problem, partly one of social criticism. In the few places where Wienbarg comes to speak of the Jews, he makes almost exclusively deprecating remarks; he had only a shrug of the shoulders for the paragraph that banned Jews from the kingdom in the Norwegian constitution he so enthusiastically admired.[42] Gutzkow's views were, as usual, more complex. Houben has written a long essay on Gutz-kow's relations with Jews, including the prominent Hamburg emancipator, Gabriel Riesser, and on his continuing concern with the Jewish problem over the years.[43] But Gutzkow was obliged to admit that he had to overcome a strong prejudice within himself when he first discovered that Heine and Börne were Jews,[44] and his otherwise admirable tragedy *Uriel Acosta* does not suggest that he had penetrated very deeply into Jewish culture; his rabbis are little more than Catholic inquisitors in disguise. Laube's special attitude toward the Jews is traceable, no doubt, partly to his good-humored and tolerant nature, partly to personal experiences. As a schoolboy in Glogau he received charity meals from a Jewish family, whose warmth and humanity he clearly appreciated; for a companion on his Italian journey with Gutzkow in 1833 he chose a Jewish businessman with whom he maintained a close friendship afterward. With one distressing exception,[45] his writings and memoirs show that, as he said, he did not have any prejudice against the Jews.[46]

This is responsible for Laube's success with the Jewish figures in *Die Krieger* — less so, perhaps, with the old, embittered Manasse, who is somewhat overdrawn and has a little too much of Shylock, than with his son Joel. Structurally, Joel is to be understood as a radical parallel figure to Valerius. Like Valerius, Joel stands between two worlds between which he cannot mediate, and this is due not to his own failings, but to the failings of the social structure. The remark that Valerius makes about Joel's situation — "O, können sie denn nie aufhören, diese grellen Kontraste der bürgerlichen Gesell-schaft"[47] — could as easily be applied to his own difficulties. Like Valerius, Joel tries to break with the old society by actively involving himself in the struggle for modern ideals, but he is obliged to recognize that he remains, despite everything, a foreign body in revolutionary Poland. Like Valerius, he loves a girl across class barriers, only to be flung ever deeper into his identity crisis. Like Valerius, he ends in profound resignation. But an important aspect of the parallel should not be overlooked. Joel undertakes his retrans-formation into a "Schacherjude" with extreme bitterness. The abandon-ment of his modern, bourgeois self-identification is a kind of symbolic suicide that is meant to chastise the inhuman order of society.

116

Valerius makes a similar decision with less aggressive bitterness and a greater capacity for rationalization:

> Es giebt nur zwei Arten, glücklich zu sein: entweder man bewegt und bevölkert sich und die Welt mit Idealen, Aussichten, neuer Zukunft, man schaukelt sich auf der wogenden Bewegung des ungezügelten Strebens, — oder man betrachtet die Welt aus einem ruhigen Herzen, freut sich des Kleinsten, hilft und fördert im Kleinsten, pflanzt mit Genügsamkeit, wartet geduldig auf das Gedeihen, gestaltet das Unbedeutende zur gefälligen Form, verlangt nichts vom Tage, als was er eben bietet, und hält den Nachbar und sein Interesse höher als das Wohl oder Wehe von Nationen.[48]

For all that Laube here begins to sound like Adalbert Stifter, Valerius' resignation, when we look closely at the process that brings it about, is not in the first instance an acceptance of a Biedermeier turn inward, but is rather something that harsh reality has forced upon him. Many years ago, Benno von Wiese spoke in this connection of the involuntary Biedermeier of the Young Germans.[49] With every recognition of the Biedermeier aspect of this process, one should not overlook the fact that it contains a reproach against a society that does not permit anything better.

But Joel's pathos is much deeper than Valerius' because the hopelessness of his situation is more radical. Valerius has the possibility of conforming to his society if he can see his way to making this capitulation, while there is no place at all in society for the emancipated Polish Jew. The scenes in which Laube shows this are among the best in the novel. Neither among the revolutionary aristocrats, nor among the democrats, nor among the rebellious people is Joel permitted to have a human relationship. Courage, kindheartedness, service in the national struggle — nothing can alter his exclusion from society. (That Laube prefigures the fate of the *German* Jews with surprising precision may be mentioned here in passing.) Valerius' growing comprehension of the hopelessness of Joel's situation contributes substantially to the erosion of his revolutionary enthusiasm. He leaves the revolutionary army out of protest against the shabby treatment Joel receives because he has dared to fall in love with the daughter of an aristocratic rebel leader. When Valerius remonstrates with Count Kicki: "Ich glaube es kaum, daß Sie mit diesen aristokratischen Bedenklichkeiten eine glückliche Revolution

117

machen,"[50] he is simply not understood. Joel's fate is thus a kind of *Bildungserlebnis* for Valerius, forcing him to the insight that "freedom," which the young German liberals propagated with insouciant imprecision, in reality can wear quite various and disquieting faces.[51]

There are some weaknesses in the characterization of Joel. The most regrettable of them is that Laube makes Joel the son of a Christian mother, whereby the symbolism of the figure becomes muddled.[52] It is likely that Laube wanted to motivate by heredity Joel's longing to escape from the narrow environment of orthodox Judaism. This fits together with a secret family relationship between Joel and his beloved, which is revealed only towards the end of the novel — an old-fashioned convention that Laube, in such a novel as this, could easily have done without. Joel's almost uninterrupted weepy self-pity, although understandable under the circumstances, seems excessive to the reader and suggests some lack of respect for the character on the author's part. More interesting is a remark that comes toward the end of the novel, after Joel has dressed himself as an orthodox "Bandjude" (a peddler of ribbons and the like): "Die Klagen des schönen jungen Mannes, welche [Valerius] so lebhaft mitfühlte, waren ihm viel würdiger erschienen, so lange der Klagende in besserer Kleidung neben ihm hergegangen war. Er schalt sich über solche Schwäche."[53] Obviously the Jew is a more pleasant phenomenon as an assimilated bourgeois. This reaction is regretted as a weakness, but is nevertheless present. A little crack in the narrative perspective opens up here, through which Valerius is seen from a critical distance. This occurs in other places in *Die Krieger* and suggests that we should be cautious with the traditional identification of Valerius with Laube himself. On the other hand, a comparison of Laube's remarks on the Jews shows that even he, to a certain degree, shared the familiar liberal hope that the Jews would abandon their separate culture and vanish into bourgeois society, a view that, twenty years later, found its ultimate formulation in the figure of Bernhard Ehrenthal in Gustav Freytag's *Soll und Haben* (1855).

Sometime a detailed comparison between *Die Krieger* and *Soll und Haben* should be undertaken; it would be quite instructive. Both novels are literary milestones in the development of the German bourgeois ideology, and not only the lines of connection, which have been stressed from time to time, but also the contrasts are of interest. In the simplest terms, one could say that, while Freytag developed the technique of realistic characterization much further, the human quality of Laube's characterization has become lost due to the hardening of the ideological position that has taken place in the meantime. One sees this above all in the treatment of the Jews. The demand for complete assimilation and *embourgeoisement*, which shows up in Laube only in hints and suggestions, has become for Freytag the absolute touchstone of human value. Freytag's Jews are not conceived as anti-Semitic caricatures; they are differentiated figures and drawn with a certain sharpness of observation.[54] But they are forced with such violence into Freytag's evaluative scheme that neither a penetration into their human substance nor a balanced judgment upon their social situation is possible. What appears in Laube as an unhappy struggle for a bearable social standpoint has become philistine conviction in Freytag. The loss of the specific virtues that appear in Laube's efforts to create Jewish characters realistically is deplorable and quite ominous for the future.

A comparison of the two novels is also suggested by the fact that both treat Polish revolutionary events. Here the difference is less striking, for. Laube's opinions of the Poles are more similar to Freytag's than his opinions of the Jews. Among the German liberals the enthusiasm for the Polish revolution is not infrequently combined with a noticeable dislike of the Polish people; Heine is a familiar example. Like most prejudices, this one is the result of observation and is strongest among those who have had the most direct experience. Laube discussed the matter at length in his memoirs:

> Ich unterschätzte diese Revolution, weil ich in Glogau und Breslau in steter Berührung mit Polen gewesen und durchdrungen davon war, daß sie in ihrem streitsüchtigen Hochmute sich nicht vertragen und nichts gestalten könnten. Der Ausdruck "polnische Wirtschaft" war in Schlesien so landläufig, daß man dort absolut nicht an die Möglichkeit eines polnischen Staates glauben mochte. Persönliche Sympathien fanden die Polen außerdem nirgends unter uns. Der Begriff einer Adelsrepublik spritzte überall aus ihnen hervor und machte sie unangenehm für unsere demokratische Empfindung. Das war ganz naturgemäß, und das gerade hat ihnen bisher jedes Gelingen erschwert. Es ist nicht ihre Schuld, es ist ihr Schicksal. Der

119

herrschende Stamm hat sich als Adelsstamm apart gehalten, hat die große übrige Bevölkerung niedergehalten. Was nützte es, daß der polnische Adel unter sich demokratische Gleichheit standhaft durchgeführt und dem ärmsten Edelmanne immer ebensoviel Ansprüche zugestanden, als dem reichsten? Die erobernde Kaste ist Kaste geblieben, hat die Emanzipation der niederen Stände, des eigentlichen Volkes, zu lange versäumt, und hat damit versäumt, ein gleichmäßig teilnehmendes Volk heranzubilden. . . . Wäre unser Feudaladel nicht vom deutschen Bürgerthume überflutet worden, so wäre es uns vielleicht ähnlich ergangen; in Polen aber ist das Bürgerthum ausgeblieben, und an dieser Lücke krankt das polnische Wesen immerdar.[55]

Laube could not even stand the Polish nobleman whom he interrogated for the novel.

In *Die Poeten*, Valerius' decision to join the Polish revolution is accompanied by similar feeling, which, characteristically for that book, he resolves aesthetically:

Ich gehe morgen nach Warschau, um für das heilige Recht eines Volkes gegen die Tyrannen zu fechten. Ich liebe das polnische Volk nicht eben sehr, aber für seine Sache will ich bluten und sterben. . . . Es ist noch viel roh Asiatisches an ihnen, aber ihre überwältigende Poesie der Vaterlandsliebe, dieses Käthchen von Heilbronn in einem ganzen Volke, ist zauberhaft, ihr Kampf ist der reinste und edelste, der gefochten werden kann.[56]

For Laube as for Freytag this dislike of the Poles is socio-politically motivated — the Poles lack the class base for a successful revolution. For both, the Polish rebellion is in the interest of a partially enlightened but also feudal and regressive nobility, while the oppressed, uncultured peasantry is incapable of judgment and lacks any real revolutionary potential. Certainly the bourgeois class consciousness is stronger and more precise in Freytag. Although both writers tend to identify specifically German virtues with those of the bourgeoisie, the nationalism of the right-wing liberal Freytag is so closely involved with his bourgeois class consciousness that his double front against the aristocracy and an uncultivated foreign peasant class remains the main concern.

For Laube, however, the unadmired Poles remain human beings.

120

In accordance with the realistic tendency to push the heroic into the background, the great leaders in Laube's novel — Skrzynecki, Prond-zynski, Krukowiecki, etc. — are more or less seen from below. Otherwise Laube seeks to differentiate among his Polish figures, and this in itself is an important example of the way the writing of fiction can enrich and complicate ideas and attitudes the author believes he holds, for, in a passage in the *Reisenovellen*, Laube denied the Poles any differentiated individuality:

> Man schildert mit *einem* Polen alle; sie haben keine absondernde Individualität, das ist auch ein Grund ihrer Größe: sie imponieren als *ein* Mann. Es ist bei allen halbzivilisierten Völkern so: ihre Bedürfnisse, Fehler, Vorzüge, sind einfach, ihre Verhältnisse nicht minder. Darum sind sie nur als Masse oder als Repräsentanten der Masse interessant; einzeln aber schnell langweilig, weil die innere Ausgebildetheit und Mannigfaltigkeit fehlt, die bei näherer Bekannt-schaft immer neue Seiten entwickelt.[57]

Fortunately, Laube did not work in *Die Krieger* according to this principle. He not only contrasts the figures with one another, but also attempts to exhibit the socially determined paradoxes in the individuals in order to expose the contradictions of the revolution. A good example of this is the careful unmasking of the aristocratic foundation in the superficially democratic attitude of one of the leaders, Count Stanislaus. Another, which is also relevant to Laube's handling of the Jews, is his treatment of the character of the popular hero, Florian the blacksmith, who is presented as sympathetic and attractive. When the rebel peasants, in an access of anti-Semitic fury, attack Valerius, Joel, and Joel's beloved, who are their allies, the blacksmith is obliged to calm them down and then remarks quietly: "Vater Kosciusco, das sind Deine Polen."[58] But when Joel, during an attack of the enemy, for his part attempts to save Florian's life by calling out his name, the latter answers as he dies: "Schweig, Jude."[59] In this way, Laube tries to penetrate into the complications of an objective social situation that would have been inaccessible to the abstract dialectics of *Die Poeten*. None of this probing sensitivity remains in Freytag. His hateful treatment of the Poles makes a mockery of any realistic intention; his Poles are no longer complex human beings, but schematic cartoons.

My remarks on *Die Krieger* are only suggestions and certainly could be refined methodologically and in regard to content. I am not contending that it is an outstanding novel; as a realistic work it is primitive enough. It is perhaps not much better than the novels that Burkhardt has asserted are the result of Wienbarg's novel theory: "Jene zahlreichen, wegen ihrer künstlerischen Unbedeutendheit längst vergessenen Zeitromane der dreißiger und vierziger Jahre des 19. Jahrhunderts."[60] But, in the Young German context, Laube's achievement takes on a relative significance. This raises another, somewhat disquieting problem: whether the original Young German radicality (using the word with all necessary qualifications) was advantageous to the development of a realistic prose art; whether, to put it another way, Laube did not *have* to fall away from his original attitude in order to write a book like *Die Krieger*. The Young German novels, beginning with Gutzkow's *Wally*, that were seeking direct confrontation, detonated some explosions at the intersection of literature and society, but do not stand up well to artistic or intellectual criticism. If we think of the names of the great realists, we find many who are quite the opposite of radical: Balzac, Flaubert, Thackeray, Fontane, Henry James, Thomas Mann. There are, of course, exceptions (Zola, Jack London, Dreiser, Dos Passos, Steinbeck), as well as others who are hard to discuss in such terms (Hugo, Dickens). But, aside from the fact that the concept of realism becomes a little difficult when applied to Dickens or Zola, it is perhaps not insignificant that Dos Passos and Steinbeck made sharp shifts rightward in later years. These remarks are offered here only as a possible starting point for the theme of "Jungdeutscher Frührealismus." For it would not be an exaggeration to claim that where we find realism, we do not find the specific Young German quality, and vice versa. This thesis seems to apply also to the drama of the *Vormärz*, as Horst Denkler has recently shown.[61]

Reality has, of course, the tendency to escape ideologically preconstructed categories, and no ingenious distinctions between *Wirklichkeit* and *Wahrheit* can prevent this. When the world is seen under relatively simply defined ideas or attitudes, art is very possible, but it will hardly be realism. For the realistic writer is wholly occupied with impressing an artistic order upon a chaotic abundance of experience and perception. This in itself obvious observation seems to me pertinent here, because it is just such reflections upon the complexity of experience, illustrated by the hard reality of the

122

Polish revolution, that play a large part in the tormenting revision of conviction that Valerius must go through. These considerations appear most succinctly in a passage that has been pointed out by Nolle, von Wiese, and Häberle,[62] and that also struck me upon a first reading:

> Und doch waren es nicht jene Freiheitsgedanken an sich, die er jetzt bezweifelte, es waren die Verhältnisse im Großen, die allgemeinen historischen Entwickelungen, die ihm den Geist mit Dämmerung bedeckten. Er ahnte das Tausendfältige der menschlichen Zustände, die tausendfältigen Nuancen der Weltgeschichte, die millionenfachen Wechsel in der Gestalt eines Jahrhunderts und in der Gestalt seiner Wünsche und Bedürfnisse. Er sah die Armuth des menschlichen Geistes, der reformiren will, neben dem unabsehbaren Reichthume, der unendlichen Mannigfaltigkeit dieser Welt und ihres verborgenen ewigen Gedankens.[63]

The theme is picked up again at the beginning of *Die Bürger*, in a more direct and resigned way: "Unsre übermüthigen Jugendpläne, die Welt umzugestalten, haben wir wohl zum Theil aufgegeben, wir sind erschrocken vor der Mannigfaltigkeit der Welt, vor der Unerschöpflichkeit ihrer Verhältnisse und Zustände."[64] These considerations seem to me not only to have some plausibility, but also to be closely connected with the conditions that permit realistic writing. It is also understandable that they should lead to a sort of resignation, a sense for the "Grenzen der Menschheit." Whether the resignation must necessarily be of the Biedermeier or conservative kind is another question. But the comparison with Freytag permits a critical judgment. Laube's frankness, his uncertainty in the face of a world difficult to apprehend with time-bound intellectual categories, permits, despite all his technical insufficiency, a beginning of an early form of realism. Freytag's technical ability, learned, for the most part, from the English novel, is much further developed, but his writing is so thoroughly determined by a chauvinistic and class-bound scheme that one can speak of his realism only with reservations. If the conditions under which Laube was writing had been a little different, perhaps beginnings like *Die Krieger* could have borne fruit that would have put an entirely different face on the German novel of the nineteenth century.

VI.   KARL IMMERMANN

The stock of Karl Lebrecht Immermann has been rising noticeably in recent years. A number of valuable studies by several scholars have now culminated in an excellent full-length critical biography by Benno von Wiese.[1] Immermann had not been in total obscurity; although he had always been something of a stepchild of literary scholarship, many creative writers over the decades expressed their admiration for him in varying degrees; von Wiese mentions Gutzkow, Laube, Heine, Eichendorff, Droste-Hülshoff, Hebbel, Conrad Ferdinand Meyer, Wilhelm Raabe, Hugo von Hofmannsthal, Jakob Wassermann, and Hermann Hesse.[2] Wilhelm Dilthey called him one of the cleverest of German writers.[3] Not all of these accolades have been without reservations, however, and indeed it is not easy to come to a firm and adequate assessment of Immermann. Martin Greiner said rather cruelly that he "gleicht einem Gastgeber, der die reichsten Vorräte in seinem Hause eingesammelt hat. Aber auf seinem Herde brennt ein so schwaches Feuer, daß er nur ein wenig davon zubereiten und seinen Gästen vorsetzen kann, während das meiste in Muff und Moder verdirbt."[4] Robert Boxberger had said many years before, more kindly, that we admire Immermann's efforts more than his achievements.[5] There certainly is a discrepancy between his talent and ambition on the one hand and the total achievement of his twenty years of literary production on the other. He possessed limited but indisputable resources of imagination and creativity, especially in the realm of satire and, in reading him, one's attention is constantly caught by passages of subtlety and strength. But other parts of his work can be dim and commonplace, partly because, like many of his contemporaries, he tried to write so much and in so many genres, and partly because, as all his modern admirers agree, his true vocation was to be a novelist and he was slow to discover this. He was misled by his obsession with the drama, which again he shared with many of his contemporaries. Unlike his friend Heine, who rather quickly got over what George Eliot called "the chicken-pox of authorship,"[6] Immermann, though he swore off the drama time and time again, could not, as Windfuhr has said, shake the "Theaterteufel" that possessed him.[7] He earned himself an honorable place in the history of the German theater by managing a "model stage" in Düsseldorf from 1832 to 1837, continuing the efforts to raise the cultural level of the theater long pursued by Lessing, Goethe, and Schiller. But his sixteen plays, even the much-noticed *Andreas Hofer* (first version, 1826; second version, 1833) and the ambitious trilogy *Alexis* (1831) are of no more than antiquarian interest.

It is significant, as Windfuhr points out, that when Immermann planned his collected edition in 1835, he intended to include only two of his works written before 1829; chronologically, as it turned out, nearly half of his writing career.[8] Not until 1836 did the major prose works begin to appear that most interest us today. Immermann died suddenly in 1840 at the age of forty-four, and there is a feeling among his modern admirers that he was just beginning to reach a level of real greatness; his death, according to Windfuhr, "beendet ein begonnenes Lebenswerk, das die ihm zugewiesene Richtung gerade erst einzuschlagen angefangen hatte."[9] But one cannot, after all, be sure. The work that occupied him at the time of his death, a modernized version of *Tristan und Isolde*, was a catastrophe in the making, so violently did he pursue the *embourgeoisement* of the material, substituting, to his friend Tieck's horror, repentence for the theme of invincible passion in the original, and garnishing the text, as was his wont, with comic and satirical whimsies. Although Immermann was clearly growing artistically and intellectually when he was so regrettably taken away, there is something in the very foundation of the man that suggests his later career might have continued to be uneasy, inconsistent, and plagued with doubt and uncertainty.

Immermann has traditionally been classified as a conservative, but modern critics have seen that this is much too facile a label to define the complexity of the man. He was raised in strict idolatry of Frederick the Great, participated with patriotic fervor in the Wars of Liberation, and was a Prussian civil servant all his life; and it is true that some of his social and political opinions have little to

125

recommend them. An anachronistic nostalgia for absolutist monarchy is among them: "Der echte Fürst," he wrote in his diary in 1832, "muß ein mythisches Gefühl seiner selbst haben, er muß sich allen andern gegenüber für ein einziges, eximirtes Wesen halten können. Hierdurch allein wird er befähigt, den Indifferenzpunkt zwischen den Persönlichkeiten und Gewalten des Staats zu machen."[10] He wrote a poem expressing scorn for the humanity of the nineteenth century that sees a brother in every rascal,[11] and of his brilliantly conceived Baron von Münchhausen, it is said that people fell for his lies as they did for the Enlightenment and the French Revolution.[12] Another constant theme is the longing for the great man, who, by the force of his personality, will cut the Gordian knot of modern dilemmas. In a letter of 7 November 1830, he comments on the July Revolution: "... die gewaltigen Ereignisse sind am Ende doch von lauter Kleinen ausgegangen — nirgends ein bedeutender Charakter, ein Held, eine wahre Apotheose der geistigen und politischen Mittelmäßigkeit — ein ungeheurer, quirlender Ameisenhaufen."[13] Although, like any writer of his time of social significance, he had trouble with the censors, he tended to support the principle of censorship.[14] He wrote a eulogy upon the death of Frederick William III in 1840 in which he incredibly calls this perjured king and terrorist of the intellectual world "Vater, Hort und Schirmherr...", redlichster Mann des Landes."[15]

Modern critics have been concerned to oppose to these opinions, which have been exploited by conservative and Fascist admirers, evidence of democratic and liberal tendencies as well. Windfuhr, in studying the manuscripts of Immermann's travel diaries, has shown how he censored his own critical observations to make them appear more legitimist, and comments that he did not have Heine's skills in masking his critique[16] — but Heine's critiques are masked only for a very obtuse reader, and Immermann, by personal ideology or public social allegiance, could not have seen any value in publishing his own. In time he did come closer to an appreciation of Young Germany; on the ban of 1835 and Wienbarg's sufferings from it he remarked: "In der That gehört jener Bannspruch, welcher die Früchte des Geistes noch ungeboren tödten wollte, zu den häßlichsten Ausgeburten eines matten Despotismus."[17] Meanwhile, his critical novels caused the Young Germans themselves to take a friendlier view of him.

126

In some respects Immermann suffered the familiar fate of a moderate man in a time of high political passion. The best example of this is an incident that occurred while he was still a student and that seriously affected his relationship to the intellectual community. Fraternity boys at Halle had administered a brutal beating to a nonconforming student, and Immermann, now a twenty-three-year-old war veteran, protested in two pamphlets and took his views directly to the king. Thus he acquired at the outset of his adult life the reputation of an informer and a pawn of the anti-patriotic forces; when his quondam literary mentor, Friedrich de la Motte Fouqué, heard of the incident some three years later, he broke off all relations with Immermann. Hans Mayer, while still employed in East Germany, judged that Immermann had acted from a genuine sense of justice but in political blindness.[18] I believe this assessment has little merit. The increasingly fanatical and chauvinistic student movement was only in a very limited sense a force for freedom, and Immermann's Prussian belief in ethical lawfulness cannot be said to have erred in this instance. The incident shows us, rather, how his fundamental orientation on principle tended to isolate him in his time and helps us to understand how he became the kind of writer he was. For his conservatism does not lie chiefly in his often half-baked political and social views, but in the simplicity of his ethical foundation: the plainness of his integrity, the moderation and normality of his principles in an immoderate and abnormal time. His ethical moderation was both unreflective and elegiac. It is more a product of instinct than of reason, and in this respect he differs from the Young Germans, who wrestled, however clumsily, for a critical, analytical approach to the moral and ideological presuppositions of life and society in their time. The result in Immermann is what E. K. Bramsted has perceptively called "negative neutrality";[19] so remote did Immermann's prosaic principles seem from anything happening in the world that his satire acquired a negative universality that was not impelled, as the satire and criticism of the Young Germans were, by allegiance to any progressive force, real or imagined, struggling to be born in this bewildered age. Both his major novels show this to a degree that has not always been fully appreciated.

Immermann's single great coup was to give a name to the malaise that beset the bourgeois intelligentsia. To the novel he worked on intermittently for a number of years and finally completed in the

127

fateful year of 1835,[20] he gave the title of *Die Epigonen*, from a Greek word meaning "descendants" or "those who come after." This is a true neologism, insofar as he gave a known word a new meaning. In Greek tradition, the *Epigonoi* were the sons of the Seven against Thebes, who conquered the city before which their fathers had perished. Thus the term had by no means a pejorative connotation, since the sons accomplished that which the fathers had been unable to do. It was Immermann who gave the word the gloomy sense it was to have ever after: it identifies a mediocre generation following on one of great brilliance, condemned to imitation and amorphousness. The word became a concept of intellectual history — one often abused — and found its way, in Immermann's sense, into other languages; in English it has never achieved much currency, although the larger dictionaries carry it. Windfuhr, in his discussion of the history of the concept, makes two important distinctions. *Epigonentum* is, first of all, not the same thing as a period of productive imitation, in which classical or traditional models have authoritative status and serve as a source of creative inspiration;[21] rather, in Immermann's time, the awareness of the overwhelming greatness of past accomplishment, whether of antiquity or the Age of Goethe, is coupled with a realization that these models cannot be plausibly recreated or imitated in the present situation. Secondly, Windfuhr distinguishes *Epigonentum* from decadence, which plays with aesthetic materials, is artistically self-conscious, esoteric, and unpopular,[22] whereas *Epigonentum*, especially when it is not as conscious of its own state as Immermann was, prepares for easy consumption what once had been vital and challenging.

There can be no doubt that Immermann caught with this concept, if perhaps somewhat obliquely, an important mood and process of his time. Von Wiese quotes Ernst Troeltsch, who in retrospect found Immermann a good guide for the atmosphere of the time and described the social and historical situation this way:

> Schon verdämmert der rationalistische Geist und wandelt sich teils in demokratische Opposition, teils in kapitalistische Unternehmungslust. Stärker dauert der humanisierte Individualismus romantischer und klassizistischer Prägung. Aber hinter alledem tauchen die alten Macht- und Standesverhältnisse wieder auf, die nicht vernichtet, sondern nur geschwächt sind, und in den Vordergrund

schiebt sich der Macht- und Gewaltbau der militärisch-bürokrati-
schen Monarchien, verbündet mit einer bei jeder Gelegenheit ein-
setzenden konfessionell-christlichen Restauration des Kirchentums.[23]

But this regressive restoration is not the only oppressive aspect of the
situation; von Wiese speaks perceptively of a troubling sense of
discontinuity in human affairs: "die wachsende Unselbständigkeit
und Unwahrhaftigkeit im menschlichen Zusammenleben, weitgehend
hervorgerufen durch das Diskontinuierliche der Geschichte, durch die
politischen Wirrnisse, die wie ein Unwetter über den Menschen
hereinbrechen und sie vor den 'Stürmen der Zeit' nirgends mehr
Schutz finden lassen, selbst dort nicht, wo es früher noch möglich
war, im privaten Dasein."[24] The age is clogged with transmitted
culture and with a civilization no longer organically involved with
the conditions of life; competing truths and absolutes resound in
a cacophony of windy debate. We have already seen this view expressed by Gutzkow and Mundt. There are, in a sense, too many
answers and not enough questions, or, as Koopmann put it, there
is "ein Zuviel an Orientierungspunkten."[25]

Because Immermann's realistic skills were greater than those of the
Young Germans, his representation of culture and society helps to
fill in the background of the situation that the Young Germans confronted with greater resources of prescriptive criticism but to which
they were generally incapable of giving convincing literary form.
It is therefore useful to examine Immermann along with the Young
Germans in order to acquire a sense of epoch. His representation of
the disjunction, diffuseness, and bewilderment of his own age helps
us to see the larger context more clearly because he does not keep
these things locked in the churning liberal intellect, as the Young
Germans generally do, but projects them, satirically or realistically,
into a narrated world. While he lacked philosophical genius and
could be obtuse in certain directions, there is no other writer of his
time who concentrates so effectively, not so much on sociological
analysis of causes and effects, but on the perceived situation itself.

The way from perception to creation, however, was a difficult
one for him, even when he came at last to the genre most appropriate
to the situation, the novel. Like the Young Germans, he leaves much
to be desired in plot construction. In *Die Epigonen* the formal resources are still very inadequate. This is due in part to the long

genesis of the novel, which started out as a quite different kind of book and went through a stage in which it was meant to be more light-hearted and comic than it turned out to be.[26] The extremely complex plot turns on secret family relationships, withheld information, lost documents, and so on, all the paraphernalia of worn-out conventions. Another problem is the influence of Goethe's *Wilhelm Meisters Lehrjahre*, to which there are many slavish parallels. The plot is improbably constructed; von Wiese, in defense of it, has argued that accident is a structural principle in the novel, accident and contradiction being among Immermann's most basic concepts.[27] But Windfuhr seems to me more convincing when he says, "Die Zufälligkeiten und Abenteuerlichkeiten der Handlung müssen auf einmal den gesetzlichen und notwendig ablaufenden Gang eines Geschichtsprozesses symbolisieren. Hier wird dem Grundschema zu viel zugemutet. Die Form hat sich nicht im gleichen Tempo mitentwickelt."[28]

Of substantial interest is the treatment of the class situation in the novel. This is also partly an inheritance from *Wilhelm Meister*, although here the theme is of much greater importance. Hermann, the hero, becomes involved in a struggle over proprietary rights between a ducal family and his own uncle, a large-scale industrialist. The question turns, rather trivially, it has seemed to some readers, on whether the duke's ancestry is purely noble or contains a peasant woman in the family tree; the problem of the documentation of this matter is part of the machinery of Immermann's complicated plot. Hermann is torn between what he perceives as the beauty of the aristocratic culture and his duty to his uncle. These forces seem at first to be irreconcilable. The downward slide of the aristocratic family has proceeded in three stages: the grandfather of the duke was frugal and gave his attention to the working of his estates; the father was a sensitive, imaginative, prodigal philanderer; the present duke is proud and strictly concerned with the restoration of a status that has no objective relevance in modern society. Hermann's capitalist uncle has no sympathy for such a restoration. He believes that wealth and property should pass to those who know how to manage and increase it in a modern way; in this regard he anticipates the attitude in Freytag's *Soll und Haben*, in which the representative of the merchant ethos and the ethos of the novel remarks that money should roll freely into other hands and the plowshare should pass to those

130

who know better how to guide it.[29] Hermann, who has practically no conscious class identity, gets himself frantically entangled in this affair from not being able to sort out his allegiances. Fancying himself enamoured of the duchess, he allies himself emotionally with the family's cause. For a time he tries to play the role of resident intellectual in the noble household.

As in *Wilhelm Meister*, however, the aristocratic milieu turns out to be a thin veneer of civilization beneath which there is much shallowness and pompous futility. No one is really interested in Hermann's evening lectures on "Poesie und Unterhaltungsliteratur," for they are stopped in the middle when dinner is served, and he must realize that nothing can be seen through to completion in this household. Immermann's critique of the aristocratic milieu proceeds through many dismaying details and weird events, and at one point explodes into a cruel grotesquerie of memorable proportions. The duchess, who has been reading and attempting to translate Scott, decides to put on a tournament with old weapons in honor of the duke's birthday. The imbecilic project is symbolic of the incongruity between phantasy and reality in the aristocratic class, and it turns into total farce. The bourgeois are to be excluded from the event, which so angers them that they decide to have their own, more expensive one. The old armor keeps falling apart and the nobles do not know how to use it. The village musicians employed play the *Marseillaise* because it is the only tune they can think of. While practicing the jousting, the horses refuse to run at one another and the men only succeed in hurting themselves. The horrified duchess cancels the jousting, which, on the day of the event, spoils the duke's pleasure, for that was the part he had been looking forward to. A disaffected participant smuggles in a disguised circus rider, who naturally outrides and outperforms all the unathletic, inauthentic "knights." The result of the affair is universal ill-humor and *blamage*. It is in such things that we see Immermann at his best. The grotesque lurked deeply in his satirical imagination, and when it was released, it could produce unforgettable results. A more imaginative and fierce deflation of aristocratic pretensions is not to be found elsewhere in the literature of the time, yet it all manages to present itself as comedy. Immermann's comedy, if not altogether what today we would call "black," is certainly of a sufficiently dark hue, for this aristocratic foofaraw is by no means all harmless nonsense. Men and horses

131

get hurt in the practice sessions, and, during the tournament, an old servant of the noble house, completely obsessed with the anachronistic ideology of loyal vassalage, attempts to assassinate the uncle who is struggling for possession of the property. The servant exhibits an internalization of what today would be called "false consciousness," a phenomenon upon which Heine had remarked a couple of years earlier in *Die Romantische Schule*.[30]

This uncle is the first modern capitalist in German fiction and *Die Epigonen* is the first German novel to describe a capitalist industrial milieu. This in itself is a breakthrough of importance, even if the industrial setting is more talked about than made palpable to us. Immermann went to some lengths to study industry where it was then most advanced in Germany, in the Wuppertal, at the time when Friedrich Engels was growing up there among the textile mills. It is known that Immermann modeled the uncle on a wealthy large industrialist of his time. He does not intend, however, as Freytag was to do twenty years later, to make his merchant prince into a hero of a healthy new class. It was Immermann's habit to caricature rather than characterize, by the systematic exaggeration of traits, and so it is also with the uncle. He is completely obsessed by rationalistic calculation; beauty, culture, even public honors mean little or nothing to him. The unpoetic rationalist is a familiar whipping-boy from the Romantic tradition, but Immermann is more subtle. For much that the uncle says and does makes genuine sense. He does not, for example, attempt to govern his diversified industries personally, but has put them in the hands of managers who have a considerable degree of executive and financial autonomy. He actually is able to issue his own currency, thus greatly increasing his credit resources, because of his insight that it is not money itself that makes wealth, but productivity. Thus the uncle gives an impression not only of rationality, but even of some degree of wisdom.

But Immermann is not buying it. His hero is impressed by the power of money, but also repelled by the "mathematische Berechnung menschlicher Kraft und menschlichen Fleißes."[31] This would be little more than an expression of Romantic anti-modernism if it were not for the observations on the condition of the workers, who are sickly and emaciated, a terrible contrast to the healthy farmers from whose families the workers have come. The description of the industrial landscape at the beginning of Book VII is a now familiar picture of a natural environment ruined by industry; a depressing pall of smoke hangs over it all. At table there is neither grace nor manners, nor is any wine served, since the uncle uses only what he himself produces; thus the furnishings are confused and without style, while the guests are served undrinkable ale and cider. What Lee B. Jennings called "the ludicrous demon"[32] is lurking here, although it does not become immediately apparent and bursts into view quite suddenly in a grotesque scene that is a fair parallel to the tournament of the aristocrats. It happens at the dedication of the mausoleum the uncle has built for himself and his late wife in the finest spirit of nineteenth-century gingerbread. The ceremony is punctuated by the sound of a machine draining away water that has flooded the building's foundations; the solemn pomposity of the occasion is disturbed in a manner that is peculiarly Immermann's. What then ensues hovers painfully between the melodramatic and the grotesque. The uncle's son Ferdinand is a ne'er-do-well who has conceived a jealous hatred of Hermann. A secret enemy fools Ferdinand into believing that lead acquired at the risk of one's life will make bullets that are infallibly fatal. Following this advice, he falls to his death from the machine draining the mausoleum during the ceremony. Now, as it happens, Ferdinand is not the uncle's son, but the product of an adulterous relationship between the uncle's wife and the prodigal nobleman who had mortgaged his estate to the uncle (this parentage accounts, presumably, for Ferdinand's dissolute uselessness; that is, blue blood can be inherited, but it is not ennobling). The uncle, meanwhile, in his purblind rationalistic way, had always believed in his marriage as a model of bourgeois virtue, and the theme of the preacher's sermon at the dedication is the perfect marriage as a symbol of true ethical purity. In the midst of this irony comes the news of Ferdinand's death. Hermann, who, for reasons too complicated to go into here, is mentally disturbed at this point, endeavors to ease his uncle's grief by explaining that Ferdinand was not his son, whereupon the uncle drops dead.

The artificial complexity of Immermann's plot structure makes analysis tedious, because it is hard to talk about details of the novel without going into endless explanation. In the scene just described, the machinery of plot creaks more deafeningly than the machinery of the water pump. But it is worth mentioning because it shows something about Immermann's peculiar strategies. Every world that he constructs houses the potential of grotesque catastrophe. The ethical underpinnings are never as they seem, and there is a disturbing incongruence between ideology and reality. Immermann should not be regarded as a humorist. A humorist shows us defects and flaws, and we can laugh at them in the shared knowledge that nothing, after all, is perfect. The failings in both the aristocratic world and the early capitalist milieu described in *Die Epigonen* are more than flaws; they are lethal incongruities. Just as the uncle dies when he discovers that a fundamental assumption of his self-understanding was a mirage, so the duke commits a dignified suicide when his claim to his estate and prerogatives turns out to be defective. This is the "negative neutrality" of which Bramsted spoke. Von Wiese says quite correctly that the only just way to see Immermann is to recognize the origin of his works in satire, which is used as a weapon against everyone.[33] Nikolaus Lenau asserted that no German writer was so sarcastic as Immermann.[34]

The universality of his caustic becomes evident in most of the details of what appears at first glance to be a moderate and leisurely book. There is, for example, the character of Wilhelmi, who, though extreme in his restorative, conservative opinions, seems in places to speak with Immermann's own voice.[35] While inducting Hermann into a new degree of a secret society, he delivers a lecture on alienation and *Epigonentum*; men today, he says, feel wretched without any specific cause for suffering; they are adrift because no one has a preordained place in society any more.[36] Hermann is overwhelmed by this wisdom, and indeed the section is often quoted by those seeking the key definition of what Immermann meant. But the ludicrous demon is again not far off; its approach is signalled at the point when Immermann speaks of his two earnest heroes as "Ritter der Wahrheit."[37] In their overexcitement they become drunk, and in an anarchic uproar make a shambles of the "temple." In Book VI, Wilhelmi delivers an anti-Semitic tirade of criticism of Madame Meyer, a Berlin salon Jewess who collects Christian art and pursues an absurd cult of pseudo-Romantic aestheticized Catholicism. "Es ist der Schachergeist ihrer Väter, welcher in der Sammelwut der Tochter fortspukt," he fulminates; Jewish emancipation is the "Erzeugnis sentimentaler Schriftsteller und schlaffer Staatsmänner"; "Im Volke hat sich vielmehr das alte Bewußtsein unzerstört erhalten, daß

134

der Jude nichts tauge"; "Jude bleibt Jude, und der Christ muß sich mit ihnen vorsehn, am meisten, wenn sie sich liebevoll anstellen. Sie sind allesamt freigelassene Sklaven, kriechend, wenn sie etwas haben wollen, trotzig, wenn sie es erlangten oder wenn sie merken, daß es nicht zu erlangen steht."[38] It happens, however, that Wilhelmi is in possession of a piece missing from an altar owned by Madame Meyer, and the result is that he marries her.

I do not think that Immermann meant here to give expression to anti-Semitic opinions — he was, after all, one of Heine's most cordial admirers — nor to suggest that anti-Semitic opinions may easily be made to disappear. Rather, we are in a situation in which any strongly held and eloquently argued opinion or principle can change overnight into its opposite. People, events, and opinions are in a constant unstable flux; many of the characters and events in the novel turn out to be not what they seem, and the boundary of the absurd is easily crossed. Contradictory styles of life and thinking are put into what seems to be a dialectical opposition, but there is no synthesis. This is true, for example, in the hilarious Book V, in which Immermann takes out after his old enemies, the radical students. It begins with the account of a student Hermann had met at the beginning of the novel, who was on his way to join the Greek war of independence, but has instead become a police commissioner who specializes in hunting the "demagogues." On the road, Hermann meets what appears to be a radical nationalist student, who tells sadly of his sufferings in jail; he asks to ride a bit on Hermann's horse, promptly gallops off with it, and turns out to be a Jewish swindler wearing a blond, long-haired wig. At an inn, Hermann finds himself among an ineffable group of radical students. While the innkeeper enhances his income by turning such fellows in to the police, his daughter, named Sophie Christine, calls herself Thusnelda instead and tries to draw Hermann into the conspiracy. The students, with sixty-three talers in their revolutionary fund, are engaged in a solemn debate to decide whether all princes should be murdered. They conclude: "Die bis zur Leipziger Schlacht teutscher Sache noch nicht beigetreten waren, sollen sterben, und denen, die vor diesem Zeitpunkte ihre Pflicht erfüllt haben, geben wir Pension oder Leibzucht, vaterländischer zu reden"; they determine on 500-800 talers a year for a king.[39] Hermann, determined to convert the students, holds a gun on them and gives a rather silly speech of his own, in which he points out that if they want to imitate the past, they should remember that in older times the young were not allowed to speak and they should therefore leave the leadership of the state to the old men.[40] At this point the police come, the students evaporate, and Hermann, of course, is arrested as the "chief demagogue." The arresting officers discuss among themselves whether the Jews or the French are responsible for these revolutionary activities and conclude with familiar folk-logic that the French are all secret Jews anyway.[41]

It is important to remember that Immermann is here treating issues of the greatest contemporary significance. In the 1820's, the years in which the action of the novel takes place, the most severe political stress in Germany was that between the authorities and the nationalistic students. Fundamentally, the rebellious students after the Wars of Liberation were pressing for the transformation of Germany into some semblance of a unified, modern state. Due, in part, at least, to the violent repression to which they were subjected, the students were radicalized into nationalistic, chauvinistic, and often wildly regressive positions that Immermann was not alone in finding ridiculous; some of the plans of Karl Follen's Giessen "Schwarze" were downright fantastic.[42] The lapsed fighter for Greek independence belongs to a context already touched upon in the chapter on Laube (see above, p. 116); from October, 1821, to November, 1822, there had been four hundred foreign volunteers in Greece, half of whom were German;[43] and in 1822 Immermann himself considered going to fight in Greece.[44] But the radicality of Immermann's satire here is striking; he allows no trace of dignity either to the conspiring students or to the political authorities, and Hermann himself cuts a pretty poor figure. Again, it is far from being a genuinely funny situation; Hermann is indeed arrested, and it is only through luck and accident, as is usual in Immermann's plots, that he is extricated from this dangerous predicament. The issues and their possible consequences are not trivial, but the human material available is inadequate to cope with them. Like the tiny hero of Immermann's mock-epic *Tulifäntchen* (1829), modern men are too small for the great challenges confronting them. Consequently, issues of grave importance find no resolution, but simply whirl about in the maelstrom of a directionless society. Similar observations could be made on other parts of *Die Epigonen*, such as a debate between two schoolteachers, one a champion of classical-

136

humanistic education, the other of relevant, practical schooling —
a large issue at the time. As usual, the representatives of the opposing
positions are obsessed to the point of idiosyncracy, and there is
neither resolution nor synthesis.[45]

A few words need to be said about Medon, the strangest character
of all. He presents himself as a champion of Machiavellian authoritarianism, arguing for a system in which people are given constitutional forms to quiet them while the rule remains as autocratic
as before.[46] He expresses the opinion that all students should be
annihilated because their minds have been poisoned for the rest of
their lives. But a police official observes ominously that Médon
exactly resembles the chief radical conspirator being sought, and,
sure enough, he is arrested as one of the leaders of the demagogues.
It turns out that the Jesuit-educated Medon was neither a radical
nor a reactionary, but what is here called a "pessimist"; pessimism
is described as "das Streben der Faktionen, durch künstliche Hervor-
bringung eines allerschlechtesten Zustandes die Menschen in eine
Wut zu stürzen, welche sie blindlings den Planen [sic] der Bösen
zutreibt."[47] He works through bad advice to create hateful conditions
for the sake of anarchy; Hermann, too, whom he had tricked into
buying a piece of land in Baden, leading him to believe that this
would qualify him for political office, was to be a victim of his
machinations, and his wife, a patriotic enthusiast, was a tool also;
he married her only to be able to open a Berlin salon to pursue his
ends.

Von Wiese calls Medon the most interesting figure of the novel.[48]
He incarnates a valueless destructiveness that seems obliquely related
to Immermann's own satirical strategies. He is a symptom of a society
in which there are no viable guidelines, and he is driven beyond
Immermann's contemplation of the absurd to a nihilistic fury. But
there is here also a representation that the unrest in society is
conspiratorially generated and manipulated for evil and destructive
ends. Medon is the only conspirator who is regarded with any serious-
ness in the novel, and he is an ideological straw man, not correspon-
ding to anything in social or political reality, and he constitutes an
evasion on Immermann's part. The society Immermann describes is
completely adrift; one looks in vain for the stable center. Medon
embraces the obsessiveness of both radical extremes of society
simultaneously and erects the lack of meaningful conviction found

everywhere in Immermann's novel into a negative philosophy; he may be meant to objectify symbolically the forces that make contemporary German life so distressing and unsatisfying. But, insofar as Immermann makes Medon wilfully evil, he obscures the dynamic of social processes that otherwise is seen with considerable perspicacity. The injection of a conspiracy theory into this novel is a blunder that misdirects the reader's attention.

The end of *Die Epigonen* has caused some unhappiness and a certain amount of critical debate. By the complexities of the plot, Hermann becomes the heir of both the noble family and his uncle. He determines to dismantle the entire industrial enterprise and return the land to agriculture:

> Jene Anstalten, künstliche Bedürfnisse künstlich zu befriedigen, erscheinen mir geradezu verderblich und schlecht. Die Erde gehört dem Pfluge, dem Sonnenscheine und Regen, welcher das Samenkorn entfaltet, der fleißigen, einfach arbeitenden Hand. Mit Sturmesschnelligkeit eilt die Gegenwart einem trockenen Mechanismus zu; wir können ihren Lauf nicht hemmen, sind aber nicht zu schelten, wenn wir für uns und die Unsrigen ein grünes Plätzchen abzäunen und diese Insel so lange als möglich gegen den Sturz der vorbeirauschenden industriellen Wogen befestigen.[49]

Most critics have taken this ending to be a withdrawal by Immermann from the issues he himself raised; in the midst of the gloom of Hermann's depressed and lacerated mental state a form of Biedermeier resignation introduces itself, a retreat into an agricultural idyll inadequate to the thrust of an innovative social novel. This view has been challenged by Franz Rumler.[50] He points out that the chronological end of the story comes not in the ninth book, but in the eighth, the correspondence between the author and the doctor concerning the accuracy of the account so far. This correspondence is dated 1835, while Book IX concludes in 1829. Rumler observes that the correspondence ends with an optimistic quote from Lamartine to the effect that, although institutions are decaying, the men of the new age are fresh and gay. From this he concludes that Immermann meant his story to end on a similarly optimistic note, that the intention to agriculturize the industrial enterprise arises out of the depression of temporarily unhappy love, which disappears with Hermann's eventual marriage, and that the flight into the idyllic is only a whim. This argument, I believe, is unconvincing. In the first place, it hardly seems a proper method of interpretation to argue from the natural chronology of events against the structure of a novel. Secondly, the peroration of Book VIII is a general statement and is not applied specifically to Hermann. Nowhere is it said that the industries were not dismantled. Nor, in my view, does it matter a great deal whether they were or not. The retreat to an agricultural idyll does end the novel on a resigned and regressive note.

Theodor Mundt criticized it for its lack of confidence in the future and for not showing, as the modern novel should, "daß die Individuen heut besser sind, als die Verhältnisse,"[51] but this simply shows the difference between the Young German notion of how to write a modern, relevant book, and Immermann's realism. The dilemma he poses at the end of the novel is a real one, and it is difficult to see what alternative resolutions were available. A socialist solution at so early a date and by such a writer is, of course, unthinkable. The only imaginable alternative would be the establishment of a cooperative industrial community like those organized by Robert Owen, but it is probably too early in Germany for such ideas. Immermann looked as far ahead as he could into the embryonic capitalist age and saw no solutions; even Hermann's despairing decision is by no means presented as a prescriptive model, for he sees clearly that the development presented by the uncle's industries is ineluctable. Immermann's intellectual honesty was too great to allow him to put an optimistic interpretation on the capitalist development.[52] The final and largest dilemma of the book is, like all the others, bereft of any positive solution.

The question now presents itself whether Immermann's other important novel, *Münchhausen, eine Geschichte in Arabesken* (1839), may also be understood in terms of the concept of "negative neutrality." Critics, as a rule, have not thought so, but I doubt that they are correct. *Münchhausen*, like *Die Epigonen*, was born in satire, but in the process of writing, Immermann decided to oppose to the bottomlessly mendacious world of the great liar Münchhausen a description of a Westphalian peasant society; this section expanded until it came to equal the Münchhausen part in size and weight. The result was a double novel, somewhat reminiscent of Hoffmann's *Kater Murr*.[53] Dimiter Statkow has recently shown that the two parts of the novel are balanced and matched artistically to a degree that had not been previously perceived.[54] Statkow has made a good case that the charge of disunity raised against the novel by older critics is largely unfounded, and that structurally and aesthetically *Münchhausen* is no mean achievement. Certainly, whether one thinks of Immermann's perceptions as genuinely dialectical or just contradictory, the wittily intertwined double novel is more appropriate to his purposes than the *Bildungsroman* scheme of *Die Epigonen*.

We cannot spend much time here with the extremely complicated Münchhausen part, which has been extensively and well analyzed by Windfuhr and von Wiese. It is to a large extent literary and cultural satire, and as such requires a good deal of commentary to be wholly comprehensible. The tendency toward exploding grotesquerie evident in *Die Epigonen* has here become a principle of narration. The quantity of sheer uproar that Immermann can generate is astounding, although the hilarity can become a trifle wearying over several hundred pages. Herman Meyer remarks that "Immermann betreibt die Konfusion mit einer Art pedantischer Gründlichkeit."[55] On the satire itself Meyer observes: "Die Bezüge zwischen der Satire und ihren Objekten sind so grob-direkt und gleichzeitig so rechnerisch-korrekt, daß sich keine plötzliche Überraschung und kein befreiendes Lachen einstellen wollen."[56] On the other hand, Meyer's criticism is too negative. For one thing, to seek for "liberating laughter" in Immermann is to regard him as a humorist, which he is not. Furthermore, the Münchhausen sections are uneven; along with much that most readers could live without, there are passages that in their wit, absurdity, and grotesqueness hardly have a parallel anywhere in nineteenth-century German letters. An example is Münchhausen's proposal to form a *Luftverdichtungsaktienkompanie*, a commercial enterprise for manufacturing building materials out of solidified air. This proposal transforms the old Baron Schnuck from a mono-maniac obsessed with the recovery of ancient privileges long since abrogated into a man possessed by the "Teufel der Industrie."[57] He begins to rehearse the role of a satanic corporation counsel, devising crooked defenses to hypothetical cases, and although he is troubled by the question whether a nobleman can lower himself to work for profit, these doubts dissolve in the intoxication of planning an empire of railroads, factories, and great industries. This is the genuine Immermann, skewering everyone and everything simultaneously, while keeping a sharp eye on social and class issues that

140

were then beginning to make their appearance. His satire on excessive complexity of narrative levels in Romantic fiction,[58] and the problem of the incongruence of consciousness and reality and of an individualism that has lost its anchor in society and become catapulted into total, solipsistic eccentricity[59] are among the significant themes that are developed with remarkable resourcefulness.

For our purposes, however, it will be more helpful to give some attention to the other part of the novel, which became widely known under the title of Book II, Chapter 3, *Der Oberhof*. About twenty years after *Münchhausen* was published, the *Oberhof* part was separated from the Münchhausen part as an independent book, and by 1930 it had seen eighty editions, as compared to twenty for the novel as a whole.[60] This procedure had an ideological motive. *Der Oberhof* stands at or near the beginning of the genre of *Dorfgeschichten*, tales of village life that in the early part of the century were worthwhile developments in realism. Hebbel said that, with *Der Oberhof*, Immermann had hurled "ein wahrer neuer Weltteil in die Literatur,"[61] and Annette von Droste-Hülshoff was pleased to have *Die Judenbuche* compared with it.[62] But, in the course of the nineteenth century, the *Dorfgeschichte* became a sentimental, mendacious form veiling rather than revealing genuine social realities, and the tradition flowed into the *Blut und Boden* literature of noxious memory. By removing *Der Oberhof* from its original context of social criticism, Immermann's work was falsified and trivialized into this direction. Men of taste and sense have naturally always deplored this. Raabe complained that "das edle deutsche Volk sich den Münchhausen aus dem Münchhausen, um ihn sich mundgerecht zu machen, gestrichen hat oder hat streichen lassen," and remarked fairly, "wir haben uns ein Unterhaltungsstücklein aus einem weisen, bitterernsten Buche zurecht gemacht."[63] Hofmannsthal called the surgery criminal and refused to include *Der Oberhof* in his anthology of great German stories.[64]

Der Oberhof is an attempt on Immermann's part to break out of his persistent negativism. He wished to oppose to the bedlam of modern mendacity and eccentricity a society still organically intact, unalienated, self-reliant, and healthy — a genuine community welded together by allegiance to tradition and not subject to interference by others in running its own communal life. For this he chose a community of prosperous Westphalian peasants, dominated by

141

the *Hofschulze*, the richest farmer, who functions as elder, guardian of tradition, master of rites, and ruler. The virtues of the *Hofschulze* and his people are strictly conservative ones: self-sufficiency, frugality, modest demands on life, harmony with the natural cycle, and resistance to all change. Windfuhr has questioned whether this dialectical strategy was successful, arguing that Immermann has again just set out unresolved dichotomies: "In der Tat führt die säuberliche Trennung der Gesellschaft in eine heile und eine kranke Hälfte zur Verzeichnung nach beiden Seiten hin: die satirische wird zur Karikatur und die bäuerliche zum Idealrefugium."[65]

This comment, however, begs an important question about the ideality of the refuge. Certainly Immermann was convinced that he was producing a positive counterweight to the negativity of his satire; he wrote to Ferdinand Freiligrath as the novel was nearing completion in 1839: "Das positive Element tritt in den folgenden Bänden immer stärker auf";[66] to his fiancée he wrote at about the same time: "Zwischen allen Fratzen grünen die Wiesen des Oberhofes, tragen als liebliche Frucht das Verständnis des Jägers und Lisbeths."[67] In another letter to her he went so far as to say, "Im Münchhausen wird positiv ausgesprochen, was in den Epigonen mehr nur angedeutet ist" and "in der süßesten Gestalt vollendet sich meine Versöhnung mit Welt und Leben, der kalte Spott zieht wie ein gebrannter Schatten in den Tartarus und der Fluch wird von meinem Haupte genommen."[68] For us to judge whether this was truly the case, Immermann would have had to live longer. The question is, can the *Oberhof* section be seen in this light? Is the curse even apparently off Immermann's head?

The fact is that critics have long tended to sense something wrong about this assessment of the *Oberhof* section, without being altogether clear about what it is. Werner Kohlschmidt, in his instructive comparison of Immermann and Gotthelf, was the first, to my knowledge, to feel uneasy. He notes how rigidly the *Oberhof* world is tied to tradition, and comments: "Nähme man der bäuerlichen Welt die Sitte, und wenn sie rational gesehen noch so unsinnig, überlebt, ja unbürgerlich gefährlich erscheinen mag, so bräche man ihr das Rückgrat. Was aber ist dann noch Halt gegen die bedrohlich aufkommende Stadt?"[69] He also points out perceptively that it is not the peasants themselves who define the meaning of the peasant community, but the local clergyman, a character who will concern us presently.[70] Von Wiese sees that there are odd, unbalanced characters in the *Oberhof* world, and that something berserk emerges in the *Hofschulze* when Oswald unwittingly upsets the order of ritual and the *Hofschulze* insists upon a duel to the death with axes.[71] Von Wiese also points out that although class propriety is maintained with fanatic insistence in the *Oberhof* world, the final marriage between the noble Oswald and the foundling Lisbeth goes directly against the rules of class and convention.[72] Windfuhr takes us a step farther by observing that Immermann gives us a picture of the peasant world through the eyes of a city man.[73] Michael Scherer has written that the *Oberhof* world is endangered, not from the outside, but from the rigidity within: "Nur scheinbar ist er [the *Hofschulze*] als Bauer gegen die schleichende Krise dieser Gesellschaft gefeit; tatsächlich gerät er hart an den Rand einer Scheinexistenz."[74] Statkow, who has defended the unity of the novel, argues that the *Oberhof* is not only ideal, but also dark and tragic and not free of conflict and criticism.[75] Finally, William McClain, while explicating the heroic stature of the *Hofschulze*, is obliged to note the "hideboundness" of his character and "the danger inherent in such a mentality."[76]

I would go a step farther than these critics and argue that the *Oberhof* section is not an ideal, but is subject to the same "negative neutrality" we have detected elsewhere in Immermann's novels, and I would regard this as significant because it is a matter of record that he did not intend it so. For he has been tripped up by his penchant for caricature. It is certainly possible to present a society living by traditional values and ritual symbols, but when these traditions and rituals are presented as surviving for their own sake alone, defended with fanatic persistence and without a clearly integrated function in the life and survival of the society, then that condition can no longer be called organic. In the *Oberhof*, the link between symbol and social reality has already been broken. The "sword of Charlemagne," which is the symbol of the *Hofschulze's* authority, is a fraud, and the *Hofschulze* forces a visiting scholar to certify it fraudulently. This is a clear case of the kind of obsessive eccentricity and mendacity that plagues the Münchhausen world; the *Hofschulze*, by knowingly maintaining a ritualistic fraud, has already departed from the naive and organic consciousness. The fanaticism with which both ritual and the authority of the *Hofschulze* are enforced is a clear sign that

143

this society is on the verge of cracking to pieces. The hierarchical relationships are maintained to such an extreme that it cannot be said they enhance humane values. The story of the so-called "Patrioten-kaspar" is a case in point; as a young man, full of egalitarian zeal, he wooed the daughter of the *Hofschulze*, an ambition to which his station did not entitle him. The son of the *Hofschulze* put out his eye, whereupon Kaspar killed him and has lived on as a vengeful pariah. It is he who creates a crisis by hiding the sword without which, the *Hofschulze* in his fetishistic rigidity believes, the governance of the community cannot be maintained. Statkow points out that Immermann, whether he intended to or not, shows here the beginning of a proletarian subclass of peasants: "Die Macht des Hofschulzen ist für Kaspar die Macht der Reichen."[77] What Immermann presents is a kind of rural Mafia, governed anachronistically by the rituals of the medieval *Vehmgericht*, rigidly stratified, egocentric, obsessed with ritual, and incapable of humane justice.

One explanation for this is found in Windfuhr's perception that Immermann viewed with the eyes of a city man. He lived in cities all his life, and, during most of his time in Düsseldorf, he made every effort to get himself transferred to Berlin; only towards the end of his life did he become reconciled to the smaller town. Windfuhr remarks that some of the most acutely observed materials in *Die Epigonen* are those in Books VI and VII dealing with Berlin society.[78] For the city man, the peasant rituals necessarily take on a quaint aspect: the ritualized, wooden moralizing; the nine vests worn by the *Hofschulze* both because tradition requires it and to show that he can afford it; the observation at the wedding scene that the bridesmaid's bouquet stinks; the general pretentiousness. In this regard the figure of the *Diakonus*, the city-born pastor who has become acclimated to the world of the *Oberhof*, is of importance. Although he participates in the wedding ritual, he has sufficient distance from it to warn Oswald not to laugh. In a curious passage in Book V, Chapter 4, it is said of the *Diakonus* that he knows about modern critical doubts in matters of religion, but he himself is untouched by them; he has made a decision in favor of conventional piety — but here, as with the *Hofschulze's* awareness of the fraudulence of the sword, one can see the fissures opening in the modern consciousness. In Book II, Chapter 10, the *Diakonus* gives a long discourse on the immortal folk, the free energies of the nation, "tiefsinnig,

144

unschuldig, treu, tapfer."[79] In the city he had suffered *Weltschmerz* and had wanted to reform Christianity, but now he has found true human relations among the peasants. Von Wiese has pointed out wryly that this discourse "hat freilich mit dem beschreibenden Realismus der Oberhofdarstellung höchstens indirekt etwas zu tun."[80] The long and the short of it is that, if Immermann intended to present the *Oberhof* as an ideological counterweight to his customary "negative neutrality," he failed; the perceptions of the modern city man intrude too easily, and the ludicrous demon is not to be exorcized by such means.

In considering the relevance of Immermann to a discussion of Young Germany, the question of realism offers itself as one possible approach. In some ways, he seems to have been more directly conscious of the issue of realism than the Young Germans were. "Realismus," as Windfuhr has pointed out, was one of Immermann's favorite words.[81] It always meant to him a turning of attention to the world without. At a very early stage he mounted a criticism of Romantic inwardness; in a draft of a review of Heine's *Tragödien, nebst einem lyrischen Intermezzo* (1823), he wrote: "Man hat dieser Zeit zum Vorwurf gemacht, daß sie, nach der Außenwelt gerichtet, sich in Oberflächlichkeit zu verlieren drohe; uns scheint jedoch, daß dieser Tadel die Dichtkunst unserer Tage wenigstens nicht treffe, daß diese vielmehr im Gegenteil sich zu einer einseitigen Innerlichkeit neige."[82] And he goes on: "der Trieb zur Selbstbetrachtung wird unwiderstehlich und gibt mehr und mehr das Material zur Dichtung her, je trüber die Augen der poetischen Psychologen für die Konstruktionen der Welt und des Lebens an sich werden."[83] Immermann himself worried a good deal whether he was in touch with this external reality. Windfuhr points out how his experience with legal affairs sharpened his sense for the logic of real events,[84] and Rumler has analyzed three realistic aspects of *Die Epigonen*: the subjective narrative perspective of the author, which yields credibility; Immermann's sense of the causal relationship between reality and literature; and "Verwissenschaftlichung," by which Rumler means Immermann's response to the scientific age in trying to be expert on what is described in the novel.[85] For example, the description of the Oberhof is prefaced by three paragraphs of a description of Westphalian peasant society quoted verbatim from a scholarly book. In the *Oberhof* section, Immermann explicitly opposes idyllic idealization of the peasant life; in Book II, Chapter 3, it is pointed out that "das ästhetische Landschaftsgefühl ist schon ein Produkt der Überfeinerung,"[86] that is, of the city man estranged from nature; it is not sensed by the peasants who actually live in nature. In another place the *Diakonus* explains to a courtier that the peasants are not "gemütlich," for they have no time and are not "Naturmenschen" in the Rousseauistic sense; they are strictly bound by tradition and caste hierarchy.[87] Even the peasant custom of premarital sex is presented, with the remark that writers of idylls had overlooked it.[88] Those who have published *Der Oberhof* separately often have overlooked it, also.

It is true, to be sure, that Immermann never made a clean break with the Romantic tradition, as his life-long orientation on Tieck as his literary model shows. But, by various means, he combatted the Romantic hypnosis from which most writers of his time suffered. The most prominent of these means is satire. An example is his parody of the Sternean tradition of the novel of confused chronology (and Pückler-Muskau's resuscitation of it) in *Münchhausen*, the first book of which begins with chapters 11-15, which are followed by a correspondence with the bookbinder discussing the faddishness that requires such confusion, whereupon Chapters 1-10 follow. Another example is the *Märchen*, "Die Wunder im Spessart," that Immermann, following Romantic practice, rather awkwardly inserted into Book V. It is, in fact, a kind of modernized anti-*Märchen*. The princess has been put under a spell by — a wicked textile mill owner! A scholar, in attempting to save her, plunges deeply into the mystical secrets of nature, but only grows mad and very old in the realm of the unreal. A knight releases her by a straightforward kiss; thus the right path is taken by the worldly knight, not by the dark seeker, who is unable to find the key to true awakening.

For a long time Immermann endeavored to maintain a link with idealism. Von Wiese comments of the period before *Die Epigonen*: "Noch scheint die Flucht aus der profanen Realität möglich zu sein, noch gibt es einen 'Immermann in der Idee', der an die eigene geistige Selbstverwirklichung glaubt. Aber die dämonische Gewalt der Natur und das Vielgestaltige und Widersprüchliche der modernen Gesellschaft sind bereits so mächtig geworden, daß die Dinge ihren eigenen Anspruch erheben und die Forderung einer wahrhaftigeren und menschwürdigeren Kunstwelt weitgehend nur ideologisch proklamiert wird."[89] Furthermore, von Wiese notes an important shift away from the Romantic function of irony: "Ironie ist bei Immermann stets der Satire verwandt. Sie zeigt den Abstand zwischen Ideal und Wirklichkeit, aber nicht zugunsten des Ideals, sondern zugunsten der Wirklichkeit. Denn das von der Wirklichkeit abgespaltene Ideal ist zur 'Lüge', zur fixen Idee, zum Wahn geworden."[90] This point is of exceptional importance and shows most clearly the parallels between Immermann and Heine. The orientation on objective, external reality is stronger and more purposeful in Immermann than it is in the Young Germans; it is a process similar to the one we noted as an exceptional example in Laube's *Die Krieger* and leads to similar virtues in the writing of fiction; Rumler has also argued that the interpenetration of social spheres with one another and a certain stylistic tendency to simultaneity of narration point ahead to Gutzkow's *Ritter vom Geiste*.[91] But it must be said on balance that Immermann's realism is a tendency, not an achievement. Hans Mayer, in drawing a parallel between Immermann and Balzac, argues that the opaqueness of the sociological situation itself was responsible for this: "die Zustände, die geschildert werden, um den Übergangscharakter dieser Epoche zu kennzeichnen, sind weitaus unreifer, schmächtiger, undeutlicher in ihrer Entwicklungsrichtung als bei Balzac. Das liegt nicht an mangelnder Kunst des Erzählers Immermann, sondern an mangelnder Schärfe der gesellschaftlichen Konturen im damaligen Deutschland."[92]

This view has already been discussed in the introductory essay. It appears to be supported empirically by the situation of the novel generally in Immermann's time. His own turn to external reality yields disparateness and chaos, manageable only by a rather atomistic satire. He lacks the disciplined, ordered consciousness that makes the social realism of Balzac, Stendhal, Flaubert possible. One might say that the Young Germans possessed a superfluity of ideological conviction and too little sense of the objective disparateness and complexity of the real world, whereas with Immermann it was the other way around. Von Wiese has made an effort to find solid ground in Immermann's mind; he argues that the resolution of accident and contradiction is in the hidden religious order in the hearts of men, in love and friendship, and in the reality of things, and that salvation in an uncertain time is in the individual who creates a new order in marriage and founding a family.[93] It is

147

true that Immermann retained a religious orientation that grew stronger toward the end of his life, and true also that both of his important novels end in love and hopeful marriage. But such views are more evasive than productive for a social realist. Von Wiese himself is obliged to point out that, except for the two denouements, the marriages in Immermann's novels tend to be very shaky,[94] as is everything else.

Despite the *Chiliastische Sonette* (1832), which gives a Christian expression to hopefulness for the future,[95] and the massive effort to formulate a philosophical world-view in his quasi-*Faust*, *Merlin*, of the same year, Immermann was a bewildered and groping thinker, without much of the prophetic gift. Herman Meyer observed that "ein anderes ist es, die Diagnose einer Zeitkrankheit zu stellen, ein anderes, diese wirklich von sich abzuschütteln."[96] Lee B. Jennings sees the nature of Immermann's perceptions as closely connected to what I, following Bramsted, have called "negative neutrality": "Immermann... recognizes the power of decay and the prevalence of chaos and is under no illusions as to their role as an integral part of all existence. This recognition makes it extremely difficult for him to gain a foothold in his struggle to attain positive values."[97] Theodor Mundt, however, saw the problem somewhat differently, in a way that shows the contrast with the Young Germans: "Sein Roman [*Die Epigonen*] hat darin eine materielle Härte, daß er, ohne bis auf die allgemeinen Zerwürfnisse und Hemmnisse der Ideen zu gehen, die Zerfahrenheit der modernen Charaktere nur als eine individuelle Haltungslosigkeit vor Augen führt. Das heißt, die Individualität einer Epoche mißachten, ohne das Wesen der Epoche selbst, ihre ehrwürdigen Schmerzen, ihre berechtigten Hoffnungen, ihre Anwartschaft auf die Zukunft, zu ergründen."[98]

Mundt is mistaken to suggest that Immermann completely individualizes epochal issues. The relationship between individuality and society in his writing is a complex and strained one that cannot be gone into here, except to say that he certainly did attempt a kind of typological representation. It is Mundt's objection to the lack of future orientation that is important for our purposes, the utopianism out of which would arise a "Prinzip Hoffnung" in Ernst Bloch's sense, and which the Young Germans, at least initially, had to a substantially greater extent. Hans-Georg Gadamer has argued that "in der Tat lebt in dem Dichter ein Glaube an die Zukunft, die sich

148

aus den abgelebten Gestalten der Vergangenheit und insbesondere aus der Reinigung von den Abstraktionen, in denen sich das erhitzte Zeitbewußtsein herumtreibt, zu einer lebensvollen Wirklichkeit erheben werde."[99] But other critics have read Immermann differently. Emil Grütter, though not the most subtle of Immermann's interpreters, has said that his world "kennt keine Zukunft. Die Gegenwart aber ist bestimmt durch eine Vergangenheit, die ihrerseits wieder nichts oder doch nur eine Schale ist";[100] and Windfuhr has drawn the comparison with Young Germany: "[Immermann] schließt sich nur während einer kurzen Phase mit seinen chiliastischen Ideen dem jungdeutschen Futurismus an,"[101] and in this I think Windfuhr is correct. The *Chiliastische Sonette* are no more than a vague expression of a secularized Messianic hope, and otherwise Immermann's utopias, like *Der Oberhof*, are not only regressive, but so clearly threatened by the ineluctable course of history that they offer scant hope for the future. Jennings is probably right in seeing the dark vision as the most fundamental one in Immermann: ". . . pessimism displays a fluctuating level of prominence in all his works, and it has the peculiar feature that it seems to consist of concentric layers. The peripheral layer manifests itself readily (as the representation of futile, incongruous life), but the more fearfully nihilistic core often remains hidden."[102] That such was probably not Immermann's intention matters little; the result shows only that his sensitivity to the torment of his age was greater than his resources for imposing a positive, forward-looking order on them.

It is likely in any case that Immermann did not share the Young German faith in the power of literature to reform or improve society. The concept of *Zeitgeist* did not mean the same thing to him, for it did not have the same pregnant, progressive, and hopeful content that it did for the Young Germans and Young Hegelians. Rumler has remarked perceptively: "Für Immermann hatte die Zeit nichts 'Offenbarendes'. Sein Zeitgeist-Begriff, inbesondere im 'Münchhausen', stand dem Zeitgeist-Begriff Gotthelfs näher, nämlich im Sinne von Zeitauswüchsen."[103] The conservative satirist measures by norms of moderation against which nearly all phenomena of an agitated time take on the quality of the absurd. On the other hand, Immermann may have had a more realistic sense of the nature of literature. He reports on a conversation with Gutzkow in which the latter argued the reform of social conditions by means of great

149

social literary works, to which Immermann replied: "Die Literatur und Poesie erzeugt die Zustände nicht, sondern sie geht aus denselben hervor,"[104] thereby aligning himself with the distinction Gutzkow himself made elsewhere between literature as "Vorrede" and as "Register" (see above, p. 15). This more modest sense of the social determinism of literature barred Immermann from the enthusiastic reformism of the Young Germans, but enabled him to move farther along the road to realism than they were able to go.

NOTES

For each chapter, first references are given in full, thereafter by short titles. Titles of unpublished dissertations are in quotation marks, those of printed dissertations are italicized. The following short titles are used throughout:

Butler, *The Saint-Simonian Religion* = E. M. Butler, *The Saint-Simonian Religion in Germany. A Study of the Young German Movement.* Cambridge, Eng.: Cambridge University Press, 1926. Reprinted, New York: Howard Fertig, Inc., 1968.

Houben, *Gutzkow-Funde* = H. H. Houben, *Gutzkow-Funde. Beiträge zur Litteratur- und Kulturgeschichte des neunzehnten Jahrhunderts.* Berlin: Arthur L. Wolff, 1901.

Houben, *JdSuD* = H. H. Houben, *Jungdeutscher Sturm und Drang. Ergebnisse und Studien.* Leipzig: F. A. Brockhaus, 1911.

Houben, *Verbotene Literatur* = Heinrich Hubert Houben, *Verbotene Literatur von der klassischen Zeit bis zur Gegenwart. Ein kritisch-historisches Lexikon über verbotene Bücher, Zeitschriften und Theaterstücke, Schriftsteller und Verleger.* 2 vols., Berlin: E. Rowohlt, 1924; Bremen: K. Schünemann, 1928. Reprinted, Hildesheim: Georg Olms, 1965.

Houben, *Zeitschriften des Jungen Deutschlands,* I = Heinrich Hubert Houben, *Zeitschriften des Jungen Deutschlands.* Veröffentlichungen der Deutschen Bibliographischen Gesellschaft, *Bibliographisches Repertorium,* Vol. III. Berlin: B. Behr, 1906. Reprinted, Hildesheim and New York: Georg Olms, 1970.

Koopmann, *Das Junge Deutschland* = Helmut Koopmann. *Das Junge Deutschland. Analyse seines Selbstverständnisses.* Stuttgart: Metzler, 1970.

Wienbarg, *Ästhetische Feldzüge* = Ludolf Wienbarg, *Ästhetische Feldzüge,* ed. Walter Dietze. Berlin and Weimar: Aufbau-Verlag, 1964.

I. INTRODUCTION

1 Harold Jantz, "Sequence and Continuity in Nineteenth-Century German Literature," *Germanic Review*, 38 (1963), 27.
2 Jost Hermand, ed., *Das Junge Deutschland. Texte und Dokumente*, Reclams Universal-Bibliothek, Nos. 8703-07 (Stuttgart: Philipp Reclam Jun., 1966).
3 Koopmann, *Das Junge Deutschland*, p. 23. Friedrich Sengle, *Biedermeierzeit. Deutsche Literatur im Spannungsfeld zwischen Restauration und Revolution 1815-1848*, I (Stuttgart: Metzler, 1971), p. 160, has come to the same conclusion.
4 Wulf Wülfing, "Schlagworte des Jungen Deutschland," *Zeitschrift für deutsche Sprache*, 21 (1965), 42-59, 160-174; 22 (1966), 36-56, 154-178; 23 (1967), 48-82, 166-177; 24 (1968), 60-71, 161-183; 25 (1969), 96-115, 175-179; 26 (1970), 60-83, 162-175.
5 Cf. Reinhold Grimm, "Romanhaftes und Novellistisches in Laubes *Reisenovellen*," *Germanisch-romanische Monatsschrift*, N.S. 18 (1968), 299-303.
6 Koopmann, *Das Junge Deutschland*, p. 71.
7 Theodor Mundt, *Moderne Lebenswirren* (Leipzig: Gebrüder Reichenbach, 1834), p. 152.
8 C. P. Magill, "Young Germany: A Revaluation," *German Studies Presented to Leonard Ashley Willoughby*, ed. J. Boyd (Oxford: Blackwell, 1952), pp. 108-109.
9 David Daiches, *Critical Approaches to Literature* (New York: Norton, 1956), pp. 266-267.
10 Magill, "Young Germany: A Revaluation," p. 109.
11 Karl Gutzkow, *Briefe eines Narren an eine Närrin* (Hamburg: Hoffmann und Campe, 1832), p. 5.
12 Karl Gutzkow, *Zur Philosophie der Geschichte* (Hamburg: Hoffmann und Campe, 1836), p. 163. It is not without interest that John Stuart Mill expressed a very similar view of the English intellectual scene in 1831. See René Wellek, *A History of Modern Criticism 1750-1950* (New Haven and London: Yale University Press, 1955-), III, 86.
13 *Zeitung für die elegante Welt*, 1 January 1833, No. 1, p. 1. Sengle has written an extremely interesting and compelling chapter on the whole subject of "Symbol, Begriffsallegorie, Naturpersonifikation, Mythologie" (*Biedermeierzeit*, I, 292-367), and on the occasional efforts of progressive writers to combat irrational symbolism. Sengle shows a reasonable respect for the tradition of rhetoric of which this problem is a part. But he is right to say that it left writers in "einer in sich selbst kreisenden Sprache" and that

the Young Germans suffered from it even more than the strictly "Biedermeier" writers (ibid., I, 407). Perhaps one of the main failures of the Young Germans was not to have put this metaphorical and organistic-symbolic style out of the world once and for all.

14 Cf. Barbara Hernstein Smith, "Poetry as Fiction," *New Literary History*, 2 (1971), 259-281.

15 Ian Watt, *The Rise of the Novel. Studies in Defoe, Richardson and Fielding* (Berkeley: University of California Press, 1967), p. 60.

16 Friedrich Sengle, "Voraussetzungen und Erscheinungsformen der deutschen Restaurationsliteratur," *Deutsche Vierteljahrsschrift*, 30 (1956), 292. Cf. Sengle, "Der Romanbegriff in der ersten Hälfte des 19. Jahrhunderts," *Arbeiten zur deutschen Literatur 1750-1850* (Stuttgart: Metzler, 1965), esp. pp. 185-186. Sengle's *Biedermeierzeit* appeared too late to have the influence on my studies that it deserves. By restricting "realism" to the programmatic realism inaugurated by Julian Schmidt and Freytag and denying that "empiricist" aspects can be a typological sign of realism (I, 257-291), Sengle insists that realism should not be spoken of before 1850 and denies it especially to Young Germany. Rather than debate this difficult matter here, I should like merely to make two points. First, the evidence accumulated in this essay ought to suggest some moderation of Sengle's strictness. Second, because of his toleration of the harmonizing, sentimentalizing, and socially accommodated character of post-mid-century realism, Sengle does not share my regret at the loss of the critical faculty in the writer's consciousness involved in this process and the resulting trivialization of much German realism. See my essay on Laube below (Chapter V, pp. 104-126).

17 Günter Bliemel, "Die Auffassung des Jungen Deutschlands von Wesen und Aufgabe des Dichters und der Dichtung" (diss. Berlin, 1955), p. 92. A similar argument concerning the lack of realism in Germany was popularized by Erich Auerbach in the chapter "Miller the Musician" in *Mimesis* (Garden City: Doubleday, 1953), pp. 398-399.

18 Walther Roer, *Soziale Bewegung und politische Lyrik im Vormärz* (diss. Münster, 1933), pp. 13, 29-30. Even in the 1840's, when literature was becoming completely politicized, there was not a very strong sense of the poor as a class: "Es schien, als ob es nur ein Zufall sei, daß es Mangel und Besitzlosigkeit gab. Ein wenig mehr Mitleid, ein wenig mehr den Beutel geöffnet, und die ganze Armut wäre aufgehoben; aber die Reichen seien hartherzig und wollten von ihren Vorrechten nicht lassen. Die Vorstellung, die man sich von den Armen machte, verrät, daß man nur an verarmte Bürgerliche dachte" (ibid., p. 178). Certain poems of Herwegh and Freiligrath are important exceptions to this generalization.

19 Quoted by Hartmut Steinecke, ed., *Theorie und Technik des Romans im 19. Jahrhundert* (Tübingen: Niemeyer, 1970), p. 3.

20 Wienbarg, *Ästhetische Feldzüge*, p. 86.

21 Ibid., p. 146.

22 Ibid., p. 16.

23 Ibid., p. 11.

24 Ibid., p. 59.

25 Ibid., p. 94.

26 Viktor Schweizer, *Ludolf Wienbarg. Beiträge zu einer Jungdeutschen Ästhetik* (diss. Leipzig, 1897), pp. 86-87.

27 Quoted ibid., p. 130.

28 Gerhard Burkhardt, "Ludolf Wienbarg als Ästhetiker und Kritiker. Seine Entwicklung und seine geistesgeschichtliche Stellung" (diss. Hamburg, 1956), p. 111.

29 Wienbarg, *Ästhetische Feldzüge*, p. 112.

30 Ibid., p. 83.

31 Ibid., p. 88.

32 Ibid., p. 130. Wienbarg's emphasis.

33 Ibid., p. 131.

34 Theodor Mundt, *Geschichte der Literatur der Gegenwart. Friedrich von Schlegel's Geschichte der alten und neuen Literatur, bis auf die neueste Zeit fortgeführt* (Berlin: M. Simion, 1842), p. 41. Mundt's phrase is derived from Schlegel.

35 Ibid., p. 306.

36 Else von Eck, *Die Literaturkritik in den Hallischen und Deutschen Jahrbüchern (1838-1842)*, Germanische Studien, No. 42 (Berlin: E. Ebering, 1926), p. 34.

37 Sengle, *Biedermeierzeit*, I, 34-47.

38 Karl Gutzkow, *Maha Guru. Geschichte eines Gottes* (Stuttgart and Tübingen: J. G. Cotta, 1833), II, 72-74.

39 Ibid., II, 131.

40 Karl Gutzkow, *Aus der Zeit und dem Leben* (Leipzig: Brockhaus, 1844), p. 115.

41 Heinrich Laube, *Gesammelte Werke in fünfzig Bänden*, ed. Heinrich Hubert Houben with Albert Hänel (Leipzig: M. Hesse, 1908-09), VI, 35-36.

42 *Zeitung für die elegante Welt*, 23 May 1833, No. 100, p. 398.

43 Ibid.

44 Ibid., 8 August 1833, No. 153, p. 609.

45 Ludolf Wienbarg, *Wanderungen durch den Thierkreis* (Hamburg: Hoffmann und Campe, 1835), p. viii.

46 Ludolf Wienbarg, *Quadriga* (Hamburg: Hoffmann und Campe, 1840), p. vii

47 Ibid.

48 Houben, *JdSuD*, pp. 194-195.

49 Ludolf Wienbarg, *Zur neuesten Literatur* (Mannheim: Löwenthal, 1835), p. 31.

50 Jeffrey L. Sammons, "Ludolf Wienbarg and Norway," *Scandinavian Studies*, 42 (1970), pp. 19-21.

51 Wienbarg, *Wanderungen durch den Thierkreis*, p. 248.

52 Ibid., p. 254.

53 Ibid, p. 256.

54 Ibid., p. 258.

55 Ibid., p. 260.

56 Ibid., p. 77.

57 Ibid., p. 80.

58 Ibid., p. 93.

59 Ibid., p. 94.

60 E.g., J. Dresch, "Schiller et la jeune Allemagne," *Revue germanique*, 1 (1905), 579; Schweizer, *Ludolf Wienbarg*, p. 55; Houben, *JdSuD*, p. 188; Butler, *The Saint-Simonian Religion*, pp. 409, 412-419; Burkhardt, "Ludolf Wienbarg," pp. 42-43; Rudolf Kayser, "Ludolf Wienbarg und der Kampf um den Historismus," *German Quarterly*, 29 (1956), 71-74.

61 Wienbarg, *Ästhetische Feldzüge*, "Anhang," pp. 311-312.

62 Wienbarg, *Zur neuesten Literatur*, pp. 8-9.

63 Sengle, *Biedermeierzeit*, I, 165-167.

64 Karl Gutzkow, *Deutschland am Vorabend seines Falles oder seiner Größe*, ed. Walter Boehlich, sammlung insel 36 (Frankfurt: Insel Verlag, 1969), p. 140.

65 Bliemel, "Die Auffassung des Jungen Deutschlands," p. 149.

66 Houben, *JdSuD*, p. 488.

67 Burkhardt, "Ludolf Wienbarg," p. 2.

68 Houben, *JdSuD*, p. 63.

69 Karl Glossy, *Literarische Geheimberichte aus dem Vormärz*. Separatabdruck aus dem *Jahrbuch der Grillparzer-Gesellschaft*, Vols. 21-23 (Vienna: C. Konegen, 1912), I, xcv.

70 See Friedrich C. Sell, *Die Tragödie des deutschen Liberalismus* (Stuttgart: Deutsche Verlags-Anstalt, 1953), p. 174.

71 Houben, *JdSuD*, p. 85.

72 Ulla Otto, *Die literarische Zensur als Problem der Soziologie der Politik* (Stuttgart: Ferdinand Enke Verlag, 1968), p. 128.

73 Ibid.

1 Koopmann, *Das Junge Deutschland,* p. 37.
2 Eitel Wolf Dobert, *Karl Gutzkow und seine Zeit* (Bern and Munich: Francke Verlag, 1968). Dietze's account of Wienbarg in Wienbarg, *Ästhetische Feldzüge,* could also be mentioned, as it tells nearly all that is known about him.
3 Butler, *The Saint-Simonian Religion,* p. 258.
4 J. Dresch, *Le Roman social en Allemagne (1850-1900). Gutzkow — Freytag — Spielhagen — Fontane* (Paris: Félix Alcan, 1913), p. 3.
5 Houben, *Gutzkow-Funde,* p. vi.
6 Dobert, *Karl Gutzkow,* pp. 61, 107-108.
7 Karl Gutzkow, *Zur Philosophie der Geschichte* (Hamburg: Hoffmann und Campe, 1836), pp. iii-iv.
8 Ibid., p. v.
9 René Wellek, *A History of Modern Criticism 1750-1950* (New Haven and London: Yale University Press, 1955-), III, 203.
10 Walter Hof, *Pessimistisch-nihilistische Strömungen in der deutschen Literatur vom Sturm und Drang bis zum Jungen Deutschland* (Tübingen: Niemeyer, 1970), p. 183.
11 Houben, *JdSuD,* p. 27.
12 Ibid., p. 29.
13 Houben, *Gutzkow-Funde,* p. 58.
14 Houben, *Zeitschriften des Jungen Deutschlands,* I, col. 58.
15 Houben, *Verbotene Literatur,* II, 299-300.
16 Karl Gutzkow, *Götter, Helden, Don-Quixote. Abstimmungen zur Beurtheilung der literarischen Epoche* (Hamburg: Hoffmann und Campe, 1838), p. 331.
17 Ibid.
18 Ibid., pp. 352-353.
19 Ibid., p. 378.
20 Ibid., p. 389.
21 Houben, *Gutzkow-Funde,* p. 56.
22 Houben, *Zeitschriften des Jungen Deutschlands,* I, col. 47.
23 Houben, *JdSuD,* p. 659.
24 Ernst Elster, "H. Heine und H. Laube. Mit sechsundvierzig bisher ungedruckten Briefen Laubes an Heine," *Deutsche Rundschau,* 135 (1908), 93-95. Whatever Heine and Laube may have written, nothing seems to have appeared in print.
25 To Varnhagen, 14 October 1835, Houben, *Gutzkow-Funde,* p. 60.

26 Karl Glossy, *Literarische Geheimberichte aus dem Vormärz*, Separatabdruck aus dem *Jahrbuch der Grillparzer-Gesellschaft*, Vols. 21-23 (Vienna: C. Konegen, 1912), I, 47. Houben (*Verbotene Literatur*, I, 264) sensationalized this information slightly by saying merely that the elderly gentlemen had been reported to be "lüstern."

27 All the page numbers in parentheses in this essay are references to the photographic reprint of the original edition of *Wally, die Zweiflerin*, ed. Jost Schillemeit (Göttingen: Vandenhoeck & Ruprecht, 1965).

28 Dobert, *Karl Gutzkow*, p. 109. In view of Dobert's harsh opinion here, it is interesting that elsewhere he finds Gutzkow's *Uriel Acosta* better structured and more realistic than *Nathan der Weise* (p. 133).

29 Houben, *JdSuD*, p. 164.

30 Karl Gutzkow, *Vertheidigung gegen Menzel und Berichtigung einiger Urtheile im Publikum* (Mannheim: Löwenthal, 1835), p. 36. What Gutzkow meant when he said in a letter of 28 October 1835 to Varnhagen that the religious side of the book was "nur Ballast und Lockspeise für die Massen" completely eludes me. See Houben, *Gutzkow-Funde*, p. 71.

31 Houben, *JdSuD*, p. 531.

32 For objections to regarding *Wally* as a Saint-Simonian novel, cf. Koopmann, *Das Junge Deutschland*, p. 35.

33 Another example is a comment on brother Jeronimo that the character is "eine widerliche Störung dieses Berichts" (p. 165), a form of narrative irony that suggests real, rather than pretended lack of control.

34 Friedrich Sengle, *Biedermeierzeit. Deutsche Literatur im Spannnungsfeld zwischen Restauration und Revolution 1815-1848*, I (Stuttgart: Metzler, 1971), p. 176.

35 Rudolf Majut, in his discussion of *Wally* in his article on the nineteenth-century novel in *Deutsche Philologie im Aufriß*, ed. Wolfgang Stammler, 2nd ed. (Berlin: Erich Schmidt, 1960), II, cols. 1429-30, is wrong to state that Wally marries Luigi because she has taken offense at Cäsar's "Bastardierung des Liebesgefühls" in this scene. Wally is moved by Cäsar's "ächt philanthropische Vorstellung" and embraces him, not out of love, but because he has made her feel part of the great chain of being and "daß diese heißen Küsse, welche Cäsar auf ihre Lippen drückte, allen Millionen gälte [sic] unterm Sternenzelt" (p. 77). The parodic allusion to Schiller adds another irony, while the primitive grammatical error in the sentence is further evidence of haste.

36 Cf. Günter Bliemel, "Die Auffassung des Jungen Deutschlands von Wesen und Aufgabe des Dichters und der Dichtung" (diss. Berlin, 1955), p. 125.

37 Houben, *JdSuD*, p. 439.

38 Karl Gutzkow, *Briefe eines Narren an eine Närrin*, (Hamburg: Hoffmann und Campe, 1832), pp. 169-170.

39 Ibid., p. 173. Cf. Gutzkow, *Zur Philosophie der Geschichte*, pp. 148-151; Dobert, *Karl Gutzkow*, pp. 71-73; and Hof, *Pessimistisch-nihilistische Strömungen*, pp. 198-199.

40 See my treatment of this theme in Heine's *Buch Le Grand* and in the poem *Doktrin* in my study, *Heinrich Heine: The Elusive Poet* (New Haven and London: Yale University Press, 1969), pp. 139-143, 212.

157

41 Ernest K. Bramsted, *Aristocracy and the Middle-Classes in Germany. Social Types in German Literature 1830-1900*, revised ed. (Chicago and London: University of Chicago Press, 1964).

42 Houben, *JdSuD*, p. 352. Cf. Ruth Horovitz, *Vom Roman des Jungen Deutschlands zum Roman der Gartenlaube. Ein Beitrag zur Geschichte des deutschen Liberalismus* (diss. Basel, 1937), pp. 45-46.

43 Friedrich Sengle, "Voraussetzungen und Erscheinungsformen der deutschen Restaurationsliteratur," *Deutsche Vierteljahrsschrift*, 30 (1956), 271. Cf. Sengle's discussion of the continuing prominence and prestige of the nobility in *Biedermeierzeit*, I, 17-20. Because he is looking at the society with a wide-angle lens, Sengle tends, in my view, to bagatellize the anti-aristocratic thrust of oppositional fiction.

44 Quored in Hartmut Steinecke, ed., *Theorie und Technik des Romans im 19. Jahrhundert* (Tübingen: Niemeyer, 1970), p. 46.

45 Ibid. On Gutzkow's later idealistic critique of realism, see Sengle, *Biedermeierzeit*, I, 290-291. Sengle does not note how sharply these polemics contrast with some of Gutzkow's own earlier insights.

46 Gutzkow thought he remembered, forty years later, that *Wally* had been influenced by the first volume of David Friedrich Strauss' *Das Leben Jesu*, which also appeared in 1835, and many interpreters and literary historians have repeated this. From the chronology of the publications, as described by Franz Schneider, "Gutzkows *Wally* und D. F. Strauss' *Das Leben Jesu*, eine Richtigstellung," *Germanic Review*, 1 (1926), 115-119, it appears that this cannot be correct. But Schneider is wrong to argue that there was no relationship between the two books; Strauss was attempting to find a middle way through the dilemmas that are adumbrated in the third part of *Wally*.

47 "Zum Lazarus," 1. Heinrich Heine, *Sämtliche Werke*, ed. Ernst Elster (Leipzig and Vienna: Bibliographisches Institut, [1887-90]), II, 92.

48 Heinrich Laube, *Die Poeten* (Mannheim: Heinrich Hoff, 1836), I, 108.

III. THEODOR MUNDT: A REVALUATION

1 Butler, *The Saint-Simonian Religion*, p. 320.
2 Ibid., p. 388.
3 Houben, *JdSuD*, p. 463.
4 Edgar Pierson, ed., *Gustav Kühne, sein Lebensbild und Briefwechsel mit Zeitgenossen* (Dresden and Leipzig: E. Pierson's Verlag, [1889]), pp. 205-206.
5 Ibid., pp. 121-122.
6 Houben, *Zeitschriften des Jungen Deutschlands*, I, cols. 167-168.
7 Jost Hermand, "Heines frühe Kritiker," *Der Dichter und seine Zeit. Politik im Spiegel der Literatur. Drittes Amherster Kolloquium zur modernen deutschen Literatur 1969*, ed. Wolfgang Paulsen (Heidelberg: Lothar Stiehm, 1970), pp. 129-130.
8 Cf. Houben, *Verbotene Literatur*, II, 389-391.
9 Houben, *JdSuD*, p. 483.
10 Ibid., p. 472. Mundt went so far as to print an anti-Semitic attack on Gutzkow's publisher Löwenthal in the October, 1835, issue of the *Literarischer Zodiacus*. See Houben, *Zeitschriften des Jungen Deutschlands*, I, col. 274.
11 Houben, *Verbotene Literatur*, II, 492-493.
12 "Rahel und ihre Zeit," *Charaktere und Situationen* (Wismar and Leipzig: H. Schmidt u. v. Cossel, 1837), I, 213-271.
13 A second edition appeared in 1843. The first edition — *Die Kunst der deutschen Prosa. Ästhetisch, literaturgeschichtlich, gesellschaftlich* (Berlin: Veit & Comp., 1837) — has been reprinted by Vandenhoeck & Ruprecht (Göttingen, 1969), with a brief commentary by Hans Düvel. This edition is used here.
14 See Georg Wilhelm Friedrich Hegel, *Sämtliche Werke, Jubiläumsausgabe in zwanzig Bänden*, ed. Hermann Glockner (Stuttgart: Friedrich Frommann, 1964-), XIII, 215-217; XIV, 395-396.
15 Cf. my tentative attempt to raise the question in *Heinrich Heine, the Elusive Poet* (New Haven and London: Yale University Press, 1969), pp. 178-179.
16 Theodor Mundt, *Die Kunst der deutschen Prosa*, p. 7.
17 Ibid., p. 20.
18 Ibid., pp. 19-20.
19 Ibid., p. 47.
20 "Deutsche Höflichkeit," *Charaktere und Situationen*, I, 329-337.
21 Mundt, *Die Kunst der deutschen Prosa*, p. 74.
22 Ibid., p. 76.

23 Ibid., pp. 94-95.
24 Mundt's view of the French language is similar to one found in a letter of Wilhelm von Humboldt to Goethe of 18 August 1799, which Goethe published in the *Propyläen* the following year under the title "Ueber die gegenwärtige französische tragische Bühne." See Humboldt, *Gesammelte Schriften*, ed. Albert Leitzmann, II (Berlin: B. Behr, 1904), 391-392.
25 Mundt, *Die Kunst der deutschen Prosa*, p. 101.
26 Ibid., pp. 119-120. Friedrich Sengle, *Biedermeierzeit. Deutsche Literatur im Spannungsfeld zwischen Restauration und Revolution 1815-1848*, I (Stuttgart: Metzler, 1971), 549-552, has a generally less admiring view of Mundt's book, pointing out the ambiguities in his critique of "Ciceronian" syntax of the *Goethezeit*.
27 Mundt, *Die Kunst der deutschen Prosa*, pp. 143-144.
28 René Wellek, *A History of Modern Criticism 1750-1950* (New Haven and London: Yale University Press, 1955-), III, 203.
29 Mundt, *Die Kunst der deutschen Prosa*, p. 272.
30 Ibid., p. 326.
31 Ibid., pp. 318-319.
32 Ibid., p. 373.
33 Theodor Mundt, *Aesthetik. Die Idee der Schönheit und des Kunstwerks im Lichte unserer Zeit.* Photographic reprint of the first edition, ed. Hans Düvel (Göttingen: Vandenhoeck & Ruprecht, 1966), p. 64.
34 Ibid., p. 58.
35 Eberhard Galley, *Der religiöse Liberalismus in der deutschen Literatur von 1830 bis 1850* (diss. Rostock, 1934), p. 55.
36 Houben, *Verbotene Literatur*, II, 408.
37 Mundt, *Aesthetik*, p. 4.
38 Ibid., pp. 4-8.
39 Ibid., p. 177.
40 Houben, *Zeitschriften des Jungen Deutschlands*, I, col. 304.
41 Mundt, *Aesthetik*, p. 83.
42 Ibid., p. 84.
43 Ibid., pp. 86-87.
44 Ibid., p. 60.
45 Ibid., p. iv.
46 Ibid., pp. iv-v.
47 "Antoniens Bußfahrten," *Charaktere und Situationen*, I, 7.
48 Mundt, *Aesthetik*, p. 2.
49 Ibid., p. 10.
50 Ibid., p. 258.
51 Ibid., pp. 4-5. Cf. Karl Marx and Friedrich Engels, *Über Kunst und Literatur*, ed. Manfred Kliem (Berlin: Dietz Verlag, 1968), II, 351.
52 Mundt, *Aesthetik*, p. 23.
53 Ibid., pp. 24-25.
54 Ibid., p. 30.
55 Houben, *JdSuD*, p. 397.
56 Ibid., p. 399.
57 Ibid., pp. 423-424.

160

58 Ibid., p. 433.
59 Karl Gutzkow, *Werke*, ed. Peter Müller (Leipzig and Vienna: Bibliographisches Institut, [1911]), III, 103.
60 Pierson, *Gustav Kühne*, pp. 22-23.
61 Ibid., pp. 24-28.
62 F. Gustav Kühne, *Weibliche und männliche Charaktere* (Leipzig: Wilh. Engelmann, 1838), I, 115-154.
63 [Theodor Mundt], *Charlotte Stieglitz, ein Denkmal* (Berlin: Veit & Comp., [1835]), p. iii.
64 There are hints in *Charlotte Stieglitz, ein Denkmal* that the sexual relationship of the Stieglitzes was not good; Mundt remarks at one point that Stieglitz' poetry made up "bei fast gänzlicher Entsagung aller andern Beziehungen der Ehe, den eigentlichen Mittelpunkt ihres Umgangs" (p. 41). Charlotte herself perceived Stieglitz' incredible series of ailments as psychosomatic (p. 201).
65 Theodor Mundt, *Madonna. Unterhaltungen mit einer Heiligen* (Leipzig: Gebrüder Reichenbach, 1835), p. 435. On the undiminished prestige of literature at this time, cf. Sengle, *Biedermeierzeit*, I, 104-106. Despite all the talk about the end of the *Kunstperiode*, "meistens tritt die zum Tempel hinausgeworfene Göttin unversehens wieder ein, in einem nationalen, demokratischen, oder religiösen Gewand" (ibid., p. 106).
66 Gutzkow, *Werke*, ed. Müller, III, 106-107, 112.
67 Houben, *JdSuD*, pp. 441-444. It is true, to be sure, that in Saxony the book was thought to be demagogic, and because of it Mundt had great difficulty getting his projects for periodicals off the ground (to Charlotte Stieglitz, May, 1834, Houben, *Verbotene Literatur*, II, 373. In Houben, *Zeitschriften des Jungen Deutschlands*, I, col. 123, the letter is misdated 1835).
68 Theodor Mundt, *Moderne Lebenswirren. Briefe und Zeitabenteuer eines Salzschreibers* (Leipzig: Gebrüder Reichenbach, 1834), pp. [1], [2].
69 Ibid., pp. 11-12.
70 Ibid., p. 17.
71 Ibid.
72 Ibid., p. 43.
73 Ibid., p. 46.
74 Mundt, *Die Kunst der deutschen Prosa*, p. 92.
75 Mundt, *Moderne Lebenswirren*, p. 126.
76 Ibid.
77 Ibid., p. 146.
78 Ibid., p. 152.
79 Ibid., p. 160.
80 Mundt, *Madonna*, p. 300.
81 Mundt, *Moderne Lebenswirren*, p. 188.
82 Günter Bliemel, "Die Auffassung des Jungen Deutschlands von Wesen und Aufgabe des Dichters und der Dichtung" (diss. Berlin, 1955), p. 96.
83 Rudolf Majut, "Der deutsche Roman vom Biedermeier bis zur Gegenwart," *Deutsche Philologie im Aufriß*, ed. Wolfgang Stammler, 2nd ed. (Berlin: Erich Schmidt, 1960), II, col. 1425.
84 Houben, *JdSuD*, pp. 438-439.

[85] Heinrich Heine, *Sämtliche Werke*, ed. Ernst Elster (Leipzig and Vienna: Bibliographisches Institut, [1887-90]), III, 74.

[86] Mundt, *Madonna*, p. 433.

[87] Houben, *JdSuD*, p. 447.

[88] Such a chapter title suggests the influence of Jean Paul, but Mundt, as appears in several passages of the book, believed Jean Paul to be obsolete and did not consciously follow him in any degree.

[89] Mundt, *Madonna*, p. 1.

[90] Ibid., p. 14.

[91] Ibid., pp. 24-25.

[92] Ibid., p. 26.

[93] Ibid., p. 281.

[94] Ibid., p. 434.

[95] Ibid., p. 79.

[96] Ibid., p. 74.

[97] *Madonna* had probably been essentially completed by that time; the first part of the MS had been submitted to the censors in November, 1834 (Houben, *Verbotene Literatur*, II, 385). But the French version of Heine's book had begun to appear in March, 1834, and his views were well known.

[98] Mundt, *Madonna*, p. 130.

[99] Ibid., p. 141.

[100] Ibid., pp. 141-142.

[101] Ibid., p. 274.

[102] Ibid., p. 365.

[103] Mundt, *Charlotte Stieglitz, ein Denkmal*, pp. 54-56.

[104] Theodor Mundt, *Geschichte der Literatur der Gegenwart. Friedrich von Schlegel's Geschichte der alten und neuen Literatur, bis auf die neueste Zeit fortgeführt* (Berlin: M. Simion, 1842), p. 388.

[105] Mundt, *Madonna*, pp. 227-228.

[106] Ibid., p. 96.

[107] For a summary of the Libussa tradition, cf. Elisabeth Frenzel, *Stoffe der Weltliteratur*, 2nd ed., (Stuttgart: A. Kröner, 1963), pp. 379-381.

[108] Mundt, *Charaktere und Situationen*, I, 3-127.

[109] Mundt, *Madonna*, p. 259.

[110] Mundt, *Charaktere und Situationen*, I, 128-210.

[111] Mundt, *Madonna*, pp. 219-220.

162

IV.   FERDINAND GUSTAV KÜHNE: *EINE QUARANTÄNE IM IRRENHAUSE*

1 Houben, *Verbotene Literatur*, II, 450-454.
2 Cf. Edgar Pierson, ed., *Gustav Kühne, sein Lebensbild und Briefwechsel mit Zeitgenossen* (Dresden and Leipzig: E. Pierson's Verlag, [1889]), pp. 175-176.
3 Ibid., p. 69.
4 Ibid., p. 20.
5 Houben, *JdSuD*, p. 65.
6 Ibid., p. 640.
7 Pierson, *Gustav Kühne*, pp. 234-235.
8 Houben, *JdSuD*, p. 638.
9 All page numbers in parentheses in this chapter are references to F. G. Kühne, *Eine Quarantäne im Irrenhause. Novelle aus den Papieren eines Mondsteiners* (Leipzig: F. A. Brockhaus, 1835). I am grateful to Professor Jost Hermand for the loan of his copy of this rare book.
10 Pierson, *Gustav Kühne*, p. 12.
11 Ibid., pp. 219-220.
12 Ibid., p. 224.
13 Ibid., p. 203.
14 Ibid., p. 159.
15 Theodor Mundt, *Charaktere und Situationen* (Wismar and Leipzig: H. Schmidt u. v. Cossel, 1837), I, 306-308.
16 *Literarischer Zodiacus*, January, 1835, p. 4, quoted Günter Bliemel, "Die Auffassung des Jungen Deutschlands von Wesen und Aufgabe des Dichters und der Dichtung" (diss. Berlin, 1955), p. 74.
17 Ruth Horovitz, *Vom Roman des Jungen Deutschland zum Roman der Gartenlaube* (diss. Basel, 1937), p. 22.

V. HEINRICH LAUBE: *DIE KRIEGER*

1 Rudolf Majut, "Der deutsche Roman vom Biedermeier bis zur Gegenwart," *Deutsche Philologie im Aufriß*, ed. Wolfgang Stammler, 2nd ed. (Berlin: Erich Schmidt, 1960), II, col. 1420.

2 Friedrich Sengle, *Biedermeierzeit. Deutsche Literatur im Spannungsfeld zwischen Restauration und Revolution 1815-1848*, I (Stuttgart: Metzler, 1971), 171.

3 Karl Gutzkow, *Vergangenheit und Gegenwart 1830-1838*, *Werke*, ed. Peter Müller (Leipzig and Vienna: Bibliographisches Institut, [1911]), III, 167.

4 Heinrich Laube, *Ausgewählte Werke in zehn Bänden*, ed. Heinrich Hubert Houben (Leipzig: Max Hesse, n.d.), I, 94.

5 Reinhold Grimm, "Romanhaftes und Novellistisches in Laubes *Reisenovellen*," *Germanisch-romanische Monatsschrift*, N.S. 18 (1968), 299-303.

6 Laube, *Ausgewählte Werke*, I, 193, 260.

7 Houben, *JdSuD*, p. 362.

8 Walter Dietze, *Junges Deutschland und deutsche Klassik. Zur Ästhetik und Literaturtheorie des Vormärz*, 3rd ed. (Berlin: Rütten & Loening, 1962), p. 89.

9 Ibid., pp. 89, 90.

10 Butler, *The Saint-Simonian Religion*, p. 200.

11 Ernst Elster, "H. Heine und H. Laube. Mit sechsundvierzig bisher ungedruckten Briefen Laubes an Heine," *Deutsche Rundschau*, 136 (1908), 448.

12 See especially the chapter, "Der Wandel in Laubes Anschauungen," in Karl Nolle, *Heinrich Laube als sozialer und politischer Schriftsteller* (diss. Münster, 1914), pp. 37-41.

13 Wilh. Johannes Becker, *Zeitgeist und Krisenbewußtsein in Heinrich Laubes Novellen* (diss. Frankfurt, 1960), p. 37.

14 The following sketch is a digest of the accounts given by Houben in Laube, *Ausgewählte Werke*, I, and *Verbotene Literatur*, I.

15 Heinrich Laube, *Gesammelte Werke in fünfzig Bänden*, ed. Heinrich Hubert Houben with Albert Hänel (Leipzig: M. Hesse, 1908-09), XL, 269-270.

16 *Zeitung für die elegante Welt*, 3 May 1833, No. 86, p. 344.

17 Houben, *JdSuD*, p. 386.

18 Butler, *The Saint-Simonian Religion*, p. 189.

19 Houben, *JdSuD*, p. 386.

20 Elster, "H. Heine und H. Laube," *Deutsche Rundschau*, 134 (1908), 80.

21 Houben, *Verbotene Literatur*, I, 481.

22 An example of what can be accomplished in this regard is Becker's study

of Laube's novellas (see above, n. 13), which elucidates the connections between form and sociological conviction more precisely than I can here; I owe his study worthwhile insights that are also applicable to Laube's novel.

23 Heinrich Laube, *Die Bürger* (Mannheim: Heinrich Hoff, 1837), p. 226.

24 Laube, *Gesammelte Werke*, XL, 184.

25 See Butler, *The Saint-Simonian Religion*, pp. 207-208.

26 Elster, "H. Heine und H. Laube," *Deutsche Rundschau*, 133 (1907), 231. My italics.

27 *Zeitung für die elegante Welt*, 23 May 1833, No. 100, pp. 398, 399.

28 Ibid., 25 July 1833, No. 143, p. 572.

29 Laube, *Gesammelte Werke*, XL, 183.

30 Ibid., pp. 182-183.

31 Karl Häberle, *Individualität und Zeit in H. Laubes Jungem Europa und K. Gutzkows Ritter vom Geist* (Erlangen: Palm & Enke, 1938), p. 41.

32 Gutzkow, *Vergangenheit und Gegenwart, Werke*, ed. Müller, III, 169.

33 Laube, *Gesammelte Werke*, XLI, 453.

34 Laube, *Die Bürger*, pp. 153-154.

35 Heinrich Laube, *Die Poeten* (Mannheim: Heinrich Hoff, 1836), [I], 113. Although this (second) edition is not explicitly in two books or volumes, there are two paginations.

36 Laube, *Gesammelte Werke*, XL, 286.

37 Quoted Eitel Wolf Dobert, *Karl Gutzkow und seine Zeit* (Bern and Munich: Francke Verlag, 1968), p. 50.

38 Ludolf Wienbarg, *Wanderungen durch den Thierkreis* (Hamburg: Hoffmann und Campe, 1835), p. 248.

39 Ibid., pp. 251-252.

40 Majut, "Der deutsche Roman," col. 1409.

41 Peter Demetz, "Zur Definition des Realismus," *Literatur und Kritik*, 2 (1967), 340.

42 Ludolf Wienbarg, *Quadriga* (Hamburg: Hoffmann und Campe, 1840), p. 136. Cf. Jeffrey L. Sammons, "Ludolf Wienbarg and Norway," *Scandinavian Studies*, 42 (1970), 21-22.

43 Houben, *Gutzkow-Funde*, pp. 144-280.

44 Karl Gutzkow, *Götter, Helden, Don-Quixote. Abstimmungen zur Beurtheilung der literarischen Epoche* (Hamburg: Hoffmann und Campe, 1838), p. 258 n.

45 Laube did once allow himself to slip into a rude tone about Jewish influence in literature, and it is characteristic of the situation of the time that the outburst was touched off by a problem of literary competition, a quarrel in 1847 concerning the subject of his drama *Struensee*, the performance of which was interfered with by the influential Giacomo Meyerbeer, whose brother Michael Beer had written a play on the same subject years before (Laube, *Gesammelte Werke,* XXIV, 130-132). The tone of these remarks is deplorable and shows how a conflict of economic interest could arouse the bacillus of anti-Semitism even in a man so thoroughly inoculated against it.

46 Examples of the nuances in Laube's judgment concerning the Jews are in Nolle, *Heinrich Laube als sozialer und politischer Schriftsteller*, pp. 46-48.

47 Heinrich Laube, *Die Krieger* (Mannheim: Heinrich Hoff, 1837), I, 157.
48 Ibid., II, 25.
49 Benno von Wiese, "Zeitkrisis und Biedermeier in Laubes 'Das junge Europa' und in Immermanns 'Epigonen,'" *Dichtung und Volkstum*, 36 (1935), 163, n. 1.
50 Laube, *Die Krieger*, I, 242.
51 To my knowledge, Wienbarg is the only one of the Young Germans to have grasped the difference between freedom as a liberal, individualistic concern and independence as a national goal (*Quadriga*, p. 140).
52 It is possible that Laube is here thinking of Heine, because he shared with Wienbarg and Johann Peter Lyser the opinion that Heine's mother was a Christian. This false information led Wienbarg in the twenty-third lecture of the *Ästhetische Feldzüge* to an assessment of Heine very much lacking in objective value. An inconclusive discussion of the possible source of this notion is in Friedrich Hirth, *Heinrich Heines Briefe* (Mainz: F. Kupferberg, 1950-51), IV, 225-226. An interesting example of how preconceptions and prejudices can interfere with direct perception is Wienbarg's description of Heine in the *Wanderungen durch den Thierkreis* (p. 150) as *black-haired*, when all other evidence is unanimous that he was blond.
53 Laube, *Die Krieger*, II, 285-286.
54 Cf. the observations in my article, "The Evaluation of Freytag's 'Soll und Haben,'" *German Life & Letters*, N.S., 22 (1968/69), 318-319.
55 Laube, *Gesammelte Werke*, XL, 135-136.
56 Laube, *Die Poeten*, [II], 186-187.
57 Laube, *Gesammelte Werke*, VI, 133.
58 Laube, *Die Krieger*, I, 127.
59 Ibid., II, 272.
60 Gerhard Burkhardt, "Ludolf Wienbarg als Ästhetiker und Kritiker. Seine Entwicklung und seine geistesgeschichtliche Stellung" (diss. Hamburg, 1956), p. 158.
61 Horst Denkler, "Aufbruch der Aristophaniden. Die aristophanische Komödie als Modell für das politische Lustspiel im deutschen Vormärz," *Der Dichter und seine Zeit — Politik im Spiegel der Literatur. Drittes Amherster Kolloquium zur modernen deutschen Literatur 1969*, ed. Wolfgang Paulsen (Heidelberg: Lothar Stiehm), pp. 134-157.
62 Nolle, *Heinrich Laube als sozialer und politischer Schriftsteller*, pp. 45-46; von Wiese, "Zeitkrisis und Biedermeier," pp. 171-172; Häberle, *Individualität und Zeit*, pp. 51-52.
63 Laube, *Die Krieger*, I, 73-74.
64 Laube, *Die Bürger*, p. 4.

166

VI. KARL IMMERMANN

1 Benno von Wiese, *Karl Immermann. Sein Werk und sein Leben* (Bad Homburg, Berlin, and Zurich: Gehlen, 1969).

2 Ibid., p. 287.

3 Ibid.

4 Martin Greiner, *Zwischen Biedermeier und Bourgeoisie. Ein Kapitel deutscher Literaturgeschichte* (Göttingen: Vandenhoeck & Ruprecht, 1953), p. 81.

5 Immermann, *Werke*, ed. Robert Boxberger (Leipzig: Dümmler, [1883]), I, vi.

6 George Eliot, "German Wit: Heinrich Heine," *Essays and Leaves from a Notebook*, ed. Charles Lee Lewes (New York: Harper & Brothers, 1884), p. 80.

7 Manfred Windfuhr, *Immermanns erzählerisches Werk. Zur Situation des Romans in der Restaurationszeit* (Giessen: Schmitz, 1957), p. 32.

8 Ibid., pp. 91-92.

9 Ibid., p. 17.

10 MS quoted by Elisabeth Guzinski, *Karl Immermann als Zeitkritiker. Ein Beitrag zur Geschichte der deutschen Selbstkritik*, Neue Deutsche Forschungen, No. 142 (Berlin: Junker und Dünnhaupt, 1937), p. 19.

11 *Werke*, ed. Boxberger, XI, 308, 310.

12 Immermann, *Werke*, ed. Harry Maync (Leipzig and Vienna: Bibliographisches Institut, [1906]), I, 16.

13 Immermann to his brother, 7 November 1830, MS letter quoted by Peter Hasubek, ed. Immermann, *Tulifäntchen*, Reclams Universal-Bibliothek, Nos. 8551-52 (Stuttgart: Philipp Reclam Jun., 1968), p. 145.

14 Cf. *Werke*, ed. Boxberger, X, 29.

15 Ibid., I, lxxxviii.

16 Windfuhr, *Immermanns erzählerisches Werk*, pp. 123-124.

17 Gustav zu Putlitz, *Karl Immermann. Sein Leben und seine Werke, aus Tagebüchern und Briefen an seine Familie zusammengestellt* (Berlin: Wilhelm Hertz, 1870), II, 234.

18 Hans Mayer, "Karl Immermanns 'Epigonen,'" *Studien zur deutschen Literaturgeschichte*, 2nd ed. (Berlin: Rütten & Loening, 1955), p. 130.

19 Ernest K. Bramsted, *Aristocracy and the Middle-Classes in Germany. Social Types in German Literature 1830-1900*, revised ed. (Chicago and London: University of Chicago Press, 1964), p. 62.

20 In fact, by coincidence, Immermann completed the novel on 12 December,

just two days after the Federal ban on the Young Germans. Cf. von Wiese, *Karl Immermann*, p. 172.

21 Manfred Windfuhr, "Der Epigone. Begriff, Phänomen und Bewußtsein," *Archiv für Begriffsgeschichte*, 4 (1959), 190.

22 Ibid., pp. 193-194.

23 Von Wiese, *Karl Immermann*, p. 174.

24 Ibid., p. 261.

25 Koopmann, *Das Junge Deutschland*, p. 96.

26 Cf. Windfuhr, *Immermanns erzählerisches Werk*, p. 139.

27 Von Wiese, *Karl Immermann*, pp. 187-188.

28 Windfuhr, *Immermanns erzählerisches Werk*, p. 140.

29 Gustav Freytag, *Soll und Haben, Gesammelte Werke*, IV (Leipzig: S. Hirzel, 1887), 561.

30 Heinrich Heine, *Sämtliche Werke*, ed. Ernst Elster (Leipzig and Vienna: Bibliographisches Institut, [1887-90]), V, 236.

31 Immermann, *Werke*, ed. Maync, IV, 22.

32 Lee B. Jennings, *The Ludicrous Demon: Aspects of the Grotesque in German Post-Romantic Prose* (Berkeley and Los Angeles: University of California Press, 1963).

33 Von Wiese, *Karl Immermann*, pp. 12, 14.

34 Ibid., p. 84.

35 Immermann complained in a letter to his brother about readers who insisted on making this assumption, despite the fact that Wilhelmi had been presented as "krank und hypochondrisch" (Putlitz, *Karl Immermann*, II, 148).

36 Immermann, *Werke*, ed. Maync, III, 135-137.

37 Ibid., p. 141.

38 Ibid., pp. 419, 421.

39 Ibid., p. 364.

40 Ibid., p. 366.

41 Ibid., p. 369.

42 See Hans-Georg Werner, *Geschichte des politischen Gedichts in Deutschland von 1815 bis 1840* (Berlin: Akademie-Verlag, 1969), pp. 55-58.

43 Ibid., p. 116; cf. the discussion of the whole subject on pp. 112-146.

44 Putlitz, *Karl Immermann*, I, 106.

45 Cf. the excellent analysis of this part of the novel by Franz Rumler, *Realistische Elemente in Immermanns "Epigonen"* (diss. Munich, 1964), pp. 106-121.

46 Immermann, *Werke*, ed. Maync, III, 406.

47 Ibid., IV, 138.

48 Von Wiese, *Karl Immermann*, p. 197.

49 Immermann, *Werke*, ed. Maync, IV, 265-266.

50 Rumler, *Realistische Elemente*, pp. 134-136.

51 Theodor Mundt, *Charaktere und Situationen* (Wismar and Leipzig: H. Schmidt u. v. Cossel, 1837), I, 276, 292.

52 Although Immermann was writing at a very early stage in the development of German capitalism, there were already signs during his time that an ideology was forming to neutralize optimistically or misdirect attention away from the depredations of capitalism that he was able to perceive. By

168

accident I have come across a book that is interesting in this regard, a German translation of Charles Babbage's textbook of capitalist industry in England of 1832, *On the Economy of Machinery and Manufactures*, translated by Dr. G. Friedenberg, *Ueber Maschinen- und Fabrikwesen* (Berlin: Verlag der Stuhrschen Buchhandlung, 1833). Of interest here is a preface supplied by one K. F. Köden, director of the Berlin Trade School. In it he raises the question whether specialized, monotonous, repetitive factory work, in contrast to obsolete craftsmanship, which made the worker responsible for a whole product, will not be harmful to the human spirit. Clearly he senses in the air the problem of what was to be called alienation. He disposes of it with ease, however, by arguing that monotonous work, rather than deadening the spirit, will free the mind to think of other things; in a characteristic, almost comic juxtaposition, he remarks that the brooding of the weavers (whose desperate conditions were to drive them, eleven years later, into the first full-scale workers' uprising in Germany) has developed in them mechanical, mystical, Pietist, and poetic talents (pp. xii-xiii). Factory work will lead men to turn inward into their souls. This being the case, however, steps must be taken to prevent workers, with so much free mental time, from developing dangerous religious and political enthusiasms, which can be accomplished by teaching them to interest themselves in the real things of their immediate world — an interesting application of Goethean principles to the class problem.

53 On the genesis of the novel, see Windfuhr, *Immermanns erzählerisches Werk*, pp. 180-181.

54 Dimiter Statkow, "Über die dialektische Struktur des Immermann-Romans 'Münchhausen.' Zum Problem des Übergangs von der Romantik zum Realismus," *Weimarer Beiträge*, 11 (1965), 200-204.

55 Herman Meyer, *Das Zitat in der Erzählkunst. Zur Geschichte und Poetik des europäischen Romans*, 2nd ed. (Stuttgart: Metzler, 1967), p. 140.

56 Ibid., p. 141.

57 Immermann, *Werke*, ed. Maync, I, 327.

58 Cf. Windfuhr, *Immermanns erzählerisches Werk*, p. 191.

59 Cf. Von Wiese, *Karl Immermann*, p. 186, and Windfuhr, *Immermanns erzählerisches Werk*, p. 84.

60 Cf. Windfuhr, *Immermanns erzählerisches Werk*, p. 183.

61 Friedrich Hebbel, *Sämtliche Werke. Historisch-kritische Ausgabe*, ed. Richard Maria Werner, XII (Berlin: B. Behr, 1903), 62.

62 Droste to Levin Schücking, 11 September 1842, *Die Briefe der Annette von Droste-Hülshoff*, ed. Karl Schulte-Kemminghausen (Düsseldorf: Eugen Diederichs, 1968), II, 77-78.

63 Quoted by Windfuhr, *Immermanns erzählerisches Werk*, p. 183.

64 Von Wiese, *Karl Immermann*, p. 11.

65 Windfuhr, *Immermanns erzählerisches Werk*, p. 202.

66 Quoted ibid., p. 181.

67 Ibid., p. 192.

68 Ibid., p. 196.

69 Werner Kohlschmidt, "Die Welt des Bauern im Spiegel von Immermanns

'Münchhausen' und Gotthelfs 'Uli,'" *Dichtung und Volkstum*, 39 (1938), 226.

70 Ibid., p. 236.

71 Von Wiese, *Karl Immermann*, pp. 228-229.

72 Ibid., pp. 241-242.

73 Windfuhr, *Immermanns erzählerisches Werk*, p. 202.

74 Michael Scherer, "Immermanns *Münchhausen*-Roman," *German Quarterly*, 36 (1963), 240.

75 Statkow, "Über die dialektische Struktur," pp. 198-199.

76 William McClain, "Karl Lebrecht Immermann's Portrait of a Folk-Hero in *Münchhausen*," *Studies in German Literature of the Nineteenth and Twentieth Centuries. Festschrift for Frederic E. Coenen*, ed. Siegfried Mews (Chapel Hill: University of North Carolina Press, 1970), pp. 55-63.

77 Statkow, "Über die dialektische Struktur," p. 208.

78 Windfuhr, *Immermanns erzählerisches Werk*, pp. 148-149.

79 Immermann, *Werke*, ed. Maync, I, 238.

80 Von Wiese, *Karl Immermann*, p. 240.

81 Windfuhr, *Immermanns erzählerisches Werk*, pp. 169-170; cf. Rumler, *Realistische Elemente*, pp. 9-11.

82 Windfuhr, *Immermanns erzählerisches Werk*, p. 247.

83 Ibid.

84 Ibid., pp. 98-99.

85 Rumler, *Realistische Elemente*, passim.

86 Immermann, *Werke*, ed. Maync, I, 183.

87 Ibid., II, 66-67.

88 Ibid., I, 269.

89 Von Wiese, *Karl Immermann*, p. 166.

90 Ibid., p. 244.

91 Rumler, *Realistische Elemente*, pp. 84-88.

92 Mayer, "Karl Immermanns 'Epigonen,'" p. 139.

93 Von Wiese, *Karl Immermann*, pp. 191-192.

94 Ibid., p. 192.

95 See Hans-Georg Gadamer, "Karl Immermanns 'Chiliastische Sonette,'" *Kleine Schriften II. Interpretationen* (Tübingen: Mohr, 1967), pp. 136-147.

96 Meyer, *Das Zitat in der Erzählkunst*, p. 136.

97 Jennings, *The Ludicrous Demon*, p. 51.

98 Mundt, *Charaktere und Situationen*, I, 278.

99 Gadamer, "Zu Immermanns Epigonen-Roman," *Kleine Schriften II*, p. 160.

100 Emil Grütter, *Immermanns "Epigonen". Ein Beitrag zur Geschichte des deutschen Romans* (diss. Zurich, 1951), p. 36.

101 Windfuhr, *Immermanns erzählerisches Werk*, p. 175.

102 Jennings, *The Ludicrous Demon*, p. 76.

103 Rumler, *Realistische Elemente*, p. 17.

104 Putlitz, *Karl Immermann*, II, 233.

BIBLIOGRAPHY

AUERBACH, ERICH. *Mimesis. The Representation of Reality in Western Literature*. Translated from the German by Willard Trask. Garden City: Doubleday, 1953.

BABBAGE, CHARLES. *Ueber Maschinen- und Fabrikwesen*, tr. Dr. G. Friedenberg. Berlin: Verlag der Stuhrschen Buchhandlung, 1833.

BECKER, WILH. JOHANNES. *Zeitgeist und Krisenbewußtsein in Heinrich Laubes Novellen*. Diss. Frankfurt, 1960.

BIEBER, HUGO. *Der Kampf um die Tradition. Die deutsche Dichtung im europäischen Geistesleben 1830-1880*. Epochen der deutschen Literatur, Vol. V. Stuttgart: Metzler, 1928.

BLIEMEL, GÜNTER. "Die Auffassung des Jungen Deutschlands von Wesen und Aufgabe der Dichtung." Diss. Berlin, 1955.

BOCK, HELMUT. *Ludwig Börne. Vom Gettojuden zum Nationalschriftsteller*. Berlin: Rütten & Loening, 1962.

BÖRNE, LUDWIG. *Sämtliche Schriften*, ed. Inge und Peter Rippmann. 5 vols. Düsseldorf: Melzer, 1964-68.

BRAMSTED, ERNEST K. *Aristocracy and the Middle-Classes in Germany. Social Types in German Literature 1830-1900*. Revised ed. Chicago and London: University of Chicago Press, 1964.

BRANDES, GEORG. *Main Currents in Nineteenth Century Literature*. Vol. VI: *Young Germany*, tr. Mary Morison. London and Paris: W. Heinemann, 1906.

BRANN, HENRY WALTER. "The Young German Movement Creates a Political Literature." *German Quarterly*, 24 (1951), 189-194.

BURKHARDT, GERHARD. "Ludolf Wienbarg als Ästhetiker und Kritiker. Seine Entwicklung und seine geistesgeschichtliche Stellung." Diss. Hamburg, 1956.

BUTLER, E. M. *The Saint-Simonian Religion in Germany. A Study of the Young German Movement*. Cambridge, Eng.: Cambridge University Press, 1926. Reprinted, New York: Howard Fertig, Inc., 1968.

COLDITZ, CARL. "Über den Denunzianten." *Modern Language Quarterly*, 6 (1945), 131-147.

DAICHES, DAVID. *Critical Approaches to Literature*. New York: Norton, 1956.

DEMETZ, PETER. "Zur Definition des Realismus." *Literatur und Kritik*, 2 (1967), 330-345.

DENKLER, HORST. "Aufbruch der Aristophaniden. Die aristophanische Komödie als Modell für das politische Lustspiel im deutschen Vormärz." *Der Dichter und seine Zeit — Politik im Spiegel der Literatur. Drittes Amherster Kolloquium zur modernen deutschen Literatur 1969*, ed. Wolfgang Paulsen. Heidelberg: Lothar Stiehm, 1970, pp. 134-157.

—. "Revolutionäre Dramaturgie und revolutionäres Drama in Vormärz und Märzrevolution." *Gestaltungsgeschichte und Gesellschaftsgeschichte. Literatur-, kunst- und musikwissenschaftliche Studien*, ed. Helmut Kreuzer und Käte Hamburger. Stuttgart: Metzler, 1969, pp. 306-337.

DIETZE, WALTER. *Junges Deutschland und deutsche Klassik. Zur Ästhetik und Literaturtheorie des Vormärz*. 3rd ed. Berlin: Rütten & Loening, 1962.

DOBERT, EITEL WOLF. *Karl Gutzkow und seine Zeit*. Bern and Munich: Francke Verlag, 1968.

DRESCH, J. *Le Roman social en Allemagne (1850-1900). Gutzkow — Freytag — Spielhagen — Fontane*. Paris: Félix Alcan, 1913.

—. "Schiller et la jeune Allemagne." *Revue germanique*, 1 (1905), 569-587.

DROSTE-HÜLSHOFF, ANNETTE VON. *Briefe*, ed. Karl Schulte-Kemminghausen. Düsseldorf: Eugen Diederichs, 1968.

ECK, ELSE VON. *Die Literaturkritik in den Hallischen und Deutschen Jahrbüchern (1838-1842)*. Germanische Studien, No. 42. Berlin: E. Ebering, 1926.

ELIOT, GEORGE. "German Wit: Heinrich Heine." *Essays and Leaves from a Notebook*, ed. Charles Lee Lewes. New York: Harper & Brothers, 1884, pp. 79-144.

ELSTER, ERNST. "H. Heine und H. Laube. Mit sechsundvierzig bisher ungedruckten Briefen Laubes an Heine." *Deutsche Rundschau*, 133 (1907), 210-232, 394-412; 134 (1908), 77-90; 135 (1908), 91-116, 232-259; 136 (1908), 233-251, 441-455.

FRENZEL, ELISABETH. *Stoffe der Weltliteratur*. 2nd ed. Stuttgart: A. Kröner, 1963.

FREYTAG, GUSTAV. *Soll und Haben. Gesammelte Werke*, Vols. IV-V. Leipzig: S. Hirzel, 1887.

GADAMER, HANS-GEORG. *Kleine Schriften II. Interpretationen*. Tübingen: Mohr, 1967.

GALLEY, EBERHARD. "Heine im literarischen Streit mit Gutzkow. Mit unbekannten Manuskripten aus Heines Nachlaß." *Heine-Jahrbuch 1966*, pp. 1-40.

—. *Der religiöse Liberalismus in der deutschen Literatur von 1830 bis 1850.* Diss. Rostock, 1934.

GEIGER, LUDWIG. *Das junge Deutschland und die preußische Censur.* Berlin: S. Schottlaender, 1900.

GLANDER, PHILIP. "K. A. Varnhagen von Ense: Man of Letters. 1833-1858." Diss., University of Wisconsin, 1961.

GLOSSY, KARL. *Literarische Geheimberichte aus dem Vormärz.* Separatdruck aus dem *Jahrbuch der Grillparzer-Gesellschaft*, Vols. 21-23. Vienna: C. Konegen, 1912.

GREINER, MARTIN. *Zwischen Biedermeier und Bourgeoisie. Ein Kapitel deutscher Literaturgeschichte.* Göttingen: Vandenhoeck & Ruprecht, 1953.

GRIMM, REINHOLD. "Romanhaftes und Novellistisches in Laubes *Reisenovellen.*" *Germanisch-romanische Monatsschrift*, N.S. 18 (1968), 299-303.

GRÜTTER, EMIL. *Immermanns "Epigonen". Ein Beitrag zur Geschichte des deutschen Romans.* Diss. Zurich, 1951.

GULDE, HILDEGARD. *Studien zum jungdeutschen Frauenroman.* Diss. Tübingen, 1931.

GUTZKOW, KARL. *Aus der Zeit und dem Leben.* Leipzig: F. A. Brockhaus, 1844.

—. *Briefe eines Narren an eine Närrin.* Hamburg: Hoffmann und Campe, 1832.

—. *Deutschland am Vorabend seines Falles oder seiner Größe*, ed. Walter Boehlich. sammlung insel, 36. Frankfurt: Insel Verlag, 1969.

—. *Götter, Helden, Don-Quixote. Abstimmungen zur Beurtheilung der literarischen Epoche.* Hamburg: Hoffmann und Campe, 1838.

—. *Maha Guru. Geschichte eines Gottes.* Stuttgart and Tübingen: J. G. Cotta, 1833.

—. *Oeffentliche Charaktere.* Hamburg: Hoffmann und Campe, 1835.

—. *Vertheidigung gegen Menzel und Berichtigung einiger Urtheile im Publikum.* Mannheim: Löwenthal, 1835.

—. *Wally, die Zweiflerin.* Mannheim: Löwenthal, 1835. Reprint, ed. Jost Schillemeit. Göttingen: Vandenhoeck & Ruprecht, 1965.

—. *Werke*, ed. Peter Müller. Leipzig and Vienna: Bibliographisches Institut, [1911].

—. *Zur Philosophie der Geschichte.* Hamburg: Hoffmann und Campe, 1836.

GUZINSKY, ELISABETH. *Karl Immermann als Zeitkritiker. Ein Beitrag zur Geschichte der deutschen Selbstkritik.* Neue deutsche Forschungen, No. 142. Berlin: Junker und Dünnhaupt, 1937.

HÄBERLE, KARL. *Individualität und Zeit in H. Laubes Jungem Europa und K. Gutzkows Ritter vom Geist.* Erlangen: Palm & Enke, 1938.

HANSON, WILLIAM P. "F. G. Kühne. A Forgotten Young German." *German Life & Letters*, N.S. 17 (1963/64), 335-338.

HARSING, ERICH. *Wolfgang Menzel und das Junge Deutschland.* Diss. Münster, 1909.

HEBBEL, FRIEDRICH. *Sämtliche Werke. Historisch-kritische Ausgabe*, ed. Richard Maria Werner. Berlin: B. Behr, 1903.

HECKER, KONRAD. *Mensch und Masse. Situation und Handeln der Epigonen. Gezeigt an Immermann und den Jungdeutschen.* Das politische Volk. Schriften zur sozialen Bewegung, Vol. II. Berlin: Junker und Dünnhaupt, 1933.

HEGEL, GEORG WILHELM FRIEDRICH. *Sämtliche Werke. Jubiläumsausgabe in zwanzig Bänden*, ed. Hermann Glockner. Stuttgart: Friedrich Frommann, 1964—.

HEINE, HEINRICH. *Sämtliche Werke*, ed. Ernst Elster. 7 vols. Leipzig and Vienna: Bibliographisches Institut, [1887-90].

HERMAND, JOST. "Allgemeine Epochenprobleme." *Zur Literatur der Restaurationsepoche 1815-1848*, ed. Jost Hermand and Manfred Windfuhr. Stuttgart: Metzler, 1970, pp. 3-61.

—. "Heines frühe Kritiker." *Der Dichter und seine Zeit — Politik im Spiegel der Literatur. Drittes Amherster Kolloquium zur modernen deutschen Literatur 1969*, ed. Wolfgang Paulsen. Heidelberg: Lothar Stiehm, 1970, pp. 113-133.

—, ed. *Das Junge Deutschland. Texte und Dokumente.* Reclams Universal-Bibliothek, Nos. 8703-07. Stuttgart: Philipp Reclam Jun., 1966.

HIRTH, FRIEDRICH, ed. *Heinrich Heines Briefe.* 6 vols. Mainz: F. Kupferberg, 1950-51.

HOF, WALTER. *Pessimistisch-nihilistische Strömungen in der deutschen Literatur vom Sturm und Drang bis zum Jungen Deutschland.* Tübingen: Niemeyer, 1970.

HOROVITZ, RUTH. *Vom Roman des Jungen Deutschland zum Roman der Gartenlaube.* Diss. Basel, 1937.

HOUBEN, H. H. *Gutzkow-Funde. Beiträge zur Litteratur- und Kulturgeschichte des neunzehnten Jahrhunderts.* Berlin: Arthur L. Wolff, 1901.

—. *Jungdeutscher Sturm und Drang. Ergebnisse und Studien.* Leipzig: F. A. Brockhaus, 1911.

—. *Verbotene Literatur von der klassischen Zeit bis zur Gegenwart. Ein kritisch-historisches Lexikon über verbotene Bücher, Zeitschriften und Theaterstücke, Schriftsteller und Verleger.* 2 vols. Berlin: E. Rowohlt, 1924; Bremen: K. Schünemann, 1928. Reprinted, Hildesheim: Georg Olms, 1965.

—. *Zeitschriften des Jungen Deutschlands.* Veröffentlichungen der Deutschen Bibliographischen Gesellschaft, *Bibliographisches Repertorium,* Vols. III-IV. Berlin: B. Behr, 1906 and 1909. Reprinted, Hildesheim and New York: Georg Olms, 1970.

HUMBOLDT, WILHELM VON. *Gesammelte Schriften,* ed. Albert Leitzmann. Vol. II. Berlin: B. Behr, 1908.

IGGERS, GEORGE G. "Heine and the Saint-Simonians: A Re-examination." *Comparative Literature,* 10 (1958), 289-308.

IMMERMANN, KARL. *Münchhausen. Eine Geschichte in Arabesken,* ed. Gustav Konrad. Frechen: Bartmann, 1968.

—. *Tulifäntchen,* ed. Peter Hasubek. Reclams Universal-Bibliothek, Nos. 8551-52. Stuttgart: Philipp Reclam Jun., 1968.

—. *Werke,* ed. Robert Boxberger. Leipzig: Dümmler, [1883].

—. *Werke,* ed. Harry Maync. Leipzig and Vienna: Bibliographisches Institut, [1906].

JANTZ, HAROLD. "Sequence and Continuity in Nineteenth-Century German Literature." *Germanic Review,* 38 (1963), 27-36.

JENNINGS, LEE B. *The Ludicrous Demon: Aspects of the Grotesque in German Post-Romantic Prose.* Berkeley and Los Angeles: University of California Press, 1963.

KAYSER, RUDOLF. "Ludolf Wienbarg und der Kampf um den Historismus." *German Quarterly,* 29 (1956), 71-74.

KISCHKA, KARL HARALD. "Typologie der Lyrik des Vormärz." Diss. Mainz, 1965.

KOHLSCHMIDT, WERNER. "Die Welt des Bauern im Spiegel von Immermanns 'Münchhausen' und Gotthelfs 'Uli'." *Dichtung und Volkstum,* 39 (1938), 223-237.

KOOPMANN, HELMUT. *Das Junge Deutschland. Analyse seines Selbstverständnisses.* Stuttgart: Metzler, 1970.

KÜHNE, FERDINAND GUSTAV. *Eine Quarantäne im Irrenhause. Novelle aus den Papieren eines Mondsteiners.* Leipzig: Brockhaus, 1835.

—. *Weibliche und männliche Charaktere.* Leipzig: Wilh. Engelmann, 1838.

KURZ, PAUL KONRAD. *Künstler, Tribun, Apostel. Heinrich Heines Auffassung vom Beruf des Dichters.* Munich: Fink, 1967.

KUTHE, OLGA. *Heinrich Laubes Roman "Die Krieger" im Zusammenhang mit der Polenbegeisterung um 1830.* Diss. Marburg, 1925.

LAUBE, HEINRICH. *Ausgewählte Werke in zehn Bänden,* ed. Heinrich Hubert Houben. Leipzig: Max Hesse, n.d.

—. *Die Bürger.* Mannheim: Heinrich Hoff, 1837.

——. *Gesammelte Werke in fünfzig Bänden*, ed. Heinrich Hubert Houben with Albert Hänel. Leipzig, Max Hesse, 1908-09.

——. *Die Krieger.* Mannheim: Heinrich Hoff, 1837.

——. *Die Poeten.* Mannheim: Heinrich Hoff, 1836.

——. ed. *Zeitung für die elegante Welt.* January, 1833 to July, 1834.

LEGGE, J. G. *Rhyme and Revolution in Germany. A Study in German History, Life, Literature and Character 1813-1850.* London: Constable, 1918.

MCCLAIN, WILLIAM. "Karl Lebrecht Immermann's Portrait of a Folk-Hero in *Münchhausen.*" *Studies in German Literature of the Nineteenth and Twentieth Centuries. Festschrift for Frederic E. Coenen,* ed. Siegfried Mews. University of North Carolina Studies in the Germanic Languages and Literatures, Vol. 67. Chapel Hill: University of North Carolina Press, 1970, pp. 55-63.

MAGILL, C. P. "Young Germany: A Revaluation." *German Studies Presented to Leonard Ashley Willoughby,* ed. J. Boyd. Oxford: Blackwell, 1952, pp. 108-119.

MAJUT, RUDOLF. "Der deutsche Roman vom Biedermeier bis zur Gegenwart." *Deutsche Philologie im Aufriß,* ed. Wolfgang Stammler. 2nd ed. Berlin: Erich Schmidt, 1960. II, cols. 1357-1535.

MARCUSE, LUDWIG. *Revolutionär und Patriot. Das Leben Ludwig Börnes.* Leipzig: P. List, 1929.

MARX, KARL, and FRIEDRICH ENGELS. *Über Kunst und Literatur,* ed. Manfred Kliem. 2 vols. Berlin: Dietz Verlag, 1968.

MAYER, HANS. *Studien zur deutschen Literaturgeschichte,* 2nd ed. Berlin: Rütten & Loening, 1955.

MAYRHOFER, OTTO. *Gustav Freytag und das Junge Deutschland.* Beiträge zur deutschen Literaturwissenschaft, No. 1. Marburg: Elwert, 1907.

MENZEL, WOLFGANG. *Geist der Geschichte.* Stuttgart: Liesching, 1835.

MEYER, HERMAN. *Das Zitat in der Erzählkunst. Zur Geschichte und Poetik des europäischen Romans.* 2nd ed. Stuttgart: Metzler, 1967.

MUNDT, THEODOR. *Aesthetik. Die Idee der Schönheit und des Kunstwerks im Lichte unserer Zeit.* Berlin: M. Simion, 1845. Reprint, ed. Hans Düvel, Göttingen: Vandenhoeck & Ruprecht, 1966.

——. *Charaktere und Situationen.* Wismar and Leipzig: H. Schmidt u. v. Cossel, 1837.

——. *Charlotte Stieglitz, ein Denkmal.* Berlin: Veit & Comp., [1835].

——. *Geschichte der Literatur der Gegenwart. Friedrich von Schlegel's Geschichte der alten und neuen Literatur, bis auf die neueste Zeit fortgeführt.* Berlin: M. Simion, 1842.

——. *Die Kunst der deutschen Prosa. Aesthetisch, literargeschichtlich, ge-*

sellschaftlich. Berlin: Veit & Comp., 1837. Reprint, ed. Hans Düvel, Göttingen: Vandenhoeck & Ruprecht, 1969.

—. *Madelon oder die Romantiker in Paris. Eine Novelle.* Leipzig: Georg Wolbrecht, 1832.

—. *Madonna. Unterhaltungen mit einer Heiligen.* Leipzig: Gebrüder Reichenbach, 1835.

—. *Moderne Lebenswirren. Briefe und Zeitabenteuer eines Salzschreibers.* Leipzig: Gebrüder Reichenbach, 1834.

NOLLE, KARL. *Heinrich Laube als sozialer und politischer Schriftsteller.* Diss. Münster, 1914.

OTT, BARTHÉLEMY. *La Querelle de Heine et de Börne. Contribution à l'étude des idées politiques et sociales en Allemagne de 1830 à 1840.* Diss. Lille, 1936.

OTTO, ULLA. *Die literarische Zensur als Problem der Soziologie der Politik.* Stuttgart: Ferdinand Enke Verlag, 1968.

PIERSON, EDGAR, ed. *Gustav Kühne, sein Lebensbild und Briefwechsel mit Zeitgenossen.* Dresden and Leipzig: E. Pierson's Verlag, [1889].

PORTERFIELD, ALLEN WILSON. *Karl Lebrecht Immermann. A Study in German Romanticism.* New York: Columbia University Press, 1911. Reprinted, New York: AMS Press, 1966.

PROELSS, JOHANNES. *Das junge Deutschland. Ein Buch deutscher Geistesgeschichte.* Stuttgart: Cotta, 1892.

PRZYGODDA, PAUL. *Heinrich Laubes literarische Frühzeit.* Diss. Berlin, 1910.

PUTLITZ, GUSTAV ZU, ed. *Karl Immermann. Sein Leben und seine Werke, aus Tagebüchern und Briefen an seine Familie zusammengestellt.* Berlin: Wilhelm Hertz, 1870.

RAS, GERARD. *Börne und Heine als politische Schriftsteller.* The Hague: Wolters, 1926.

ROER, WALTHER. *Soziale Bewegung und politische Lyrik im Vormärz.* Diss. Münster, 1933.

RUMLER, FRANZ. *Realistische Elemente in Immermanns "Epigonen."* Diss. Munich, 1964.

SAMMONS, JEFFREY L. "The Evaluation of Freytag's 'Soll und Haben.'" *German Life & Letters,* N.S. 22 (1968/69), 315-324.

—. *Heinrich Heine: The Elusive Poet.* New Haven and London: Yale University Press, 1969.

—. "Ludolf Wienbarg and Norway." *Scandinavian Studies,* 42 (1970), 14-30.

SCHERER, MICHAEL. "Immermanns *Münchhausen*-Roman." *German Quarterly,* 36 (1963), 236-244.

SCHERER, WINGOLF. "Heinrich Heine und der Saint-Simonismus." Diss. Bonn, 1950.

SCHNEIDER, FRANZ. "Gutzkows *Wally* und D. F. Strauss' *Das Leben Jesu*, eine Richtigstellung." *Germanic Review*, 1 (1926), 115-119.

SCHÖNFELD, MARGARETE. *Gutzkows Frauengestalten. Ein Kapitel aus der literarhistorischen Anthropologie des 19. Jahrhunderts.* Germanische Studien, No. 133. Berlin: E. Ebering, 1933. Reprinted Nendeln/Liechtenstein: Kraus Reprint, 1967.

SCHWEIZER, VIKTOR. *Ludolf Wienbarg. Beiträge zu einer Jungdeutschen Ästhetik.* Diss. Leipzig, 1897.

SELL, FRIEDRICH C. *Die Tragödie des deutschen Liberalismus.* Stuttgart: Deutsche Verlags-Anstalt, 1953.

SENGLE, FRIEDRICH. *Arbeiten zur deutschen Literatur 1750-1850.* Stuttgart: Metzler, 1965.

—. *Biedermeierzeit. Deutsche Literatur im Spannungsfeld zwischen Restauration und Revolution 1815-1848.* Vol. I. Stuttgart: Metzler, 1971.

—. "Voraussetzungen und Erscheinungsformen der deutschen Restaurationsliteratur." *Deutsche Vierteljahrsschrift*, 30 (1956), 268-294.

SMITH, BARBARA HERNSTEIN. "Poetry as Fiction." *New Literary History*, 2 (1971), 259-281.

STATKOW, DIMITER. "Über die dialektische Struktur des Immermann-Romans 'Münchhausen.' Zum Problem des Übergangs von der Romantik zum Realismus." *Weimarer Beiträge*, 11 (1965), 195-211.

STEINECKE, HARTMUT, ed. *Theorie und Technik des Romans im 19. Jahrhundert.* Tübingen: Niemeyer, 1970.

STORCH, WERNER. "Die ästhetischen Theorien des jungdeutschen Sturms und Drangs." Diss. Bonn, 1926.
[Upon my inquiry, I was informed that this dissertation was lost during World War II. Dietze, however, refers to it several times, so that this information may not be correct. An abstract of the dissertation is in *Jahrbuch der philosophischen Fakultät der Rheinischen Friedrich Wilhelms-Universität zu Bonn*, 3 (1924/25), 141-147.]

WATT, IAN. *The Rise of the Novel. Studies in Defoe, Richardson and Fielding.* Berkeley: University of California Press, 1967.

WELLEK, RENÉ. *A History of Modern Criticism 1750-1950.* New Haven and London: Yale University Press, 1955-.

WERNER, HANS-GEORG. *Geschichte des politischen Gedichts in Deutschland von 1815 bis 1840.* Berlin: Akademie-Verlag, 1969.

WIENBARG, LUDOLF. *Ästhetische Feldzüge*, ed. Walter Dietze. Berlin and Weimar: Aufbau-Verlag, 1964.

—. *Der dänische Fehdehandschuh, aufgenommen von Ludolf Wienbarg.* Hamburg: Hoffmann und Campe, 1846.

—. *Das dänische Königsgesetz oder das in Dänemark geltende Grundgesetz.* Hamburg: Hoffmann und Campe, 1847.

—. *Geschichtliche Vorträge über altdeutsche Sprache und Literatur.* Hamburg: Hoffmann und Campe, 1838.

—. *Holland in den Jahren 1831 und 1832.* Hamburg: Hoffmann und Campe, 1833.

—. *Menzel und die junge Literatur. Programme zur deutschen Revue.* Mannheim: Löwenthal, 1835.

—. *Quadriga.* Hamburg: Hoffmann und Campe, 1840.

—. *Soll die plattdeutsche Sprache gepflegt oder ausgerottet werden? Gegen Ersteres und für Letzteres.* Hamburg: Hoffmann und Campe, 1834.

—. *Wanderungen durch den Thierkreis.* Hamburg: Hoffmann und Campe, 1835.

—. *Zur neuesten Literatur.* Mannheim: Löwenthal, 1835.

WIESE, BENNO VON. *Karl Immermann. Sein Werk und sein Leben.* Bad Homburg, Berlin, and Zürich: Gehlen, 1969.

—. "Zeitkrisis und Biedermeier in Laubes 'Das junge Europa' und in Immermanns 'Epigonen.' " *Dichtung und Volkstum,* 36 (1935), 163-197.

WINDFUHR, MANFRED. "Der Epigone. Begriff, Phänomen und Bewußtsein." *Archiv für Begriffsgeschichte,* 4 (1959), 182-209.

—. *Immermanns erzählerisches Werk. Zur Situation des Romans in der Restaurationszeit.* Giessen: Schmitz, 1957.

WÜLFING, WULF. "Schlagworte des Jungen Deutschland." *Zeitschrift für deutsche Sprache,* 21 (1965), 42-59, 160-174; 22 (1966), 36-56, 154-178; 23 (1967), 48-82, 166-177; 24 (1968), 60-71, 161-183; 25 (1969), 96-115, 175-179; 26 (1970), 60-83, 162-175.

UNIVERSITY OF NORTH CAROLINA
STUDIES IN THE GERMANIC LANGUAGES
AND LITERATURES

Initiated by RICHARD JENTE (1949–1952), *established by* F. E. COENEN (1952–1968)

Publication Committee

SIEGFRIED MEWS, EDITOR

For other volumes in the "Studies" see page ii and following pages.

Send orders to: (U.S. and Canada)
The University of North Carolina Press, P.O. Box 2288
Chapel Hill, N.C. 27514
(All other countries) Feffer and Simons, Inc., 31 Union Square, New York, N.Y. 10003

UNIVERSITY OF NORTH CAROLINA STUDIES IN THE GERMANIC LANGUAGES AND LITERATURES

initiated by RICHARD JENTE (1949–1952), established by F. E. COENEN (1952–1968)

Publication Committee

For other volumes in the "Studies" see preceding and following pages and p. ii

UNIVERSITY OF NORTH CAROLINA
STUDIES IN THE GERMANIC LANGUAGES AND LITERATURES

Initiated by RICHARD JENTE (1949–1952), *established by* F. E. COENEN (1952–1968)

Publication Committee

SIEGFRIED MEWS, EDITOR

For other volumes in the "Studies" see preceding pages and p. ii